EMBODIED

EMBODIED

Living as Whole People
in a Fractured World

GREGG R. ALLISON

BakerBooks
a division of Baker Publishing Group
Grand Rapids, Michigan

© 2021 by Gregg R. Allison

Published by Baker Books
a division of Baker Publishing Group
PO Box 6287, Grand Rapids, MI 49516-6287
www.bakerbooks.com

Printed in the United States of America

Library of Congress Cataloging-in-Publication Data
Names: Allison, Gregg R., author.
Title: Embodied : living as whole people in a fractured world / Gregg R. Allison.
Description: Grand Rapids, Michigan : Baker Books, a division of Baker Publishing Group, [2021] | Includes bibliographical references.
Identifiers: LCCN 2020042358 | ISBN 9781540900050 (paperback) | ISBN 9781540901743 (casebound)
Subjects: LCSH: Human body—Religious aspects—Christianity.
Classification: LCC BT741.3 .A335 2021 | DDC 233/.5—dc23
LC record available at https://lccn.loc.gov/2020042358

Unless otherwise indicated, Scripture quotations are from the Christian Standard Bible®, copyright © 2017 by Holman Bible Publishers. Used by permission. Christian Standard Bible® and CSB® are federally registered trademarks of Holman Bible Publishers.

Scripture quotations labeled ESV are from The Holy Bible, English Standard Version® (ESV®), copyright © 2001 by Crossway, a publishing ministry of Good News Publishers. Used by permission. All rights reserved. ESV Text Edition: 2016

Scripture quotations labeled NASB are from the New American Standard Bible® (NASB), copyright © 1960, 1962, 1963, 1968, 1971, 1972, 1973, 1975, 1977, 1995 by The Lockman Foundation. Used by permission. www.Lockman.org

Scripture quotations labeled NIV are from the Holy Bible, New International Version®. NIV®. Copyright © 1973, 1978, 1984, 2011 by Biblica, Inc.™ Used by permission of Zondervan. All rights reserved worldwide. www.zondervan.com. The "NIV" and "New International Version" are trademarks registered in the United States Patent and Trademark Office by Biblica, Inc.™

Italics added to Scripture quotations reflect the author's emphasis.

Some names and details have been changed to protect the privacy of the individuals involved.

This publication is intended to provide helpful and informative material on the subjects addressed. Readers should consult their personal health professionals before adopting any of the suggestions in this book or drawing inferences from it. The author and publisher expressly disclaim responsibility for any adverse effects arising from the use or application of the information contained in this book.

21 22 23 24 25 26 27   7 6 5 4 3 2 1

To my wife, Nora.

For well over two decades, I've intended to write this book
and dedicate it to you.
In the meantime, other books have consumed my attention.
But I never lost sight of one day writing the book
I've always longed to write, and the book
you've inspired and patiently waited for me to write.
That day has come, and I joyfully dedicate
Embodied: Living as Whole People in a Fractured World to you!

You, as God's embodied gift to me, are the best wife, friend,
and partner I could ever imagine.

CONTENTS

ACKNOWLEDGMENTS

I am grateful to a number of family members and friends who provided extensive comments on an original draft of this book. Their insights and suggestions were invaluable and make this book better than what it would have been. Of course, I, not they, am responsible for any inaccuracies and errors. Family members are my wife, Nora; my son, Luke; my daughter, Hanell Schuetz; and my son-in-law, Michael Schuetz. Friends are Morgan DeLisle, Chad Gahafer, Gracilynn Hanson, Kelly Nall, Lindsay Simpson, Torey Teer, Andrew Walker, Laura Wierenga, the folks at Love Thy Neighborhood, and former students in my Theology of the Body courses over the past two decades at Western Seminary and The Southern Baptist Theological Seminary.

Special thanks also to Baker Books, especially Brian Vos, who as a friend believed in this project and as an editor shepherded this book from beginning to end. And thanks to Amy Nemecek, who copyedited the manuscript, engaged me in dialogue about several important points of content, and tended to the many details of publication.

INTRODUCTION

Why This Book?

Drake was usually a self-assured, steady, and social person.

But not that day when he came to my office.

Seemingly impatient with the small talk that began our conversation, he leaped at the first chance to address why he had come to see me: "I'm not doing well. I'm not doing well at all," he doubly announced.

A bit shaken because of his directness, I asked him what was bothering him.

Drake rehearsed a list of disconcerting physical problems: He had difficulty sleeping. He was experiencing stomach problems and constipation. He was lethargic, barely having energy for normal life activities. He had spied blood in his urine. He found it difficult to pay attention in conversations. He couldn't remember the ideas he had just read in books.

So here he was in my office. He wondered what spiritual causes could lie at the heart of these physical symptoms, and he wanted my advice about how to become well again.

I didn't need to probe much, but my questions caught him off guard because they focused on physical matters.

What are you eating? Drake was consuming a large and regular amount of junk food, living like a couch potato.

Are you scheduling rest periods? He explained that he was too busy for relaxation.

How are you exercising? Drake dismissed that question because he had no need for workouts.

Are you getting good sleep? Perturbed, he reminded me that one of his problems was insomnia.

Drake was clearly becoming irritated with my line of questioning, and he offered the following: because his body was going to be sloughed off at death anyway, he didn't need to be concerned about eating well, resting well, exercising well, and sleeping well. All those bodily matters were irrelevant—and useless.

I countered with an observation. His body was (literally) breaking down before his eyes. If he kept it up, he would soon be no good for himself, his family, and the church ministry for which he was preparing. And, I added, I thought the problem was a physical one, not a spiritual one.

To put it mildly, Drake was not pleased. My response wasn't the answer a "spiritually minded" Christian like him was accustomed to hearing—or wanted to hear. Besides, he had come to me with an expectation that I'd share something with him from the Word of God.

With an angry huff, Drake stormed out of my office.

My lack of preparedness for that encounter with Drake started me on a journey. As a theologian, I've spent the past two decades working out an understanding of life in the human body that is well-grounded biblically and sound theologically.

This book is the fruit of that journey prompted by Drake's crisis.[1]

---

1. An earlier version of this story was published in Gregg R. Allison, "Toward a Theology of Human Embodiment," *Southern Baptist Journal of Theology* 13.2 (2009): 4.

What This Book Is About

This book is about human embodiment. Simply put, embodiment is the condition of being a body or having a body.

A moment's reflection will reveal that in reading this book, you as an embodied person are engaged in a bodily activity. With your eyes, you're reading the words that I've written on this page. With your brain, you're processing and understanding those words. With your hands, you're holding the book or electronic device containing my words. In all likelihood, you're sitting at a desk with your feet on the floor, your behind nestled in a chair, and your back nice and straight for good posture. Or, maybe you're reading while running on a treadmill to exercise your legs and arms and to strengthen your core.

You are an embodied person engaging in a bodily activity.

Human beings aren't unique in being embodied. Birds are embodied with wings and feathers. Lizards are embodied with legs and scales. Bears are embodied with claws and fur. Fish are embodied with fins and scales.

We could say that all living things are embodied.

But that wouldn't be completely true. Angels are living things, but they aren't embodied. Well, unless they take on a human body so they can rescue wayward Lot or imprisoned Peter. And subatomic particles—electrons and quarks, the basic components of living things—aren't embodied either.

But our concern isn't with angels and particles that aren't embodied. Nor are we concerned about owls and frogs and lions and salmon.

This book is about human embodiment.

What Human Embodiment Is

To understand life in the human body, we need to know a few basic concepts. *Body* is the material aspect of human nature. It's composed of five essential organs—the heart, brain, kidneys, lungs, and liver—and thirteen systems, including circulatory (blood), respiratory (oxygen), reproductive (sperm and eggs), skeletal (bones), digestive (nutrition and waste), and muscular. The body is one of two aspects of human nature, the other— often called the soul or spirit—being the immaterial aspect. So we human beings are complex people, consisting of both a material aspect and an immaterial aspect.[2]

This book focuses on the body.

Embodiment has two definitions. In the first sense, it's simply having or being in a body. Embodiment is the proper state of human existence. This statement simply refers to the reality that people have or are in a body. In this earthly life, if we aren't embodied we don't—even more, we can't—exist.

In a second sense, embodiment is a field of study that explores how people are present bodily and engage physically in the world.

2. To avoid confusion and anticipate questions that may arise from my focus on the body, a couple of comments about the soul or spirit are in order at the start of this book. Scripture affirms that human beings are complex creatures. Our immaterial element is called a soul or a spirit. Our material element is a body. In this earthly existence, we are a body-soul or body-spirit unity. That is, I affirm some type of dualism and reject all forms of monism, which asserts we are only material (a body) or only immaterial (a soul or a spirit). Additionally, the church historically has held to some form of dualism: we consist of both a material and an immaterial aspect. As I will discuss later, the intimate connection of our material and immaterial elements makes it impossible to assign certain actions and functions to either our body or to our soul. Neuroscience confirms this intimate unity. Our mind and brain, for example, are so connected that if we experience brain trauma, our mind is significantly damaged.

What, then, happens when we die and go into the presence of the Lord in heaven? Traditionally, we say that our body is sloughed off and put in a grave or cremated while our soul or spirit continues to live with Christ. This description is fine. My preference, however, is to express life in the intermediate state in this way: we as disembodied people continue to live with Christ in heaven. It is I, not a mere aspect of myself—a soul or a spirit—that will praise God and rest from my labors. Moreover, because the proper state of human existence is embodiment, as (strangely) disembodied people in heaven, we will long for and anticipate the resurrection of our body. Then, and only then, will our salvation be complete. Then, and only then, will we be restored to our proper state of human existence, with this twist: our proper state will be that of glorified embodiment.

Thinking, feeling, willing, purposing, moving, and acting are common activities, all of which include some bodily component. Many of these expressions are observable, so embodiment as a field of study requires alertness to lived embodied experience. We can pay attention to how people actually live and experience life in their body. Familiarity with neuroscience, physiology, genetics, and other related sciences can also be of help. The most important elements that this book brings to this field of study are Scripture—the inspired, truthful, and authoritative Word of God—and sound theology—Christian beliefs and practices that arise from Scripture. This book develops a theology of human embodiment.

Why This Book Is Needed

A theology of human embodiment is important for many reasons. It intersects with other important Christian doctrines. As part of the doctrine of creation, a theology of human embodiment helps us understand God's creation of human beings and his design for human flourishing. As an aspect of the doctrine of humanity (technically called "theological anthropology"), embodiment theology addresses the composition of human nature. In relation to the doctrine of sin, a theology of embodiment traces the bodily effects of the fall and sin. With respect to the doctrine of Christ, embodiment speaks to the nature of the incarnation. Connecting to the doctrines of the Holy Spirit and salvation, a theology of embodiment helps us understand the Spirit's indwelling of, and divine action through, redeemed people. In relation to the doctrine of future things, embodiment theology highlights the strangeness of disembodiment in the intermediate state (the period between our death and the return of Christ). It also fosters hope in the completion of God's redemptive work through the resurrection of the body.

Beyond touching on these other important Christian doctrines, a theology of human embodiment addresses numerous contemporary moral and social issues: human personhood, gender dysphoria, transgenderism, heterosexuality and homosexuality, dehumanization and objectification, body image, the obesity epidemic, anorexia and bulimia, compulsive exercise, orthorexia, body modification, selfie dysmorphia, and more. Embodiment theology isn't a cure-all when it comes to caring for people who wrestle with these and other issues. But it does provide the proper theological foundation on which Christians and the church should construct their mercy and caring ministries.

Finally, a theology of human embodiment exposes the devastating impact of Gnosticism/neo-Gnosticism on the American society and church. Gnosticism/neo-Gnosticism underscores that material things (like the body) are inherently evil or at least not as important as spiritual things. If this view is true, then our body is at least insignificant, if not the major cause of sin and the key hindrance to Christian maturity. But if God's design for his image bearers is that we are embodied, then we will need to rethink and reject this far too prevalent perspective that diminishes or demonizes human embodiment.[3]

In other words, a theology of human embodiment will help us live as whole people in a fractured world. We'll be more connected with God and his design for us. We'll be better prepared to face the cultural challenges around us. And we'll be more integrated and sound—not divided—people for ourselves and for others.

For these reasons, this book is needed—maybe even long overdue.

How This Book Unfolds

This book consists of thirteen chapters, each of which is structured in the following way: topic, big idea, and application, that

---

3. For further discussion of Gnosticism as the theological foundation of contemporary social developments such as same-sex marriage and transgenderism, see Robert P. George, "Gnostic Liberalism," *First Things* (December 2016): 33–38. Available at https://www.firstthings.com/article/2016/12/gnostic-liberalism.

is, how to concretely live out the topic. Additionally, if you want to do a deeper dive into the topic, each chapter concludes with a section titled "For the Curious." For example, you can do some extra thinking about relationships with the other gender, lust and masturbation, same-sex attraction, gospel liturgy, tattoos, traditional burial versus cremation, and phantom limbs.

Chapter 1 is about the *creation* of the body. The big idea is that embodiment is the proper state of human existence. God's design for his image bearers is that we are embodied people. I affirm, "I am my body." The application question is, Are you thankful for God's creation of you as an embodied human being?

Chapter 2 addresses *sex/gender* (I'll clear up this distinction in the chapter). The big idea is that an essential given of human existence is maleness or femaleness.[4] God's design for his image bearers is that we are sexed/gendered people. The application question is, Are you thankful for the gender that God created you?

Chapter 3 discusses *particularity*. The big idea is that an essential given of human existence is particularity, which is defined as the condition of being an individual. God specifically designs and creates each human being to be a particular gendered embodied individual. The application is to map out who you are as a particular person designed and created by God.

Chapter 4 raises the issue of *sociality*. While some people use the word "sexuality" for this category, I'll explain why I avoid that term and use instead "sociality." The big idea is that an essential given of human existence is sociality, the condition that tends to bring individuals together. God's design for his image bearers is that we are social people who express our sociality in appropriate interpersonal relationships and, in the case of marriage, through sexual activity. The application question is, How

---

4. When I use the expression "essential given," I refer to a necessary fact, a reality established as it is by God himself.

are you expressing your sociality in God-honoring, self-valuing, and others-respecting ways?

Chapter 5 is about *sexuality*. The big idea addresses one particular aspect of sociality: sexual activity. God's design for his image bearers is that, as social people, we express our sociality in the case of marriage through sexual activity. The application question is, How are you expressing your sexuality in God-honoring, self-valuing, and spouse-respecting ways?

Chapter 6 is about the *incarnation* of the Son of God as Jesus Christ. The big idea is that the incarnation is about God the Son becoming embodied. The triune God's design was for the eternal Son of the Father to become the God-man by virtue of the Holy Spirit's uniting him to a human nature just like ours. The purpose of this embodiment was so the Son, without spot or blemish and perfectly prepared for his mission, would be the once-and-for-all embodied sacrifice for sin. The question for application is, How does the embodiment of the Son of God instruct you about your existence as an embodied person?

Chapter 7 treats the *sanctification* of the body. The big idea is that maturing as Christ's followers is not only about spiritual and moral progress but physical development as well. God's design for his embodied image bearers is that we are holistically sanctified, which includes growing in holiness in our body. Such progressive embodied sanctification fights against "deadly" sins of the body—lust, gluttony, and sloth. It also pursues physical wellness through sleep and rest. The question for application is, How should you progress in sanctification as an embodied believer?

Chapter 8 addresses bodily *blessing and discipline*. The big idea is that through the physical senses, human embodiment brings blessings that are too numerous to count. At the same time, it also demands bodily discipline. God's design for his embodied image bearers is that we live physically blessed and disciplined lives in areas such as regular exercise, good nutrition, fasting, and feasting. The application is to design a personal program of bodily discipline that you consistently follow.

Chapter 9 connects human embodiment with *worship*. The big idea is that embodied worshipers properly render worship to God through whole-body devotion to him, expressing praise, thanksgiving, confession, repentance, joy, obedience, faith, lament, and love. God's design for his people gathered to worship him is that we express bodily what is transpiring in our heart and mind. The question for application is, How can you ensure that your physical posture and bodily activity during worship expresses what is transpiring in your heart and mind?

Chapter 10 explores some implications of human embodiment for *clothing*. The big idea is that clothed embodiment is the proper state of human existence after the fall. God's design for his embodied image bearers after sin entered the world is that we are clothed for the purpose of covering the shame of nakedness. The only exception is nakedness between husband and wife.[5] Moreover, clothing expresses something important about human beings. The application is a call to thoughtfulness with respect to the clothes we choose to wear.

Chapter 11 is about *suffering and healing*. The big idea is that suffering is part and parcel of embodied existence, and that suffering may persist, worsen, or improve, perhaps even be healed. God's design for his embodied image bearers after the fall is to permit us to suffer the physical consequences of living in a fallen world. Moreover, he calls Christians to suffer for the sake of Christ, even to the point of martyrdom. At all times, God's grace is sufficient to sustain his people, and sometimes he will physically heal us or rescue us from persecution. The question for application is, How should you face suffering and how should you seek healing as an embodied Christian?

---

5. There are other occasions—e.g., during a physical exam by a doctor—when nakedness is permitted, and these will be addressed in that chapter.

Chapter 12 is a consideration of the *death* of the body. The big idea is that human existence plays itself out from conception through eternity. Death is an enemy intruder that, at the end of our earthly existence, results in the cessation of the body's proper functioning. God's design for his embodied image bearers after the fall is to permit us to die as a physical consequence of living in a fallen world. Because of their salvation through Christ, Christians are able to face death with hope and not fear. The application question is, How should we face death?

Chapter 13 addresses the *future* of the body. The big idea is that after death, which is a temporary separation from our body, we live in an abnormal condition of disembodiment. At the return of Christ and the accompanying event of bodily resurrection, we will be re-embodied. God's design for his embodied image bearers is that as we are in this earthly life, so we will be for all eternity: embodied. The application question is, How does the resurrection (with eternal physical life) confirm our first big idea that embodiment is the proper state of human existence?

 Finally, I conclude with an invitation to embrace our embodiment.

CHAPTER 1

THE CREATED BODY

Consider

"I am my body." Do you agree or disagree with this statement, and why?

Big Idea

Embodiment is the proper state of human existence. God's design for his image bearers is that we are embodied people.

Application Question

Are you thankful for God's creation of you as an embodied human being?

Our Contemporary Context and Problems with Embodiment

We are troubled by our body.

I'm not just talking about the physical illnesses that beset us and the increasing aches and pains that come with age. The trouble I refer to is more subtle and insidious than those evident problems.

21

We are troubled by our body because we find our value in accordance with cultural expectations of physical appearance. Men, for example, are to be chiseled with steel-like abs. They should be tall, dark, and handsome, preferably young and muscular, and have thick hair. Women likewise are to be shaped according to a certain ratio between breasts, hips, waist, and legs. They should be beautiful, young, and fit, and have a glowing face.

These norms dictate what our body—our perfect body—should be like in order for us to have value, feel successful, be accepted, enjoy relationships, and be appreciated. And more often than not (never?), our body doesn't match up to these cultural norms.

This disconnect between our society's expectations for our outward appearance and our actual physical self creates a problem for our body image. And, to say the least, an inordinately high percentage of people today suffer from the problem of body image.

By *body image* I mean the subjective picture or mental image of your own body, how you see yourself when you look in the mirror or when you picture yourself in your mind. As a mental representation that you create, it may or may not bear close resemblance to how others see you. Importantly, body image, as a perception, leads to thoughts, feelings, and behaviors about that perception. These thoughts, feelings, and behaviors can be positive, negative, or both.

Let's break down body image into four categories: perceptual, affective, cognitive, and behavioral.

Perceptual body image is how you *see* your body. This perception isn't necessarily a correct representation of how you actually look. For example, a woman may view herself as overweight when she is actually underweight.

Affective body image is how you *feel* about your body. This aspect relates to the amount of satisfaction or dissatisfaction you feel about your shape, weight, and individual body parts. For example, a man may be disappointed with his physique, even though his body is well sculpted.

Cognitive body image is how you *think* about your body. Such thinking can lead to an unhealthy preoccupation with body shape and weight. For example, a woman may think that if others see the real her, they will be repulsed by that appearance.

Behavioral body image is the way you *act* as a result of your body image. Such behavior may bear little or no connection to how you actually appear. For example, a man may be displeased with the way he looks and thus isolate himself from others, even though they find him attractive.

Importantly, when our body image is distorted, it often leads to mistreatment of the body, which takes on many forms of abuse or harm, including negative emotions (fear, shame, insecurity), eating disorders (binge eating, anorexia, and bulimia), compulsive exercise, body modification, substance abuse, and selfie dysmorphia (using filters to embellish your social media image, then undergoing cosmetic surgery to conform your actual appearance to your filtered image). Though you may think women struggle with negative body image more than men do, estimates suggest as high as 95 percent of both men and women suffer from negative body image.[1]

The following narrative of the struggle with body image represents the tragic experience of millions of girls and women:

> As a participant on a competitive swimming team starting at 6 years old, I practiced intensely every day. My favorite part was the excited, heart-racing feeling I'd get before every race. Unfortunately, it didn't take long before that anxious, heart-pounding started to stem from the way I thought I looked in my swimming suit, rather than my performance. In third grade, I stood in front of a full-length mirror, noticed one dimple in the side of my little girl thigh and desperately felt the need to cover up. I vowed to remind myself to keep my left hand covering the dimple on my left thigh at all possible moments I wasn't in the water.

1. "The Body Project," Bradley University, https://www.bradley.edu/sites/body project/male-body-image-m-vs-f/.

My newly heightened awareness of my looks quickly gave way to a relentless preoccupation with weight loss, starting around age 11. Journals and notebooks filled with weight-loss goals, motivating thoughts and tips, food logs, and my most depressing thoughts were lined up in my home bookshelf, stacked next to piles of teen magazines. For a long time, my weight defined my days—either successful or a waste. One step closer to happiness or another day of worthless disappointment.

I wasn't alone. My friends suffered the same preoccupation with weight and appearance. Heather, the president of the ballroom dance team, could tell you her weight from any given day of the previous years. One of our most popular friends cut out dozens of lingerie models from Victoria's Secret catalogs and stuck them all over the back of her door for "motivation." Another friend, a cheerleader, bragged to everyone that all she had eaten in days was five Doritos. I wondered how she found the motivation to be so strong. We were all middle-class white girls from Idaho, with happy, successful families of all shapes and sizes, but we all shared the deep-seated idea that the only way to attain happiness, popularity and love was to be as thin and beautiful as possible. . . .

Being stifled by a preoccupation with my appearance was not a natural part of me. I learned to hate my body from sources surrounding me, including peers, family, media, and cultural messages. When I became more worried about the dimple in my thigh than my race time, I stopped excelling as a swimmer. When I am fixated on keeping my clothes in the most flattering position and everything sucked in just right, I can't concentrate on anything else at all. I was overwhelmed just thinking of the number of activities I could have excelled at, the relationships I could have cultivated, the goals I could have pursued, and the girls feeling the exact same way I did that I could have helped if I hadn't spent so much of my life preoccupied with the way I looked.[2]

---

2. Lexie and Lindsay Kite, *More Than a Body* (Boston: Houghton Mifflin Harcourt, 2020), forthcoming. Used by permission. Because the narrative is told from Lindsay's perspective, I've slightly altered the story to be told from the first person singular. For an online version of the story see https://beautyredefined. org/body-anxiety-to-body-image-activism/.

This heartbreaking story of the struggle with negative body image is a tragedy that repeats itself over and over again.

We are troubled by our body.

An Old Problem with a New Look

A second, totally different worldview contributing to our struggles with our physicality is Gnosticism. Unlike body image problems that flow from an overemphasis on the body, Gnosticism flows from an underemphasis on the body. With roots in ancient (pre-Christian) philosophy, Gnosticism is the perspective that spiritual, immaterial realities are inherently good, while physical, material realities are inherently evil. As we will learn, this view is strongly contradicted by Scripture, and because it's so wrong, the early church condemned it as a heresy—false doctrine to be avoided at all costs.

In early Christian times, Gnosticism clashed with key doctrines. For example, because of its scorn for physical matters, Gnosticism denies that the Son of God became incarnate. How could God, who is holy, become embodied by taking on material human nature, which is inherently evil? How could the Word of God become flesh? Gnosticism rejects the incarnation, believing instead that Jesus only appeared to be a man; he is certainly not God the Son incarnate. As another example, because of its rejection of all things physical, Gnosticism believes that salvation consists of the escape of the soul—the immaterial aspect of human nature—from the body. The body is like a prison in which the soul is confined. So salvation is the soul casting off the chains of imprisonment and breaking out of the body.

Sadly, Gnosticism continues to infect us today and leads to disregard for the body. Some of us may equate biblical references to the flesh with the body. For example, Paul complains, "I am of the flesh, sold as a slave to sin" (Rom. 7:14), adding, "Those who are in the flesh cannot please God" (Rom. 8:8). If "the flesh" equals our body, then by all means let's seek to subdue our body by mistreating it! However, in these contexts the flesh refers not to our body but to our sinful nature. It's that tendency toward sin that infects not just our body but also our entire being. It's our sinful nature that we should war against and seek to overcome. Others of us reason that because our body is going to stop functioning and be discarded at death, we should give no attention whatsoever to it now. Our body doesn't matter, so any concern for it is a complete waste of time.

Neo-Gnosticism continues this early heresy in new forms today. It continues to infect the church, leading to disregard for, distancing oneself from, or disparagement of the body.

Because of neo-Gnosticism, we sometimes view the body as an instrument, not dismissing it as inherently evil but diminishing its importance. We may even consider the body as good, but not as good as the soul. So we spend our time pursuing "spiritual" disciplines while viewing "physical" disciplines as only serving an instrumentalist purpose: to keep our body functioning well so we can engage in the more important matter of spiritual growth, which is unrelated to our body. Others of us imagine that human embodiment is a mistake. For example, C. S. Lewis quipped that "the fact that we have bodies is the oldest joke there is."[3]

Such ambivalence toward embodiment may manifest itself as indifference toward proper nutrition (potato chips for couch potatoes), dismissal of proper exercise (CrossFit is for gym rats, not for people), disdain for rest and sleep (I'll sleep when I'm dead), and a general apathy for embodied existence (Why bother at all?).

Thankfully, the church has confronted and continues to confront Gnosticism and neo-Gnosticism. God's creation of the physical universe challenges the notion that matter is inherently evil.

3. C. S. Lewis, *The Four Loves* (New York: Harcourt Brace, 1960), 101.

God's creation of embodied image bearers contradicts the idea that the human body is sinful in and of itself. The mandate in Genesis 1:28 to engage in procreation ("be fruitful and multiply and fill the earth"; ESV) and vocation ("and subdue [the earth] and have dominion"; ESV) emphasizes that life in this physical reality is a divinely given responsibility. For the sake of our salvation, the Son of God became incarnate, a miracle that could not be possible if Gnosticism's rejection of physicality is correct. And if embodiment is evil, why would Jesus's resurrection be a bodily resurrection? And how could the Holy Spirit indwell us if we weren't embodied Christians? Even our future bodily resurrection and the physicality of the new heaven and new earth contradict Gnosticism and neo-Gnosticism.[4]

So, following Scripture, the church has always denounced and continues to contradict the heretical worldview that material reality is inherently evil. Human embodiment—life in a physical, material body—is the proper state of human existence.

To summarize our discussion to this point: We are troubled by our body for various reasons. It may be due to struggles with body image. Our perception of our body may become distorted, and we may be obsessed with our outward appearance. Oppositely, we may totally dismiss our body or, if we don't go to that extreme, we may relegate our embodiment to secondary status. As the pendulum swings from one side to the other—overemphasizing or underemphasizing our body—Scripture challenges both errors by emphasizing that the proper state of human existence is embodiment. And it calls us to live as whole, embodied people in the midst of a fractured, body-troubled world.

---

4. In a humorous summary of the Gnostic error of elevating the soul and scorning the body, Wendell Berry offered that Gnostic-influenced preachers thought "that the soul could do no wrong, but always had its face washed and its pants on and was in agony over having to associate itself with the flesh [body] and the world. And yet these same people believed in the resurrection of the body." Wendell Berry, *Jayber Crow* (Berkeley: Counterpoint, 2001), 49.

Biblical Affirmations

In one sense, Scripture assumes from beginning to end that human existence is properly an embodied existence. It specifically addresses this matter in its opening chapter:

> Then God said, "Let us make man in our image, after our likeness. And let them have dominion over the fish of the sea and over the birds of the heavens and over the livestock and over all the earth and over every creeping thing that creeps on the earth."
>
> So God created man in his own image,
> in the image of God he created him;
> male and female he created them.
>
> And God blessed them. And God said to them, "Be fruitful and multiply and fill the earth and subdue it and have dominion over the fish of the sea and over the birds of the heavens and over every living thing that moves on the earth." (Gen. 1:26–28 ESV)

This passage comes at the climax of the creation narrative. Everything that has been brought into existence thus far—light, the expanse, dry land, vegetation, the sun and moon and stars, water creatures and flying birds and wildlife of the earth—has been created in preparation for, and anticipation of, this climactic moment.

This creative event is preceded by a divine deliberation (v. 26). The Father, the Son, and the Holy Spirit determine to create a being that is more like God than any other creature.[5] God plans to create human beings in the divine image, according to his likeness, and to give them certain responsibilities. Then he actualizes this

---

5. Though v. 26 doesn't specify that this divine deliberation is trinitarian, Genesis 1 indicates that the Creator is (at least) God the Father and God the Holy Spirit, and later Scripture affirms the creative agency of the Word, who is God the Son (John 1:1–3; Col. 1:16; Heb. 1:2). Appropriately, early confessions of faith such as the Nicene-Constantinopolitan Creed (AD 381) affirmed creation as the work of the three Persons of the Trinity.

plan (v. 27). God creates human beings in his image, with a crucial qualification: his image bearers are either male or female. That is, God creates men in his image and women in his image (we will return to this distinction in genders in the next chapter). Finally, to his image bearers, God announces a blessing and mandate (v. 28). These divinely created male and female image bearers are to reproduce other image bearers and to produce an ordered society. That is, in accordance with the divine deliberation to create human beings as divine image bearers who have a specific purpose and responsibility, God creates such image bearers with that purpose and for that responsibility.

Human beings, as divine image bearers, are embodied beings by divine design. This point is confirmed in Psalm 139:13–16, which poetically presents God's creation of individuals as embodied human beings:

> For it was you who created my inward parts;
> you knit me together in my mother's womb.
> I will praise you
> because I have been remarkably and wondrously made.
> Your works are wondrous,
> and I know this very well.
> My bones were not hidden from you
> when I was made in secret,
> when I was formed in the depths of the earth.
> Your eyes saw me when I was formless;
> all my days were written in your book and planned
> before a single one of them began.

Not only did God once create an original pair of human beings, and not only does God continue to create human beings; God also personally creates each and every individual.[6] He is intimately

---

6. I am thankful for the small but growing scholarship that addresses a theology of creation and the reality of disabilities. Michael S. Beates, *Disability and the Gospel: How God Uses Our Brokenness to Display His Grace* (Wheaton: Crossway,

engaged in each and every aspect, the minute and large details, of embodied creation, which include the following: (1) a mental component, associated with intellect, cognition, the mind, thinking, memory, and reasoning; (2) an emotional component, associated with feelings, sentiments, the heart, passions, motivations, and affections; (3) a volitional component, associated with the will, judgment, decision-making, purposing, and choosing; (4) a moral component, associated with the conscience, ethical awareness, scruples, a sense of right and wrong, and feelings of guilt/innocence, shame/honor, and fear/power; (5) a physical component, associated with the body, action, agency, and effecting change.

Importantly, these components can't be sequestered into discrete parts of human nature, some pertaining to the soul and others to the body. Rather than thinking in terms of isolation or even of influence, we should think in terms of interconnectivity. All of these aspects are inextricably linked together. For example, grief over the loss of a loved one or trauma due to verbal abuse doesn't only affect one's soul; it's carried physically. These bodily manifestations may not occur for months or years after the grief and trauma, but when they exhibit, they come with a vengeance: insomnia, digestive problems, fidgetiness, lack of mental clarity, proneness to disease, chronic fatigue, migraines, uncontrollable sobbing, and much more.[7] Our

---

2012); Amos Yong, *The Bible, Disability, and the Church: A New Vision of the People of God* (Grand Rapids: Eerdmans, 2011); Deborah Creamer, *Disability and Christian Theology: Embodied Limits and Constructive Possibilities* (New York: Oxford University Press, 2009); Joni Eareckson Tada and Steve Bundy, *Beyond Suffering: A Christian View on Disability Ministry* (Agoura Hills, CA: The Christian Institute on Disability, 2011). I'll have more to say about disabilities in the chapter on suffering.

7. For further discussion of grief and its effects, see Elisabeth Kübler-Ross and David Kessler, *Grief and Grieving: Finding the Meaning of Grief through the Five Stages of Loss* (New York: Scribner, 2005). For further discussion of trauma and its effects, see Bessel van der Kolk, *The Body Keeps the Score: Brain, Mind, and Body in the Healing of Trauma* (New York: Penguin, 2014). My thanks to Gracilynn Hanson and Colleen Ramser for their insights into grief and trauma.

mental, emotional, volitional, moral, and physical components are dependent on one another and together are determinative for human existence, whether for suffering and misery or for flourishing and happiness.

And it is embodied individuals whom God designs and creates.

Theological Reflections

On the basis of these biblical affirmations, an important theological reflection is that embodiment is an essential feature of God's creation of us as human beings. It should be recalled that another realm of created beings is immaterial: angels don't have bodies or any other material element. While they may appear in human form, these temporary manifestations are exceptions to the normal existence of angels as spiritual or immaterial beings.[8] But human beings are material. We are embodied beings by divine design. As whole people, we face this fractured world.

What about the intermediate state, the period of existence between our death and the return of Jesus Christ (with its accompanying event of our bodily resurrection)? In this state, believers are disembodied. True, we are full of joy, worship God as we see him face-to-face, and enjoy rest from our earthly labors and troubles. Still, we exist without our body. It has been sloughed off and laid in a tomb or grave, cremated, buried at sea, or some other means

8. Beyond this created realm is God himself, who is immaterial. Thus, given the reality of the immateriality, or lack of embodiment, of both God and angels, William Alston is correct: what is essential to acting is not bodily movement (God doesn't have a body), only that "an agent with knowledge and purposes wills, or intends, to produce certain effects in the pursuit of those purposes." But in this case, what is true of God and angelic beings is not true of human beings. Bodily movement is indeed essential to human activity. The purposeful effects that human beings will or intend to produce require a body. By God's design, human beings are embodied creatures. William Alston, "How to Think about Divine Action," in Brian Hebblethwaite and Edward Henderson, eds., *Divine Action: Studies Inspired by the Philosophical Theology of Austin Farrar* (Edinburgh: T&T Clark, 1990), 57.

by which it becomes separated from us. Doesn't this disembodied existence contradict the big idea of this chapter that the proper state of human existence is embodiment?

Actually, this temporary disembodiment provides support for our big idea. This condition isn't the way human existence is supposed to be. As he considers the intermediate state and its consequence of disembodiment, Paul shudders in horror: he doesn't want to be "naked" or "unclothed," that is, without his body (2 Cor. 5:1–9). Thus we shouldn't allow this unusual condition to define what we are as human beings. Rather, embodiment is the proper state of human existence. It is so during our earthly existence, and it will be so for eternity following our re-embodiment as we are resurrected at Christ's return. The temporary state of disembodiment does not—cannot—contradict our essential reality as embodied human beings.

A second theological reflection concerns the purpose of this creation of embodied human beings as divine image bearers. It can be summed up in two interrelated aspects, both leading to human flourishing. The first aspect is procreation, underscored by the mandate to "be fruitful and multiply and fill the earth" (Gen. 1:28 ESV). This responsibility means that the majority of people will be married, and that the majority of married couples will have children. That some of us remain single doesn't signify that we somehow miss God's purpose for us, that he's punishing us in any way, or that we cannot be whole people. On the contrary, Paul commends the state of singleness, explaining that it's a divine gift with numerous personal benefits. Single people enjoy freedom to focus on their relationship with God and have opportunity to serve him with undivided attention (1 Cor. 7:25–35). Moreover, some couples experience infertility and are unable to have children. Still others decide not to have children out of concern, for example, that a pregnancy will put the wife at very high risk for serious physical problems or even death. In these cases of childlessness, the couples aren't shirking their divinely given responsibility and

This is good

32

aren't somehow outside God's purpose for them as married image bearers.[9]

The second aspect of human purpose is vocation, highlighted by the mandate to "subdue [the earth] and have dominion" over the rest of the created order (Gen. 1:28). This responsibility means that able-bodied people will work. Rather than a burden to endure or a curse from which to escape by exerting minimal effort, work is a purposeful human activity. It comes with great dignity and produces concrete results: personal fulfillment, creative expression, as well as support for oneself, one's family, one's church, and the poor.

At the heart of human life are procreation and vocation. Importantly, this divinely given purpose—the so-called cultural mandate, or the duty to build human society—is accomplished by, and only by, embodied image bearers.

The particular place that God designed for the beginning of this civilization building was the garden of Eden: "The LORD God took the man and placed him in the garden of Eden to work it and watch over it" (Gen. 2:15). He was joined by Eve, with whom he would begin to expand the human race through procreation and to build human society through vocation. Together they would carry out the task of "Edenizing" the world—enlarging the small space and budding society into all the parts of the world. Genesis 4 presents the beginning of the fulfillment of this mandate: "The man was intimate with his wife Eve, and she conceived and gave birth to Cain. She said, 'I have had a male child with the

9. The church must show compassion to and not marginalize members who are experiencing infertility or, for medical reasons, decide to forego having biological children. The couple's suffering is already great. For example, an infertile wife may view her body as a failure or be angry at her situation. An infertile husband may feel sadness over his brokenness or struggle with contentment. When church members, even with good intentions, pass on trite advice like "Just trust God" or "Just wait and you'll have children someday," they compound the heartache. Rather, church members should join infertile couples in mourning their loss and lamenting before the Lord. My thanks to Lindsay Simpson for her insights into this topic.

Who else shouldn't we marginalize?.

LORD's help.' She also gave birth to his brother Abel. Now Abel became a shepherd of flocks, but Cain worked the ground" (Gen. 4:1–2). Here is both procreation and vocation. And the story continues, with people being engaged in both procreation—"she conceived," "he fathered"—and vocation: shepherding, farming, city building, tending livestock, musical artistry, and tool making (4:17–22). Genesis narrates the initial fulfillment of the original mandate to human beings to "be fruitful and multiply and fill the earth and subdue it and have dominion over" all other earthly creatures.

To contemporize the ongoing fulfillment of this divine mandate, we build civilization through generating (reproducing and raising) about 130 million new human beings worldwide each year and by engaging in politics, education, business, construction, arts, athletics, science and technology, economics, agriculture and food preparation, clothing and fashion, city planning, and much more. As beings created in the image of God, we are designed for procreation and vocation and are given the responsibility to build society for human flourishing.

Again, this divinely given purpose is accomplished by, and only by, embodied image bearers.

In summary, embodiment is the proper state of human existence. God's design for his image bearers is that we are embodied people.

Application

Are you thankful for God's creation of you as an embodied human being?

To press in a bit more, how can you embrace the goodness of your physical nature and distance yourself from wrongful attitudes toward your body?

In what ways have you been troubled by your body?

How do you see yourself when you look in the mirror or when you picture yourself in your own mind?

Have you ever found yourself thinking of your body as inherently evil? Or not as good and valuable as your soul? Or as the ultimate source of sin? Or as necessarily a hindrance to your spiritual and moral development? Or as being outside God's purposes and plans for you? How can this chapter help you to overcome these wrongful attitudes?

As a whole person living in a fractured world, how can you reject the dictates of our culture concerning body image so as not to be conformed to our society's definition, norm, and expectation of your body/embodiment?

When you think about our human responsibility to build society, how does that apply to you particularly as married or single, with children or without, and as working in a job or ministry?

Part of refuting the cultural trend includes embracing your two (intimately connected) identities. The first is your created identity as a divine image bearer. The second is your re-created identity in Christ as an image bearer who is being transformed more and more into his image. How would your struggle with body image be different if you valued these two identities above everything else?

For the Curious

"I am my body." Did you agree or disagree with this opening statement? (Remember, I'm not asking about your agreement or disagreement with the statement "I am *only* my body." That can't be true—so you'd better not agree!—because we exist as disembodied people in the intermediate state. But our focus is on human embodiment, so I frame the statement to highlight being embodied.) I agree with the opening statement, and this chapter provides support for affirming it, or something like it. Put differently as a question: "Am I who I am principally in virtue of the fact that I have the body I have?"[10] I respond positively. Put as another statement: "Without this body I do not exist, and I am myself as my body."[11] I agree. This position contradicts the popular contention that "You don't have a soul. You are a soul. You have a body."[12] This view seems to reflect the influence of Gnostic thought, which privileges the immaterial aspect of human nature—the soul—over the material aspect—the body. Rejecting such influence, I affirm to the contrary, "I am my body."[13]

Still, there is a way to affirm that "I have a body." As Luke Timothy Johnson explains, "Whereas there is some truth to the claim that I *have* a body, since I can in fact dispose of it in a number of ways, there is at least equal truth to the claim that I *am* my body. I cannot completely dispose of my body without at the same time losing myself. In strict empirical terms, when my body disappears, so do I."[14] I would slightly modify Johnson's view by contending that the statement "I *am* my body" is the ground for the statement "I *have* a body."

Let me illustrate Johnson's point. Because I *have* a body, I can sacrifice certain parts of it for the sake of others. For example, I can donate one of my kidneys so that someone whose kidneys are failing may, by organ transplantation, live. But if I sacrifice too much of my body, which I *have*—for example, if I donate both kidneys for the sake of others—then I (and I *am* my body)

10. Justin E. H. Smith, "Introduction," in *Embodiment: A History*, ed. Justin E. H. Smith (Oxford: Oxford University Press, 2017), 2.

11. As expressed by the Russian philosopher Vladimir Iljine. Quoted without bibliographic detail in Elisabeth Moltmann-Wendel, *I Am My Body: A Theology of Embodiment*, trans. John Bowden (New York: Continuum, 1995), 2.

12. This sentiment is often attributed (as I myself have done) to C. S. Lewis, but careful research demonstrates that he isn't responsible for it. Rather, George MacDonald seems to have expressed the basic idea with similar wording in chap. 28 of his *Annals of a Quiet Neighborhood* (London: Hurst and Blackett, 1867).

13. Again, this affirmation isn't a denial of the soul or immaterial part of human nature.

14. Luke Timothy Johnson, *The Revelatory Body: Theology as Inductive Art* (Grand Rapids: Eerdmans, 2015), 80.

no longer exist (that is, I'm dead). Thus "I *am* my body" is the ground for "I *have* a body."[15]

So do you agree or disagree with this statement, and why? "I am my body."

If you agree, an implication to be drawn is to stop viewing your body as an instrument, an object to be used and stewarded. When my wife and I were on the staff of Campus Crusade for Christ (now called Cru), one of our regular topics in discipling Christians was stewardship, which is defined as "the careful and responsible management of something entrusted to one's care."[16] Ideas that were included under this subject were the stewardship of our time (how we work our schedule), the stewardship of our treasures (how we manage our money), the stewardship of our talents (how we invest our abilities and gifts efficiently and fruitfully), and the stewardship of our body. It was this last item that always caught my attention, because it seemed like it belonged in a different category than the other topics. For example, our money and possessions are disconnected from us, but our body isn't outside of us. We have a different relationship to our body than we do to our abilities and gifts. We use our intelligence. We put our skills to work. We lend our insights to counsel others. But, as I propose, we are our body.

Still today I often hear people talk about the stewardship of their body. It appears in statements like, "I need to exercise in

15. For further discussion, see Moltmann-Wendel, *I Am My Body*, 1. She further illustrates this point:

"I've a fever," "my stomach's on strike," "my back's out of action"—that's how we first perceive our illnesses. We keep them from us, see them as an isolated defect which can be remedied in isolation, until one day we have to say, "I'm sick." Then we are saying something that we do not normally say of ourselves: that our destiny is to be bound up with our bodies. In a variety of situations we can distance ourselves from our bodies, but at some point they get hold of us and will not let go. "I am my body." . . . It is not only my body that is sick; I am sick. I am in my body. I have no other identity. (21–22)

16. *Merriam-Webster Dictionary*, s.v. "stewardship," https://www.merriam-webster.com/dictionary/stewardship.

order to keep my body functioning at peak performance" or "I prefer to eat only certain foods in order to fuel my body properly." These expressions, while valid in one sense, can appear to regard our body as a mere instrument to leverage, a machine to tune up, a tool to keep sharp.

But is this the right way to view our body? It is certainly common to do so. But the fact that God designed and created us to be his embodied image bearers weighs against this view. As Frederica Mathewes-Green offers, "The initial impression that we stand critically apart from our bodies was our first mistake. We are not merely passengers riding around in skin tight racecars; we are our bodies. They embody us."[17]

17. Frederica Mathewes-Green, "The Subject Was Noses: What Happens When Academics Discover That We Have Bodies," *Books and Culture* (January/ February 1997): 14–16.

CHAPTER 2

THE GENDERED BODY

Consider

"I'm glad that God created men and women as complementary—similar yet different—kinds of people." Do you agree or disagree with this statement, and why?

Big Idea

An essential given of human existence is maleness or femaleness. God's design for his image bearers is that we are gendered people.

Application Question

Are you thankful for the gender that God created you?

Our Contemporary Language Development

Since the middle of the twentieth century, two words that are important for our discussion here—*sex* and *gender*—have undergone quite a development. Before the 1950s they were interchangeable words. For example, if you filled out a job form or application, either term was fine to use. My sex is male. My gender is male.

Still today, couples expecting a baby may host gender-reveal parties disclosing the biological sex of their fetus: a girl or a boy.

So up until the recent past, sex = gender.[1] Half our population was the male sex, the other half was the female sex. Alternatively, half our population was the male gender, the other half the female gender.

Such language convention has now significantly changed: sex and gender are not synonymous but refer to two different concepts, so that sex ≠ gender.

Sex refers to "the physical, biological, and anatomical dimensions of being male or female (including chromosomes, gonads, sexual anatomy, and secondary sex characteristics)."[2] Sex is the assigned biological label written on one's birth certificate. Genetically, men are composed of XY chromosomes and women of XX chromosomes. For clarity's sake, some people use the expression "biological sex" or "natal male" and "natal female." Sex is a matter of human DNA and anatomy.

Gender, which is now a complex term, can still refer to sex but more commonly refers to gender expression or gender identity. Generally speaking, gender refers to the "psychological, social, and cultural aspects of being male and female."[3] More specifically, *gender expression* is the set of attitudes and behaviors conveyed by people, significantly influenced by their society's expectations for (generally speaking, male and female) persons. Gender stereotypes

1. In this discussion, *sex* refers to being male or female. It doesn't refer to sexual activity, which is the subject of a later discussion.
2. Craig L. Frisby and William T. O'Donohue, eds., *Cultural Competence in Applied Psychology* (New York: Springer, 2018), 578. This notion of sex is at the heart of Todd Wilson's book *Mere Sexuality: Rediscovering the Christian Vision of Sexuality* (Grand Rapids: Zondervan, 2017). He uses the word *sexuality* "to refer to the state or condition of being biologically sexed as either male or female" (33).
3. Mark Yarhouse, *Understanding Gender Dysphoria: Navigating Transgender Issues in a Changing Culture* (Downers Grove, IL: IVP Academic, 2015), 16–17, quoted in Julie Roys, *Redeeming the Feminine Soul: God's Surprising Vision for Womanhood* (Nashville: Thomas Nelson, 2017), 57.

abound and differ from culture to culture. For example, men drive trucks, smoke cigars, and never ask for directions. Women multitask, are highly relational, and express gentle compassion.

Gender identity concerns how people perceive or feel about their sexual identity. The term *cisgender* refers to people whose sex and gender identity match: a biological male identifies as a man, and a natal female identifies as a woman. The term *gender dysphoria* refers to people whose sex and gender identity don't correspond: a person whose sex assigned at birth is male doesn't perceive himself as a man but feels like a woman. A person who is a female according to her birth certificate doesn't perceive herself as a woman but feels like a man. Such gender incongruence may lead to transgenderism, including the use of puberty blockers (in the case of prepubescent children), hormone treatment, and sex-reassignment surgery.

I'll have more to say about this development later in this chapter. For the sake of clarity, I'll use the expression "gendered human beings" or "gendered embodiment," with *gender* being synonymous with *sex* and both terms referring to genetic identity.

We turn first to a discussion of male and female image bearers according to the opening chapters of Genesis.

Biblical Affirmations

As we've already seen, the opening chapter of the Bible presents God's creation of human beings in his image. This narrative of human creation underscores the divine deliberation concerning, and the divine actualization of, image bearers who are either male or female (Gen. 1:26–28).

This point is confirmed in the subsequent narrative of God's creation of the first man and the first woman (Gen. 2:7, 18–25). As for Adam's creation: "Then the LORD God formed the man out of the dust from the ground and breathed the breath of life into his nostrils, and the man became a living being" (Gen. 2:7).

Having constructed Adam's physical framework from the dust of the ground (Martin Luther calls it a "lump of clay"[4]), God breathes into his nostrils the breath of life. Some people understand this action to be the impartation of the soul, the immaterial aspect of human nature. As I prefer, this divine breathing is the conveyance of the spark of life (the energizing principle) that courses through all living beings (Gen. 1:30; 7:22). Adam is an embodied human being made alive by God himself.[5]

This creation of the first man is followed by the formation of the first woman. To achieve the divine design for male image bearers and female image bearers (Gen. 1:27), and to fill the emptiness of Adam, whose aloneness is "not good" (Gen. 2:18), God himself undertakes the completion of human creation. "So the LORD God caused a deep sleep to come over the man, and he slept. God took one of his ribs and closed the flesh at that place. Then the LORD God made the rib he had taken from the man into a woman and brought her to the man" (Gen. 2:21–22). Out of Adam's physicality, God forms Eve as an embodied woman. The originators of the human race, from whom we derive our existence, were designed and created to be embodied beings.

Having created Adam as the first embodied man, God places him in the physical garden of Eden. Next, God forms Eve from Adam's physicality. Thus she becomes the first embodied woman

4. Martin Luther, "Enemies of the Cross of Christ," section 34, *The Sermons of Martin Luther*, vol. 8 (Grand Rapids: Baker, 2000), 302.

5. For further discussion, see Peter Gentry, "Sexuality: On Being Human and Promoting Social Justice," *Christian Psychology* 8, no. 1 (2014): 49–57. In the conclusion of his exegesis of Gen. 2:7, Gentry states, "This basic text is not specifying the soul as an aspect or component of a human being, but denotes the body animated with the life of God as a whole" (p. 50). This position interprets that text as an affirmation that Adam, the man formed by God of the dust of the ground, became a living being when God breathed the breath of life (or animating principle) into his embodied form. God took what he had formed out of dust—the material component or body of Adam—and energized it into a living person through the impartation of the actualizing principle, or breath of life, that which courses through all living beings, not just human beings (Gen. 1:24, 30; 2:19; 6:17; 7:15, 22; Job 27:3; 34:14–15; Eccles. 3:18–21; 12:7; Isa. 42:5).

and joins Adam in the garden. Together and indispensably, they begin to engage in the cultural mandate involving procreation and vocation for human flourishing. They're able and obligated to carry out the mandate to build society because of, and only because of, their complementary genderedness. Adam and Eve are embodied human beings, and as such, they're fundamentally male and female.

This creation of human beings as male or female isn't unique or surprising, for it follows the pattern of binary creation that is narrated in the first two chapters of Genesis:[6]

Nothing and something

Creator and creature

Heaven and earth

Light and darkness

Day and night

Evening and morning

Waters above and waters below

Dry land and waters

Sun and moon

Work and rest

Tree of life and tree of knowledge

Good and evil

Importantly, the creation of human beings as male or female follows this pattern of binary creation: God created humanity as male and female. This common design underscores the fundamental

---

6. While not commonly discussed, this created binarity is the subject of a fascinating children's book: Danielle Hitchen, *Let There Be Light: An Opposites Primer* (Eugene, OR: Harvest House, 2018). A scholarly work that develops the topic is Megan DeFranza, *Sex Difference in Christian Theology: Male, Female, and Intersex in the Image of God* (Grand Rapids: Eerdmans, 2015). As noted below, she takes this created binarity in a different direction than I do.

genderedness of human beings. There is, and there is only, maleness and femaleness. There is no such thing as an agendered—that
is, genderless or androgynous—human being. No dimension other
than maleness and femaleness exists.[7] Moreover, given the divine
assessment of the created order upon its completion—"And God
saw everything that he had made, and behold, it was very good"
(Gen. 1:31 ESV)—gendered embodiment is beautiful and gestures
beyond itself, prompting belief in the goodness of God its Creator.[8]

7. I disagree with DeFranza, who argues that the Gen. 1 account isn't binary in
nature but presents a spectrum. For each created thing there are two terms (e.g.,
night and *day*) representing the two poles or ends of the spectrum. Each spectrum,
then, features many intermediate created realities not mentioned in the text (e.g.,
dusk and dawn in between night and day). Thus human gender/sex includes not
only male and female but also all varieties in between these two poles. DeFranza,
Sex Difference in Christian Theology.
   Important to consider is the language of "separation": (1) "And God *separated*
the light from the darkness" (Gen. 1:4). (2) "And God said, 'Let there be an expanse
in the midst of the waters, and let it *separate* the waters from the waters'" (1:6 ESV).
(3) "And God said, 'Let there be lights in the expanse of the heavens to *separate*
the day from the night . . . to *separate* the light from the darkness'" (1:14, 18 ESV).
   The text also sounds a strong note of distinction of "kinds": (1) "And God
said, 'Let the earth sprout vegetation, plants yielding seed, and fruit trees bearing
fruit in which is their seed, *each according to its kind*, on the earth.' And it was
so. The earth brought forth vegetation, plants yielding seed *according to their
own kinds*, and trees bearing fruit in which is their seed, *each according to its
kind*" (1:11–12 ESV). (2) "So God created the great sea creatures and every living creature that moves, with which the waters swarm, *according to their kinds*,
and every winged bird *according to its kind*" (1:21 ESV). Importantly, the latter
creatures were endowed with the ability and given the responsibility to "be fruitful
and multiply" (1:22), a task that requires the binarity of male and female tuna
and male and female osprey. (3) "And God said, 'Let the earth bring forth living
creatures *according to their kinds*—livestock and creeping things and beasts of
the earth *according to their kinds*.' And it was so. And God made the beasts of
the earth *according to their kinds* and the livestock *according to their kinds*,
and everything that creeps on the ground *according to its kind*" (1:24–25 ESV).
My conclusion is that the language of the creation narrative emphasizes discon-
nection and distinction, not the intermediate notion that figures so strongly in
DeFranza's position.
   8. This thought expands on Lesley-Anne Dyer Williams's critique of Gnosticism: "The Gnostic does not consider that the beautiful nature of a work reflects
the good intention of its maker. The beauty of ensouled and enformed bodies
in the universe is the primary justification that a person might have to believe in
a good creator. For this reason, in stark contrast with the Gnostics, bodies . . .

Theological Reflections

Wonderfully, human beings are male and female embodied beings—gendered—all the way down.[9] Each cell in our body consists of twenty-three pairs of chromosomes. Twenty-two pairs are autosomal chromosomes. They are identical in both men and women. Through patterns of genetic inheritance, different possible combinations produce ranges of traits from blue eyes to brown eyes and dimples to smooth skin. All these traits are inherited in the same manner, regardless of one's sex.

One pair is the sex chromosome. Every cell in a woman's body has an XX sex chromosome. Every cell in a man's body has an XY sex chromosome. Unlike autosomal chromosomes, which combine to produce a range of traits, the sex chromosome determines that a person is either a woman or a man. There are no other combinations.[10] Importantly, recent research has found that sixty-five hundred genes—parts of chromosomes—are expressed differently in men and women, again emphasizing that gendered

---

reveal the good intent of the maker of the universe." Lesley-Anne Dyer Williams, "Beautiful Bodies and Shameful Embodiment in Plotinus's *Enneads*," in *Embodiment: A History*, ed. Justin E. H. Smith (Oxford: Oxford University Press, 2017), 81. In addition to being beautiful, gendered embodiment, specifically gender difference, is pleasant. As Frederica Mathewes-Green offers, "For large segments of the world, gender differences are pleasant, appealing, and enjoyable, and practical application of theory—reproduction itself—is hardly a chore. (The subtitle of a Dave Barry book put it winningly: 'How to make a tiny person in only nine months, with tools you probably have around the home.') Yes, most cultures note and highlight gender differences, because most people find them delightful, as well as useful in producing the next generation." Frederica Mathewes-Green, "The Subject Was Noses: What Happens When Academics Discover That We Have Bodies," *Books and Culture* (January/February 1997): 14–16. Her reference is to Dave Barry, *Babies and Other Hazards of Sex* (New York: Rodale Books, 2000).

9. As Emil Brunner expressed this notion, "We cannot say that humanity is divided into the 'sanguine' and the 'choleric' temperament, into extraverts and introverts, into white or coloured races, into geniuses and non-geniuses, but humanity certainly is divided into men and women, and this distinction goes down to the very roots of our personal existence, and penetrates into the deepest 'metaphysical' grounds of our personality and our destiny." Emil Brunner, *Man in Revolt: A Christian Anthropology*, trans. Olive Wyon (London: Lutterworth, 1939), 345.

10. We will discuss the genetic phenomenon of intersex later in this chapter.

embodiment is crucial to the identity of human beings as men and women.[11] This means that human rationality, cognitive abilities, emotional make-up, volitional faculties, motivations, and purposing are gender-determined and expressed. Gender is the most fundamental given of human embodied existence.

This point means that I experience myself as an embodied man, I relate to others as an embodied man, and as an embodied man I relate to God. Similarly, my wife, Nora, experiences herself as an embodied woman, she relates to others as an embodied woman, and as an embodied woman she relates to God. Try as I might, I can't experience life from my wife's perspective, from a female point of view, and vice versa. We are perspectively gendered embodied human beings.[12] We view and experience all life through male or female eyes.[13]

While this perspective may sound like gender essentialism—that men and women are of distinctly different natures—it's not, or it's

11. That is 6,500 out of approximately 20,000 genes. The differences appear mostly in sexual organs, particularly the mammary glands, but also include the adipose (fat), skeletal, muscle, skin, and heart tissues. Medically, these differences express themselves in male-prevalent and female-prevalent diseases (e.g., the prevalence of Parkinson's disease in men) and male-prevalent and female-prevalent reactions to certain drugs. Moran Gershoni and Shmuel Pietrokovski, "The Landscape of Sex-Differential Transcriptome and Its Consequent Selection in Human Adults," *BMC Biology* 15 (2017): 7.

12. Smith raises the issue of "the extent to which subjectivity is determined by embodiment—that is, the extent to which one's own subjective experience of the world is forged or inflected by the particular sort of body one has." Smith, "Introduction," *Embodiment: A History*, 5. The big idea of this chapter proposes that human sex/gender maps completely onto human embodiment; thus a woman's subjectivity—her subjective experience of the world—is completely forged or inflected by the female body she has. The same is true for a man's subjectivity.

13. See an illustration of this point as it pertains to female epistemological development: Jennifer Kintner, "Assessing Epistemological Development among Women in Evangelical Seminaries" (EdD diss., The Southern Baptist Theological Seminary, 2018). Another way to know this gendered perspectivism is by simple observation: men and women offer different perspectives and, as we will see shortly, express common human capacities and properties in a different manner. It is seen in popular books such as John Gray, *Men Are from Mars, Women Are from Venus: The Classical Guide to Understanding the Opposite Sex* (New York: HarperCollins, 1992).

certainly a significantly modified notion.[14] Rather, my view maintains that there are no particular capacities and properties (obviously, outside of reproductive capabilities) that belong exclusively to women or that belong exclusively to men. There are, instead, common human capacities and properties that are—indeed, given gendered embodiment, will naturally be—expressed by women in ways that are fitting to women and expressed by men in ways that are fitting to men. Men and women uniquely express common human traits as men and as women.[15] Thus while my view affirms that gender is essential for human embodiment, it diverges from the common idea of gender essentialism.

To illustrate this view, capacities such as reasoning, emotion, will, and purposing aren't gender-specific but are common human capacities that are and will inherently be expressed by women and men in ways that reflect their femaleness and maleness.[16] To further illustrate, properties such as gentleness, courage, initiative, nurturing, patience, and protectiveness aren't gender-specific but are common human properties—some would be Christian

---

14. My thanks to Gracilynn Hanson for helping me to clarify this point. While some studies show a correlation between gender essentialism and gender inequality/discrimination, the view affirmed here repudiates any and all bias and mistreatment of men and women that is supported by gender essentialism. Lea Skewes, "Beyond Mars and Venus: The Role of Gender Essentialism in Support for Gender Inequality and Backlash," *PLoS One* 13, no. 7 (2018): e0200921. Available at https://www.ncbi.nlm.nih.gov/pmc/articles/PMC6057632/.

15. My thanks to Luke Allison for helping me with this section.

16. According to a study published in the *Journal of Clinical and Diagnostic Research*, "Mental skills or cognitive abilities include attributes like perception, attention, memory (short-term or working and long-term), motor, language, visual and spatial processing, and executive functions. These cognitive attributes are different in males and females. Generally, females show advantages in verbal fluency, perceptual speed, accuracy and fine motor skills, while males outperform females in spatial, working memory and mathematical abilities." The conclusion to be drawn is that capacities such as mental skills and cognitive abilities are common human capacities that are and will naturally be expressed in gender-specific ways. Namrata Upadhayay and Sanjeev Guragain, "Comparison of Cognitive Functions between Male and Female Medical Students: A Pilot Study," *JCDR* 8, no. 6 (June 20, 2014), BC12–15. Available at https://www.ncbi.nlm.nih.gov/pmc/articles/PMC4129348/.

virtues, some would be the fruit of the Holy Spirit—that are and will innately be expressed by women and men in ways that reflect their femaleness and maleness.

As an application, when we consider the common human property of self-sacrifice, we shouldn't think primarily of husbands in relation to their wives. In this case, self-sacrifice in loving their wives is a biblical injunction associated with a marital role. Nor should we think primarily in terms of wives in relation to their husbands. In this case, self-sacrifice in submitting to their husbands is a biblical injunction associated with a marital role. Rather, we should think in terms of siblings in Christ, all of whom are called to self-sacrifice on behalf of their brothers and sisters as a shared human quality (1 John 3:16).[17]

Two examples suffice. Though Steve is given the opportunity to pursue his ten-year dream of becoming a missionary to Serbia, he foregoes the chance in order to finish discipling a group of university students who have another year before they graduate. Though misunderstood and criticized by her friends for intervening, Briana speaks up to condemn the bullying of her lesbian and homosexual coworkers in her office. Both express the common human property of self-sacrifice, but Steve does so as a man and Briana does so as a woman.

Accordingly, people mistakenly speak of the masculine attributes of God and the feminine attributes of God. (We will avoid getting sidetracked by the fact that God is agendered. He can't be male or female, because gender maps onto embodiment, and God isn't embodied.)[18] Taking it a step further, people mistakenly speak of the masculine and feminine attributes of Jesus. Some examples of his so-called feminine side are Jesus's washing the

17. My appreciation to Gracilynn Hanson for underscoring the presence of mutual self-sacrifice in marital roles.
18. Furthermore, to affirm that God is gendered contradicts the doctrine of the simplicity of God. Being simple rather than complex, the divine nature cannot be divided into masculine and feminine characteristics.

disciples' feet, healing the sick, showing compassion to the Syrophoenician woman, weeping over dead Lazarus, and gently treating children. But servanthood, a healing touch, compassion, lamentation, and gentleness aren't properties that pertain exclusively to women or to men. Rather, they concern all human beings.[19]

To repeat: there are no particular capacities and properties that belong exclusively to women or exclusively to men. There are, instead, common human capacities and common human properties that are—indeed, will naturally be—expressed in gendered ways.

Please note that I've said nothing about roles and authority. There are hundreds of books and thousands of articles about the roles of men and women, but this perspective emphasizes the essence of human gender, not gender roles and authority structures. It's certainly possible to embrace this perspective about gender and still affirm a difference in roles and authority structures for men and women in the home and in the church—indeed, even affirm a traditional view of role differences.[20]

Additionally, the fact that we are gendered in the totality of our perspectives is a key reason we desperately need each other. Men need women and women need men, and not just in terms of marriage, to be transported beyond our own limited viewpoint so as to experience life in a multifaceted way. Moreover, creation as male image bearers and female image bearers is indispensable for us to carry out our divinely given mandate to build society. And this necessity isn't just for procreation but also for vocation,

---

19. For further discussion, see Marc Cortez, *ReSourcing Theological Anthropology* (Grand Rapids: Zondervan, 2017), 203.

20. Without getting into the discussion of egalitarianism and complementarianism (and its spectrum of applications), the latter (traditional) position minimally holds that (1) one aspect of the relationship between husbands and wives is that of authority and submission, and (2) the office of pastor/elder/bishop/priest is reserved for qualified men and not open to women.

which requires both men and women to work and contribute to human flourishing.

In summary, an essential given of human existence is maleness or femaleness. God's design for his image bearers is that we are gendered people.

Application

Are you thankful for the gender that God created you? Why or why not?

To press in a bit more, is there anything holding you back from fully embracing your maleness or femaleness? What are some proper ways to respond to your own genderedness? What are some improper responses?

Do you agree or disagree with my proposal that we all share common human capacities and common human properties? Do you agree or disagree that we naturally express them as either a man or a woman in accordance with whether we're a man or a woman?

In regard to others: as all human beings are created in God's image, and as all human beings are created as either male image bearers or female image bearers, how do we live out our relationships with those of the complementary gender? With those of the same gender?

For the Curious

If this perspective on embodied genderedness is correct—that is, well-grounded in Scripture and sound theologically—then it has important implications. We will focus on its applications for the looming and disconcerting contemporary movement that detaches maleness and femaleness from biological sex (XY and XX, or the sex that is assigned at birth). In place of the givenness of sex, now there is genderedness, one's self-identification as either male or female, regardless of one's genetic identity.[21]

The disconnect between sex and gender results in *gender dysphoria* or, in current terminology, *gender incongruence* (I will use both terms). In terms of definition, it is "the tension a person feels when their gender experience/identity does not correspond to their biological sex."[22] In more detail, "Gender dysphoria involves a conflict between a person's physical or assigned gender and the gender with which he/she/they identify. People with gender dysphoria may be very uncomfortable with the gender they were assigned, sometimes described as being uncomfortable with their body (particularly developments during puberty) or being uncomfortable with the expected roles of their assigned gender."[23]

Such tension may express itself in various ways, from cross-dressing to sex-reassignment surgery. This surgery is the hormonal and surgical transformation of a biological woman into a man (e.g., Charity Bono, daughter of Sonny and Cher, who became Chaz Bono) or of a biological man into a woman (e.g., Olympic decathlon champion Bruce Jenner, who became Caitlyn Jenner).

At the heart of gender incongruence leading to transgenderism is a denial of the big idea of chapter 1: "I am my body." As an example, actor Jessica Savano transitioned from being a man to being a woman. His failed Kickstarter campaign sought financial backing for a documentary titled "I Am Not My Body." Clearly, Savano's motto contradicts that big idea and is rooted in the detachment of maleness and femaleness from biological sex.

21. Though I won't do it now, I could use this biblical-theological perspective to address unigenderism and all other forms of nonbinary genderedness.
22. Scott B. Rae, *Moral Choices: An Introduction to Ethics*, 4th ed. (Grand Rapids: Zondervan, 2018), 337.
23. "Help with Gender Dysphoria," American Psychiatric Association, https://www.psychiatry.org/patients-families/gender-dysphoria.

Gender dysphoria rejects basic genetic facts. And by its neglect or rejection of embodiment, living as whole people in a fractured world becomes a significant challenge.

Gender incongruence must be clearly distinguished from an unusual physical condition that actually *is* a matter of genetics. In rare cases, "a child is born with an ambiguous gender, and it is not clear whether the child is male or female. One form of this is known as intersex. Ambiguous gender results from a genetic abnormality, and normally the parents select a gender at birth, which then requires corrective surgery and hormone replacement therapy."[24] Whereas intersex is a physical matter, gender dysphoria and transgenderism is a matter of perception or feeling.

Some gender incongruence is typical of adolescents. Typically (and there are many exceptions) gender confusion is experienced by teenage girls who are socially awkward, outliers in their schools, often anxious and depressed, and starved for acceptance and relationships. Once they come out as trans, they experience much adulation, encouragement, and recognition (especially on social media).[25] With the help and guidance of a loving community of family, friends, teachers, and church, the vast majority of adolescents will grow out of those feelings. For example, according to the American Psychiatric Association's *Diagnostic and Statistical Manual of Mental Disorders* (DSM-5), among gender-confused adolescents, 98 percent of boys and 88 percent of girls accept their biological sex after puberty.[26]

---

24. Rae, *Moral Choices*, 339.

25. At the same time, the suicide rate of trans youth is appallingly high. The American Academy of Pediatrics lists the rate among female-to-male adolescents to be 50 percent, among male-to-female adolescents to be 30 percent, and among nonbinary adolescents to be 42 percent. Russell B. Toomey, Amy K. Syvertsen, and Maura Shramko, "Transgender Adolescent Suicide Behavior," *Pediatrics: The Journal of the American Academy of Pediatrics* (October 2018), https://pediatrics.aappublications.org/content/142/4/e20174218.

26. American Psychiatric Association, *Diagnostic and Statistical Manual of Mental Disorders*, 5th ed. (Arlington, VA: American Psychiatric Association, 2013), 451–59. Page 455 addresses the rates of persistence of gender dysphoria. For further

In many cases, "the experience of gender dysphoria is real, and the pain and distress it causes should not be underestimated."[27] Specifically, "People with gender dysphoria may often experience significant distress and/or problems functioning associated with this conflict between the way they feel and think of themselves (referred to as experienced or expressed gender) and their physical or assigned gender."[28] A diversity of opinions exists for managing such tension. What follows is some practical counsel for addressing gender incongruence and transgenderism.[29]

Based on the presentation in this chapter, the theological grounding for handling gender confusion and transgenderism must be the fundamental givenness of God's design for the sex with which he created his image bearers. Still, living with the incongruity between biological sex and gender identity requires care, self-control, and relentless struggle on the part of those who experience gender dysphoria. Such personal action is to be matched by love, kindheartedness, and persevering companionship on the part of those in relationship with them. In particular, the church's marginalization of people experiencing gender dysphoria needs transformation into Jesus-like compassion.

The church's compassionate, firm, and theologically grounded voice is needed to contrast with the pro-transgenderism voices that exert pressure to conform to this trend. In addition to the church's expression of concern, other voices—for example, some

discussion, see Paul Rhodes Eddy, "Reflections on the Debate concerning the Desistance Rate among Young People with Gender Dysphoria," Center for Faith, Sexuality and Gender (April 2020), https://centerforfaith.com/sites/default/files /eddy_on_the_desistance_rate_of_gender_dysphoric_youth_2.pdf.

27. Rae, *Moral Choices*, 339.

28. American Psychiatric Association, "Help with Gender Dysphoria."

29. For further discussion, see Nancy Pearcey, *Love Thy Body: Answering Hard Questions about Life and Sexuality* (Grand Rapids: Baker, 2018), chap. 6; and Andrew T. Walker, *God and the Transgender Debate* (Charlotte, NC: Good Book Company, 2018).

feminists—sound warnings about transgenderism.[30] An example is Kellie-Jay Keen-Minshull, who believes that transgenderism threatens feminism.[31] Her warning can be expanded to illustrate the risks that transgenderism causes women when transgendered men insist on competing in women's sports and on using women's bathrooms, locker rooms, showers, and changing rooms in clothing stores. In the first case, transgendered men, with their masculine physicality, gain a significant advantage over their women competitors. The other scenarios put women's privacy at risk and increase the likelihood of physical abuse.[32]

Practically speaking, the church should avoid the following unhelpful steps in coming alongside people who wrestle with gender incongruence and transgenderism. We shouldn't stereotype masculinity and femininity according to fundamentalist Christian cultural norms or so-called Christian patriarchy. "It is precisely those rigid stereotypes that drive gender nonconforming young people into the arms of the transgender . . . communities in their search for a sense of belonging and acceptance."[33] For example,

30. One such group is labeled "transgender exclusionary radical feminists" (TERFs) and it claims that transgendered women aren't truly women. Often used pejoratively, this label is an attempt by transgender proponents, including other feminists, to silence TERFs, the most famous of whom is J. K. Rowling. Bringing attention to TERFs and their rejection of transgenderism doesn't constitute an endorsement of any hate and ostracism that the group may express toward transgendered women. For a story about Rowling, see Dawn Ennis, "J.K. Rowling Comes Out as a TERF," *Forbes*, December 19, 2019, https://www.forbes.com/sites/dawnstaceyennis/2019/12/19/jk-rowling-comes-out-as-a-terf/#583182c5d70e.

31. "Feminist Blogger Believes Trans-Women Aren't Real Women," *This Morning*, September 28, 2018, https://www.youtube.com/watch?v=fDSOP_j7HZE.

32. The increasing danger of this trend can be seen in the case of transgendered men who, being confined to prison after committing a crime, rape women inmates. For example, see David Emery, "Did a Male Rapist Who Identifies as Female Transfer to a Women's Jail and Assault Female Inmates?," Snopes, November 30, 2018, https://www.snopes.com/fact-check/male-rapist-transfer-womens-jail/; Zachary Evans, "Female Inmate Claims She Was Raped by Transgender Inmate Who Was Placed in Illinois Women's Prison," *National Review*, February 21, 2020, https://www.nationalreview.com/news/female-inmate-claims-she-was-raped-by-transgender-inmate-who-was-placed-in-illinois-womens-prison/.

33. Pearcey, *Love Thy Body*, 218.

we need to stop viewing men as "feminine" when they act in common human ways like crying or being hygienic, or viewing women as "masculine" when they express common human traits such as ambition or courage. We dare not accuse men and women of "acting against their gender" when they act humanly.[34]

The church shouldn't support people's request for hormone treatment and sex-reassignment surgery. Tragically, such procedures permanently mar the body of trans people, rendering them sterile. Additionally, these surgeries don't ultimately resolve the problem. First, "Transgendered men do not become women, nor do transgendered women become men. All (including Bruce Jenner) become feminized men or masculinized women, counterfeits or impersonators of the sex with which they 'identify.' In that lies their problematic future."[35] Second, "It is a little reported fact that people who undergo sex re-assignment surgery do not, statistically, report higher levels of happiness after the surgery."[36] Moreover, this radical step will come back to haunt them and others when their level of exhaustion from living as trans people reaches the

34. My thanks to Morgan DeLisle for these illustrations.

35. Paul McHugh, "Transgenderism: A Pathogenic Meme," *The Public Discourse*, June 10, 2015, https://www.thepublicdiscourse.com/2015/06/15145/. "Furthermore, it's incredibly controversial whether cosmetic changes actually give one the biological substrate that one desires, especially since gender reassignment surgery does nothing to alter the DNA and/or chromosomal structure of a human person. . . . Furthermore, it's objectionable that simply acting like a stereotypical woman and surgically changing one's body would be sufficient to make anyone a woman." Benjamin H. Arbour and John R. Gilhooly, "Transgenderism, Human Ontology, and the Metaphysics of Properties," Evangelical Philosophical Society Article Library, https://www.epsociety.org/userfiles/Arbour%20and%20Gilhooly_Transgenderism%20(Final2019-1).pdf, 20–21.

36. Walker, *God and the Transgender Debate*, 67. He references Paul McHugh, "Transgender Surgery Isn't the Solution," *Wall Street Journal*, May 13, 2016, https://www.wsj.com/articles/paul-mchugh-transgender-surgery-isnt-the-solution-1402615120. Other studies come to the opposite conclusion that the quality of life of people who undergo male-to-female sex-reassignment surgery improves. Géraldine Weinforth, Richard Fakin, Pietro Giovanoli, and David Garcia Nuñez, "Quality of Life Following Male-to-Female Sex Reassignment Surgery," *Deutsches Ärzteblatt International* 116, no. 15 (April 12, 2019): 253–60.

breaking point. When they give up and "desist" or "detransgen-der" (transition back to their original sex), they will wreak havoc upon parents, doctors, psychologists, and churches who were com-plicit in their now-denounced transgender experiment.[37]

Finally, the church shouldn't place trans people in the category of unredeemable sinners and treat them as being an evil influence on church members. The gospel changes everything—including gender dysphoria and transgenderism. To categorize trans people and those suffering from gender incongruence in this dismissive way may lead to horrible consequences for them. On the contrary, "To see the full dignity of a transgendered person means to abhor or reject any mocking humor that would demean them. It means to stand up and defend them against bullies or abuse."[38]

In terms of some helpful steps to take: "Christians ought to weep for people so confused about their identity—people who . . . think their body is just a piece of matter that gives no clues about who they are as persons; who think their identity as male or female has no special dignity or meaning; who view their body negatively as a limitation on their authentic identity. By contrast, . . . Christianity gives the basis for a high and humane view of the person as an integrated whole."[39] Compassion for their dilemma is appropriate. They are real people and fellow image bearers who suffer real pain, and they are going to destroy their lives.[40] In our expression of compassion, we imitate Jesus Christ, who embodied what was prophesied of himself as the Suffering Servant: "He will

37. This warning doesn't begin to address the rightness or wrongness of trans-gendered people detransgendering to their original gender.
38. Walker, *God and the Transgender Debate*, 96.
39. Pearcey, *Love Thy Body*, 204.
40. Pearcey, *Love Thy Body*, 207. This statement reflects a biblical-theological perspective and is aware that some transgendered people sense that their lives are better after hormone replacement therapy and sex-reassignment surgery. For further discussion, see Justin Sabia-Tanis, "Holy Creation, Wholly Creative: God's Intention for Gender Diversity," in *Understanding Transgender Identities: Four Views*, ed. James K. Beilby and Paul Rhodes Eddy (Grand Rapids: Baker Academic, 2019), 195–222.

not break a bruised reed, and he will not put out a smoldering wick, until he has led justice to victory" (Matt. 12:20). "Jesus will not let fragile people crumble or collapse beneath the weight of their struggle."[41] And neither should we.

The church should embrace a spectrum of masculinity and femininity to prevent men and women who don't fit the traditional notions from feeling as though they must be the wrong sex and thus seek transgenderism as the solution to their feelings.[42] For example, certain mathematical skills are more commonly associated with men, but that doesn't mean that women who possess those skills to a high degree are "males," are "like men," or are "less feminine." In those skilled areas, they have a mathematical inclination and aptitude that, while more prominent among men, is found in a lower percentage of women. If you've seen the movie *Hidden Figures*, we are all indebted to those women who did the calculations (using slide rules!) and invented math equations that put the first man on the moon. And they weren't "acting like men"! On the contrary, they were acting as gifted, intelligent women.[43]

The church should work with people who are wrestling with their gender identity and are considering transitioning and help them to accept themselves as what they are—boys/men or girls/women—with their identity corresponding to their body.[44] We can

41. Walker, *God and the Transgender Debate*, 13–14.
42. For further discussion of the distribution of sex-related personality and behavioral differences, see William J. Malone, Colin M. Wright, and Julia D. Robertson, "No One Is Born in the 'Wrong Body,'" *Quillette*, September 24, 2019, https://quillette.com/2019/09/24/no-one-is-born-in-the-wrong-body/.
43. Affirming a spectrum of masculinity and femininity doesn't endorse being naïve or promote unigenderism or deny that there are expressions of one's sex that are outside the spectrum. While the church needs to avoid stereotyping men and women according to restrictive, fundamentalist standards, it can discern wisely when gender expression is beyond the bounds.
44. Discussions of authenticity (not in a philosophical sense but in a common-sense approach) can become very divisive. For example, an adolescent girl claims that she is being authentic to her true self by transitioning to a boy, and others hotly dispute her claim. Still, the category of authenticity shouldn't easily be abandoned. The biblical emphasis on human beings as male embodied image

remind them that "the entire range of human personality traits is open to both sexes—[thus] it is okay to be different from prevailing social norms." And we can "encourage them to value their unique temperament and to resist pressure to interpret it as evidence they must be transgender."[45] By so doing, we aim at helping them to live as whole people in a fractured world.

Finally, the church should be prepared to care for and support trans people, even long-term. This view may entail us coming to grips with the possibility that they may never be completely restored to wholeness in this lifetime. "Also it should not be assumed that greater Christlikeness is the same as having experiences of gender dysphoria abate. Rather, many people who know and love Christ have besetting conditions that have simply not resolved as a result of their belief in Christ as their Savior. It may very well be that it is in the context of these enduring conditions that God brings about greater Christlikeness."[46] In that case, because of their suffering and post-traumatic growth, they may become compassionate and capable ministers of the gospel to other trans people.[47]

---

bearers and female embodied image bearers provides a foundation for calling people to authenticity based on God's design for them. My thanks to Rachel Bell Hamm for her thoughts on acceptance of one's authentic self, which is the person whom God made.

45. Pearcey, Love Thy Body, 217, 224.
46. Yarhouse, Understanding Gender Dysphoria, 148.
47. Pearcey, Love Thy Body, 226–27.

CHAPTER 3

THE PARTICULAR BODY

Consider

Respond to this question: Who are you as a particular individual created by God?

Big Idea

An essential given of human existence is particularity, which is defined as the condition of being an individual. God specifically designs and creates each human being to be a particular gendered embodied individual.

Application

Map out who you are as a particular person created by God.

Our Contemporary Context and Problems with Individuality

We face three problems with our individuality. The first is being lost as a particular person. Given the statistic that the world's population is about eight billion, some of us feel lost among that inconceivable number of others. What am I amid that teeming horde of people? What significance could I possibly have? If I didn't exist, what difference would it make? It seems that our particularity is lost in the immense crowd.

A second problem is overestimating our individuality. Call it pride or conceit. Identify it as a sense of superiority or an inflated self-esteem. Blame it on narcissism or being spoiled or not being held accountable. In any case, some of us go around with an exaggerated sense of self. I'm special, and the other eight billion people either know it or need to know it. And I go out of my way to emphasize my particularity by standing out in terms of my hair color and style, tattoos and piercings, empire building (huge corporations or megachurches), gender conformity or nonconformity, mansions and luxury cars, sexual preferences (straight, gay, bi, fluid), surgical alteration ("fixing" one's nose), personal entourage of "yes" servants, tanning or lightening my skin, philanthropic works, and more.[1]

A third problem is intersectionality.[2] Some people divide the world into haves and have-nots. Those in the former category are people of privilege, and those in the latter category are marginalized. Examples of the first category of individuals are wealthy, straight, educated, English-speaking, native-born, white, Christian males. Examples of the second are poor, lesbian (or transgendered), uneducated, non-English-speaking, born elsewhere, Muslim women of color.[3]

1. In most of these cases, there is nothing inherently wrong with the pursuit or the expression. My concern is to point out that people infected with hyperindividuality may seek to stand out by these means.
2. The origin of intersectionality is commonly traced to Kimberle Crenshaw, "Demarginalizing the Intersection of Race and Sex: A Black Feminist Critique of Antidiscrimination Doctrine, Feminist Theory and Antiracist Politics," *University of Chicago Legal Forum*, vol. 1989, issue 1, article 8.
3. Descriptors are pulled from the intersectionality score calculator, https://intersectionalityscore.com/recent. It should be noted that intersectional identities are a mixture of ontological elements (e.g., biological man or woman), ethnic elements (e.g., Cuban- or British-born), economic elements (e.g., wealthy

According to intersectionality, people exist along a spectrum of identities. Those with more prized characteristics (the first category) are individuals possessing power and prestige. They snub and sideline the others, or they simply live in such a way that they are blind to the many privileges they enjoy. Those with more disfavored characteristics (the second category) lack access to power; they are disenfranchised by the others and should claim their right to protest against their oppressors. Key to intersectionality is its emphasis on differences among individuals rather than commonalities shared by them.[4]

In this chapter, our emphasis on particularity is intended to help those who feel lost as individuals, as well as to remind those with an exaggerated sense of self, that all they are and have comes from God their creator. The goal is to enable people to live as whole people in a fractured world. Additionally, though the ideas presented here bear some resemblance to discussions of intersectionality, they address human embodiment in a different way.

Particularity and Its Particularities

By *particularity* I mean that each person is an individual. God explicitly designs and creates each human being to be a particular gendered embodied individual. Specifically, each person is a particularity in terms of their ethnicity/race, family/kinship, temporality,

---

or impoverished), and social elements (e.g., urban dweller or rural resident). Accordingly, people are *born* with some identities (as the intersectionality calculator notes), while other identities are due to *being born* into a particular social system. My thanks to Chad Gahafer for his insights into these points.

4. A positive impulse that may arise from intersectionality is the championing of access to equal opportunities and wellness for all human beings. Biblically speaking, creation in the image of God signifies that all people—whatever their intersectionality score—should be accorded respect and treated with dignity. My thanks to Morgan DeLisle for her help with this point.

spatiality, context, and story.[5] Each of these six particularities will be briefly defined and illustrated (when appropriate).

(1) *Ethnicity/race*. Each gendered embodied individual is characterized by a particular ethnicity or race.[6] The distinction between these two terms is notoriously difficult to settle.[7] For simplicity's sake, this property isn't a matter of self-identification—for example, whether one considers oneself to be Black or African American. Rather, ethnicity is a matter of one's origin,[8] specifically one's shared language(s), customs, religion(s), and nationality. I am, for example, a Caucasian male of Scottish/Irish ancestry.

(2) *Family/kinship*. Each gendered embodied individual is characterized by a particular family background and by particular kinship ties. The first property concerns one's family of origin or, in the case of adoption/fostering, one's family/families of nurture. It also includes one's birth order, birthplace, siblings, and intact parental unit or parental divorce (with or without remarriage and blended family). Kinship concerns, in the case of adults, either singleness (including widowhood) or marriage (in most cases with biological and/or adopted children), and perhaps includes the responsibility of caring for aging parents. For example, I was born in Chicago, am the firstborn son of Roy and Winifred Allison (both

5. As Justin Smith notes, "Embodiment is the product of a mostly local, particular history." Justin E. H. Smith, "Introduction," *Embodiment: A History*, ed. Justin E. H. Smith (Oxford: Oxford University Press, 2017), 7.

6. I affirm that ethnicity/race is a second order characteristic, with embodied genderedness being the primary order characteristic. Sex/gender is more fundamental than race/ethnicity. Genesis 1 narrates the creation of human beings as divine image bearers who are fundamentally either male or female. The development of distinct ethno-linguistic groups or nations is narrated later in Genesis. The conclusion I draw, then, is that gender is primary and ethnicity is secondary. Still, both are by divine design. As God creates human beings as male and female, he creates human beings as diverse ethnicities (Acts 17:26–27).

7. In the United States, "race" often has reference to an appearance-based grouping. This is due in large measure to our shameful history of discrimination based on appearance. My thanks to Laura Wierenga for her insights into this topic.

8. This point doesn't dispute self-identification. The US Census Bureau defines "race" in those terms.

of whom are deceased), and have one younger brother. And I am married to Nora, with whom I have three adult children and ten grandchildren.

(3) *Temporality.* Each gendered embodied individual is characterized by a particular time and age. This property has to do with both mathematical time and subjective time, along with birth date and perceived age. Mathematical time is the same for all people. For example, as I write this sentence the clock informs me that it is 5:12 p.m. Eastern Standard Time. This corresponds to 11:12 p.m. Greenwich Mean Time (too late for me to call my five grandchildren in France) and 2:12 p.m. Pacific Standard Time (too early for me to Skype with my four grandchildren in school in Washington State). Subjective time (time as one perceives it) varies among people. For example, time passes by more quickly for me as a sixty-seven-year-old than it does for my thirty-one-year-old son, Luke. Moreover, being born in 1954, I am part of the aging baby-boomer crowd that is characterized by the impact of certain key historical events (e.g., the Cold War and the threat of nuclear destruction; the civil rights movement), the ever-quickening advancement of technology (e.g., cell phones, Alexa) and medical technology (e.g., CT scans, MRIs, organ transplantation), and the seemingly unstoppable movement toward retirement. Yet one's perceived age may differ, even significantly, from one's chronological age. For example, I consider myself to be a "young" sixty-seven.[9]

(4) *Spatiality.* Each gendered embodied individual is characterized by a particular space and place. The body is "the place in which we are in the world. Existence is always 'being a body in the world.'"[10] To be embodied is to be emplaced, located according to several

9. Context exerts an influence on subjective age. Erica L. O'Brien et al., "Context Influences on the Subjective Experience of Aging: The Impact of Culture and Domains of Functioning," *The Gerontologist* 57, no. S2 (August 2017): S127–37. Available at https://academic.oup.com/gerontologist/article/57/suppl_2/S127/3913328.

10. Elisabeth Moltmann-Wendel, *I Am My Body: A Theology of Embodiment*, trans. John Bowden (New York: Continuum, 1995), 99. Her citation is

axes.[11] Being born in the city of Chicago, I am a Midwesterner by upbringing and thus characterized by common Midwestern traits such as friendliness, hard work, and aversion to change. For the past twenty-seven years I've taught in educational institutions. My profession challenges me in the areas of communication and listening skills, knowledge acquisition, and preparedness. Being a Northern evangelical at a Southern Baptist seminary situates me in a particular culture that is quite foreign to my spatiality prior to 2003, the year I joined the faculty.[12] In one sense then, I am a product of my environment—that is true in general, and it's also true with particular reference to how my workplace has shaped me.[13]

⑤ *Context.* Each gendered embodied individual is characterized by a particular context. "Context" is defined as the interrelated conditions or settings in which human beings live, act, and understand their experiences. Any human context includes socioeconomic, political, educational, cultural, and religious factors. The socioeconomic category crosses the spectrum from the generational poor to the ruling rich. The political category in the United

---

from F. J. J. Buytendijk, *Woman: A Contemporary View* (Glen Rock, NJ: Newman Press, 1968).

11. For an excellent theology of human emplacement, see Craig G. Bartholomew, *Where Mortals Dwell: A Christian View of Place for Today* (Grand Rapids: Baker Academic, 2011).

12. The relevancy of the following affirmation for me has become clearer through the past seventeen years: "We move through places every day that would never have been if not for those who came before us. Our workplaces, where we spend so much time—we often think they began with our arrival. That's not true." As spoken by Ruby to Eddie, in Mitch Albom, *The Five People You Meet in Heaven* (Westport, CT: Hyperion, 2003), 123.

13. The debate between nature and nurture continues almost unabated. Are human beings basically determined by their genetic makeup, the culture and environment in which they were raised and in which they now live, or a combination of the two factors? "The field of epigenetics is quickly growing and with it the understanding that both the environment and individual lifestyle can also directly interact with the genome to influence epigenetic change. These changes may be reflected at various stages throughout a person's life and even in later generations." "Epigenetics: Fundamentals," What Is Epigenetics?, https://www.whatisepigenetics.com/fundamentals/.

States encompasses the two major parties as well as a wide range of political ideologies, such as communism, socialism, and libertarianism. The educational category focuses on attainment of knowledge and skills. It runs the gamut from illiteracy to the doctor of philosophy and encompasses different educational approaches (e.g., Montessori and Waldorf). The vast category of culture encompasses food, clothing, the arts, entertainment, communication, traditions, transportation, leisure, environment, and health. The category of religion includes not only the major faith traditions like Roman Catholicism, Eastern Orthodoxy, Protestantism, Islam, and Buddhism, but also various spiritualities (e.g., nature worship, meditation) and nonreligious persuasions (e.g., secularism, agnosticism, atheism). This multifaceted context exerts numerous and strongly felt influences on how human beings communicate using language and gestures; how they reason and express emotions; how they assess actions with respect to morality, amorality, and immorality; how they engage in personal behaviors and social events; and much more.

Story. Each gendered embodied individual is characterized by a particular story. This property is concerned with "the storied nature of human conduct."[14] Narratives identify us, and we communicate with others through the narratives we tell. We know, experience, process, remember, relate, feel, and decide according to our specific narrative. From our earliest recollections to the final moments of our life, we frame and recount the stories of our infancy, childhood, adolescence, young adulthood, mature adulthood, old age, and impending death. Especially prominent in our narrative is our face-off with hardship and suffering. "In telling the story of how you became who you are, and of who you're on your way to becoming, the story itself becomes part of who you are."[15] We weave together,

14. Theodore R. Sarbin, ed., *Narrative Psychology: The Storied Nature of Human Conduct* (Westport, CT: Praeger, 1986).
15. Julie Beck, "Life's Stories: How You Arrange the Plot Points of Your Life into a Narrative Can Shape Who You Are—and Is a Fundamental Part of Being

emphasize, diminish, and cut out elements from the particularities of our ethnicity/race, family/kinship, temporality, spatiality, and context.[16] Our particularity prompts us to find or create a space in our world through social media, for example, by which we tell our stories.[17]

As explained at the start of this chapter, this idea of particularity is quite different from intersectionality. Yes, intersectionality treats many of the same particularities that I'm discussing—gender/sex, race, social background and class, culture, and the like. But, at least in some cases, intersectionality emphasizes how these particularities divide, privilege, and disenfranchise certain human beings from other human beings. By contrast, the particularity I'm presenting focuses on the reality of human embodiment: as a matter of fact, all human beings are characterized by ethnicity/race, family/kinship, temporality, spatiality, context, and story. What people do with that reality is another matter. In step with Scripture, they may emphasize that God designed and created all such human beings to be his image bearers (Gen. 1:26–28). In this case, intersectionality may be helpful in uncovering the brokenness that destroys unity among people. Oppositely, intersectionality may emphasize divisions among different categories of people so as to privilege one group while disenfranchising another.

The idea of particularity may overlap with, but doesn't endorse, intersectionality.

Human," *The Atlantic Daily*, August 10, 2015, https://www.theatlantic.com/health/archive/2015/08/life-stories-narrative-psychology-redemption-mental-health/400796/.

16. Words and terms such as "spin," "embellishment," "contextualization," "redemptive arc," "false humility," "selective memory," "autobiographical reasoning," and "idealized self" are associated with the creation and telling of narratives, both to oneself and to others. One pathology—narcissism—is characterized by the tendency to invent false narratives that deflect from holding narcissists accountable, contradict the truth about their sorry reality, protect them from threats to expose their shame and guilt, etc.

17. My thanks to Hanell Schuetz for her insights into social media storytelling.

Biblical and Theological Affirmations

This presentation of the particularities of ethnicity/race, family/kinship, temporality, spatiality, context, and story may sound like we've taken some pages out of a sociology or anthropology textbook. In one sense, this could be the case, as these individual human realities can be largely a matter of simple observations, cultural research, and demographic studies. In another sense, particularity is grounded in Scripture and sound theology.

As noted in chapter 1, Psalm 139:13–16 highlights God's careful, intricate work in creating each person according to his particular design:

> For you formed my inward parts;
>> you knitted me together in my mother's womb.
> I praise you, for I am fearfully and wonderfully made.
> Wonderful are your works;
>> my soul knows it very well.
> My frame was not hidden from you,
> when I was being made in secret,
>> intricately woven in the depths of the earth.
> Your eyes saw my unformed substance;
> in your book were written, every one of them,
>> the days that were formed for me,
>> when as yet there was none of them. (ESV)

God is intimately engaged in each and every aspect, the minute and large details, of embodied creation. Moreover, "From one man he has made every nationality to live over the whole earth and has determined their appointed times and the boundaries of where they live" (Acts 17:26). In other words, God designs and determines the particular ethnicity/race, family/kinship, temporality, spatiality, context, and story of his image bearers.

This particularity is emphasized elsewhere in Scripture in relation to the incarnation and work of redemption: "When the time came to completion, God sent his Son, born of a woman, born under the law, to redeem those under the law, so that we might receive adoption as sons. And because you are sons, God sent the Spirit of his Son into our hearts, crying, '*Abba*, Father!' So you are no longer a slave but a son, and if a son, then God has made you an heir" (Gal. 4:4–7).

The particularity of the incarnation reinforces what this chapter is about. The one and only true God, the God of Abraham, Isaac, and Jacob, Yahweh of Israel, purposed to rescue his people, the people of Israel, whom he had chosen for particular favor among all the nations of the world. In the wisdom of this eternally existing triune God, the Father sent forth his only begotten—or, according to some renderings, unique, or one and only—Son to become incarnate by the power of the Holy Spirit. At the proper, particular moment—in the fullness of time, at the climax of ages of preparation for this specific moment—the Son was sent, and he came. All history is registered as either before this time—before Christ (BC)—or after this time—*anno domini* (AD), in the year of our Lord.

In becoming incarnate, the Son took on the human nature of those he came to save. He became not a generic representative of humanity in general but a particular man. He lived as a real and fully human being. Specifically, he was born of a woman who was uniquely chosen for this role: he was Jesus ben-Mary, the son of a teenage girl. At his birth he was nineteen inches long, six pounds fourteen ounces, Apgar score 9, with a good set of lungs, as his mother, who heard his first cries, could attest (using our sanctified imagination). She was a faithful Jew, as was Jesus's adopted father, Joseph, so on the eighth day after their son's birth, they brought him to the temple in Jerusalem where they had him circumcised according to Jewish custom. Jesus was born under the law of Moses, and as a circumcised member of the Abrahamic covenant, he was charged with the responsibility to obey the Ten Commandments, submit to the holiness code of conduct, and avoid violating any of its prohibitions. His delight was to be in the law of the Lord. Being of the lineage of David, he was charged with the duty of heeding the Davidic covenant. He was to relate to God his loving Father as an obedient son and, what is more, rule over the house and kingdom of David forever. No small task for a baby born in Bethlehem, who would soon move to Egypt, then back to Israel in the region of Galilee, where he would finally settle in the unimportant town of Nazareth. So he became known as Jesus the Nazarene.

The particularity of Jesus's work of redemption further reinforces what this chapter is about. The mission on which he was sent was to redeem those under the law of Moses. This point reminds us that Jesus's ministry was almost exclusively to his own people: "I was sent only to the lost sheep of the house of Israel" (Matt. 15:24). Likewise, Jesus launched his disciples in ministry to the Jewish people, instructing them to avoid gentiles and Samaritans (Matt. 10). Even the initial stages of church evangelism and expansion focused on the Jews (Acts 1–7). Only after some time did Jesus's words of global commission (Matt. 28:18–20; Luke 24:44–49; Acts 1:8) find their initial fulfillment in the redemption of many gentiles (Acts 11:19–25). What began as a particular ministry eventually developed, in accordance with divine purpose, into a worldwide redemptive movement.

This redemption has special reference to adoption, the legal and relational choice to take as family members those who were formerly far off. Adoption as "sons"—the term, which to our contemporary sensibilities connotes sexism, includes both men and women—brings with it the wealth of the family inheritance and the honor of the family name. The redeemed become sons and daughters of God the Father, through the work of God the Son, by means of God the indwelling Holy Spirit.

Accordingly, our point concerning particularity is well supported both biblically and theologically, appearing even in the incarnation and work of redemption. The particular God. The particular incarnate Son. The particular work. The particular redemption. As Paul reminds us elsewhere, "For there is one God, and there is one mediator between God and men, the man Christ Jesus" (1 Tim. 2:5 ESV). In summary, an essential given of human existence is particularity, which is defined as the condition of being an individual. God specifically designs and creates each human being to be a particular gendered embodied individual characterized by their ethnicity/race, family/kinship, temporality, spatiality, context, and story.[18]

Application

Map out who you are as a particular person created by God. For each of the particularities, identify who you are as a divinely created individual.

Ethnicity/race

- shared language(s), customs, religion(s), and nationality

Family/kinship

- family of origin or, in the case of adoption/fostering, family/families of nurture
- birth order, birthplace, siblings, intact parental unit or parental divorce (with or without remarriage and blended family)
- kinship in terms of either singleness (including widowhood) or marriage, biological and/or adopted children, the care of aging parents

Temporality

- mathematical time, subjective time, birth day, age, and perceived age

18. As Marc Cortez rightly underscores, "each of these expressions of particularity is also the kind of constraint that we associate with being finite creatures, which means that limit/constraint/finitude is a good thing and not the obstacle to human flourishing that we often describe it as being." Personal correspondence, August 16, 2019.

Spatiality
- location(s) in the past and present, home and work environments

Context
- socioeconomic factors
- political factors
- educational factors
- cultural factors
- religious factors

Story
- narratives of infancy, childhood, adolescence, young adulthood, mature adulthood, old age, impending death (choose which categories apply to you)

Having completed your map as a particular individual created by God, revisit each created particularity and do another map: your map as a particular individual being *re-created* by God. That is, through his redemptive work, how is God changing your story? For example, how does the Word of God address the relationships with your parents, siblings, spouse (if married), and children (if applicable)? In what ways is the Spirit of God sanctifying you in your work environment and enjoyment of entertainment? How is the Lord helping you to live as a whole person in a fractured world?

For the Curious

When you've completed your map, share it with others.

As you do, and in preparation for the next topic, think through the particularities of others with whom you have relationships: friends, work colleagues, parents, siblings, spouse (if married), and children (if applicable). What is it that moves you to desire their friendship? Why do you want to bond with them? How do you express your camaraderie with others? When the pandemic prevented you from hanging out with your friends and family, what could account for the loneliness and sense of isolation you experienced? What is it about community that it suffers when it is inhibited?

While particularity focuses on us as individuals, sociality opens us up to others and moves us toward community.[19] We now turn to that topic.

19. Philosophically speaking, this emphasis on particularity and individuality must never be allowed to devolve into solipsism, that is, the idea that only the self exists. Solipsism may express itself as "I alone am real; everything else exists in my mind." Our next section on sociality is, among other things, an antidote to solipsism.

CHAPTER 4

THE SOCIAL BODY

Consider

Respond to this question: Why are relationships with others so important?

Big Idea

An essential given of human existence is sociality, the condition that tends to bring individuals together. God's design for his image bearers is that we are social people who express our sociality in appropriate interpersonal relationships and, in the case of marriage, through sexual activity. (The next chapter will address the sexual body.)

Application Question

How are you expressing your sociality in God-honoring, self-valuing, and others-respecting ways?

Definitions and Terminology

Sociality is the universal human condition of desiring, expressing, and receiving human relationships. You and I desire to bond with other people and become close friends in ways that our tendency to isolation and our pain of loneliness vanish in the light of truly being known. We express our sociality by joining with others in community in which we expect to experience unconditional love, steadfast care for one another, the sharing of prayers and burdens, and confession of sin that is met by extending forgiveness. We are receptive of other people's companionship when our suspicion of them yields to trust and when our fears of betrayal and being disappointed by them give way to dependence on them. So when they do indeed fail us, we are shaken but not shocked by the revelation of their sin.[1]

To tie in with earlier chapters, as male-gendered embodied individuals and female-gendered embodied individuals, men and women express their sociality differently. To avoid misunderstanding, sociality is a personal and relational reality, not a physical activity. It's not sexiness, seductiveness, or eroticism. Rather, it is the universal human state of being oriented toward others. Sociality is expressed in the giving and receiving that lead to and characterize human relationships.

In a limited way, sociality is associated with sexual activity. As one type of expression of human sociality, *sexual activity* refers to any physical event or movement between people that is intended to arouse erotic desires and sensations. The sexual body is the topic of the next chapter.

Naming this aspect of embodiment raises the problem of language. Until recently, my practice has been to use the term *sexuality*. But with its many associations (particularly an emphasis on physical activity), the word causes an unacceptable amount

---

1. Living under quarantine and observing social distancing during the COVID-19 pandemic drove home this point about sociality: we deeply long for embodied community and experience painful loss when we're constrained to remove ourselves from the physical presence of other people. And we know that Zoom conversations aren't as meaningful as person-to-person encounters. My thanks to Hanell Schuetz for noting how the pandemic underscored human sociality.

of confusion.[2] Instead, I will use the word *sociality* and define it as the universal human condition of desiring, expressing, and receiving human relationships.[3]

Biblical Affirmations

From its outset, Scripture presents human beings as people in community. When the triune God creates the human race, the divine image bearers are male and female. Together they are tasked

2. I still respect those who have used, and continue to use, the term *sexuality* to name this universal human condition. For example, Stanley Grenz, commenting on Gen. 2:18–25, offers:

> The narrative indicates that individual existence as an embodied creature entails a fundamental incompleteness or, stated positively, an innate yearning for completeness. This sensed incompleteness is symbolized by biological sex—that is, by existence as a particular person who is male or female. The incompleteness is related to existence as a sexual creature and therefore to human sexuality. Sexuality, in turn, is linked not only to the incompleteness each person senses as an embodied, sexual creature but also to the potential for wholeness in relationship to others that parallels this fundamental incompleteness. . . . Hence, sexuality is the dynamic that forms the basis of the uniquely human drive toward bonding. (Stanley J. Grenz, *The Social God and the Relational Self: A Trinitarian Theology of the Imago Dei* [Louisville: Westminster John Knox, 2001], 277–78)

What is for Grenz the idea of human sexuality—"the impulse toward bonding" (280)—is for me the idea of human sociality.

3. Other terms that were considered but rejected for one reason or another are *relationality*, *alterity*, and *sexuate installation*. (1) *Relationality* may be close, but as this word is also used in connection with the covenantal bond between God and human beings, its broadness works against it. *Sociality* is restricted to the human-to-human domain. (2) *Alterity* is a word that has to do with others or otherness, yet not as persons in themselves but as persons in relationship to me, persons as I perceive them. While this term captures some of what I'm trying to express in my idea of sociality, it is a rather rare word and thus not all that helpful. (3) *Sexuate installation* is a phrase invented by the Spanish philosopher Julián Marías to express the condition of men and women that prompts them toward friendship and companionship by means of the giving of themselves through their differences. While this phrase expresses some of what I'm trying to communicate in this chapter, it is an expression that is unknown outside the technical field of philosophical anthropology, so not at all helpful. Julián Marías, *Metaphysical Anthropology: The Empirical Structure of Human Life* (University Park, PA: Penn State University Press, 1971).

with the responsibility of marrying and having children, as well as working to build human society (Gen. 1:26–28). Genealogical lists record the generations of families (Gen. 5, 10). Even when dispersed by divine judgment, people scatter as nations (Gen. 11) according to divine design (Acts 17:26).

Whereas the ancient world was divided into Jews and gentiles, in the church these two distant groups are brought together in Christ (Eph. 2:11–22). The rivalry between other adversaries— men and women, slave and free—is overcome by the cross as well. Accordingly, "There is no Jew or Greek, slave or free, male and female; since you are all one in Christ Jesus" (Gal. 3:28). Genuine sociality becomes a reality in the church.

Theological Reflections

Sociality links to creation and the fall, the first two chapters in the overall biblical narrative of creation, fall, and redemption. Sociality comes with both a design and a capacity. The first aspect has just been covered: it is by divine design that all embodied people desire, express, and receive relationships. Women are to enjoy friendships with other women and men. Men are to enjoy friendships with other men and women. These relationships are to be life-giving and pure, helping us to live as whole people in a fractured world.

The second aspect is the human capacity to desire, express, and receive relationships in either a positive way or a negative way. As for the positive manner, you and I do indeed engage in relationships with others according to divine design. The bonds we form and the community in which we engage are character- ized by love, care, empathy, and the like. As for the negative man- ner, some of us pervert relationships through both unconscious ways (e.g., a genetic propensity for antisocial behavior or an addiction to pornography that hinders genuine relationships) and conscious ways—that is, willful rebellion against the divine order.[4]

Sociality and Siblingship

In addition to the biblical themes of creation and the fall, sociality also connects to the story of redemption, which makes it so that men and women in the church can and should be friends. Better still, they are brothers and sisters in Christ and need to act according to who they are (1 Tim. 5:1–2). Positively, sociality prompts us in the church to know, love, respect, cherish, encourage, and care for one another as siblings. Scripture is our guide and the indwelling Holy Spirit is our empowerment for holy living and pure relationships. As Christian brothers and sisters then, we live and champion exemplary, godly friendship. We honor and respect one another, promote and give preference to one another, and teach and admonish one another.

Negatively, this idea undoubtedly raises concerns. Wisdom dictates that before we jump too quickly to the potential dangers and pitfalls present in the relationships between Christian sisters and Christian brothers who aren't spouses, we should first consider the many benefits and privileges such other-gendered, nonromantic, nonmarital relationships offer. There are many advantages. In keeping with Jesus's new commandment for his disciples (John 13:34), these relationships provide opportunities for us men and women to express Christlike love. Closely related are the many "one another" passages in Scripture. These relationships offer occasions for us men and women to pray for one another, accept one another, forgive one another, confess sins to one another, serve one another, submit to one another, and be hospitable to one another. We must not allow the potential pitfalls of other-gendered

---

4. My appreciation to Gracilynn Hanson for providing the concept of, and language for, design and capacity for this chapter.

relationships to chill the care and concern envisioned by these commands to love one another.

Additional benefits include being drawn outside of ourselves and gaining the perspective of the complementary gender. We are gendered all the way down, so we view all of life from our male or female perspective. As difficult—even impossible—as it may be for us to see things from the other gender's viewpoint, relationships between men and women push us to stop focusing solely on our perspective and to listen to others around us: "Friendship between the sexes may take us not out of ourselves but beyond ourselves and may make us more whole, balanced and sane than we could otherwise be."[5]

Moreover, as people to whom the Holy Spirit has granted spiritual gifts, men and women are blessed and built up by one another's gifts. It should be recalled that there are no gender-specific gifts. To men and women alike are given the gifts of teaching, leading, exhortation, giving, faith, helps, and, from a continuationist position, prophecy, speaking in tongues, word of wisdom, and more.[6] The church is edified as we men and women exercise our spiritual gifts together and toward one another. As for leadership roles, in an egalitarian church with a female pastor, these relationships provide opportunities for her to teach, disciple, and equip key men in the church for all ministries. Similarly, in a complementarian church with a male pastor, these relationships provide opportunities for him to teach, disciple, and equip key women in the church for all nonpastoral ministries.

5. Gilbert Meilander, "Men and Women—Can We Be Friends?," *First Things*, June 1993, https://www.firstthings.com/article/1993/06/men-and-womencan-we-be-friends.

6. This reminder isn't to be confused with the proper exercise of those gifts, which is another matter. From a complementarian position, women aren't permitted to teach or to exercise authority over the men of the church (1 Tim. 2:12). However, older women are to teach younger women (Titus 2:3–5) and deaconesses possess the necessary authority to engage in their servant leadership of various ministries.

Accordingly, we affirm many benefits and privileges that other-gendered, nonromantic, nonmarital relationships offer. If we lose sight of these advantages, the potential pitfalls into which such relationships may fall will sour men and women from engaging in such friendships.

Perhaps it goes without asking, but what are such pitfalls? Some of these hazards are lust, fantasies, inappropriate closeness, mistrust, and sexual intercourse with someone other than one's spouse. All such immorality is precluded (1 Cor. 6:12–20). Moreover, if one's marriage is already strained or collapsing, such relationships may weaken or destroy it. This strain may manifest itself in jealousy, as the friends' spouses are resentful of the relationship. The strain may reveal itself as rivalry, as the nonparticipating spouses wonder, "Does my spouse find the other person more attractive? Easier to talk to? More relationally captivating? Funnier or more competent or satisfying?" Such relationships may exacerbate existing problems in an already troubled marriage.

When these other-gendered, nonromantic, nonmarital relationships fail, the damage they cause perpetuates the terrible reputation that has been (sadly, but rightly) earned by Christians and churches because of sexual scandals. For this reason alone, some people denounce these relationships because of the mere appearance of evil they present. This avoidance for appearance sake is a controversial matter, because just about anything can be misconstrued as being evil. For example, witnessing a Christian buying a six-pack of bottled root beer at a party store where liquor is sold can appear sinful to those who abstain from alcohol.

These potential dangers aren't to be minimized. Still, the poem "Lovers Apart" by Madeleine L'Engle reminds married people, "We may not love in emptiness; / We married in a peopled place."[7] Beautifully then, marriage enhances the lives of others with whom

7. Madeleine L'Engle, "Lovers Apart," *The Ordering of Love: The New and Collected Poems of Madeleine L'Engle* (Colorado Springs: WaterBrook, 2005), 141.

the couple interact. While marriage is an exclusive covenant between a man and a woman, their relationship shouldn't isolate them from others. Sadly, some marriages suffer from unrealistic expectations that one spouse can supply all that the other spouse needs. Indeed, "many marital relationships bend and break under the weight of trying to provide all the emotional, social, cultural and intellectual needs of both partners."[8] On the contrary, sociality underscores the divine design for human beings to give and receive relationships—not just one, but many.

Being mindful of the traps into which we may fall, we can put structures in place so that the many benefits and privileges of other-gendered, nonromantic, nonmarital relationships may prevail and the potential snares may be avoided. First and foremost (and not to be dismissed easily), married men and women should be faithful to their spouse. Physical expressions toward other-gendered friends should be measured, and should not go beyond what is appropriate between siblings or cross boundaries that would cause a spouse to object. On a spectrum from intimacy, which is reserved for marriage, to independence, which characterizes proper friendships, the two other-gendered friends should target their relationship toward individuation, not identification.

Figure 4.1

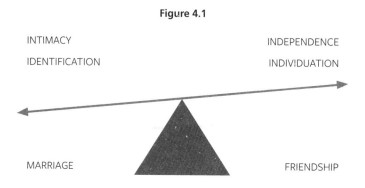

8. Richard Faris and Jeanne Finley, "Eros and Friendship," *The Christian Century* 114, no. 6 (February 19, 1997): 195.

Holiness and purity should be pursued, and prayer for God-honoring friendships should characterize these relationships. Meetings should be in public places, not behind closed doors in isolated offices. In the case of married people, the nonparticipating spouse should be made aware of the meetings and the nature of the conversations. If attraction arises or an emotional bond begins to form, it should be addressed openly between the man and woman and a course correction should be made. Accountability partners should also be alerted to this pull.

If this is the wise approach at the one-to-one level, wisdom also dictates that the church should avoid incorporating a worldly hypersexualization into its treatment of other-gendered relationships. When it suspects such relationships of always being oriented toward sexual activity, the church views them as inherently dangerous and to be avoided at all costs. In doing so, the church unintentionally trains its members to view one another as little more than sex objects.[9] For Christian men to treat Christian women as temptresses, seductresses whose only intention is to engage in sex with every man, is to fantasize and thus degrade their sisters in Christ. Likewise, for Christian women to view Christian men as sexual predators, slaves of their sexual impulses and thus incapable of pursuing holiness in relationships with women, is to objectify and thus dehumanize their brothers in Christ. It's not our right to falsely assign intent of sinful sexual activity to others, thereby stripping away their value and dignity. If one Christian dehumanizes another Christian, then we no longer have two redeemed human beings.[10] Reprehensibly then, we destroy the possibility of obeying the scriptural injunction to live as brothers and sisters in Christ. We spoil sociality.

In summary, an essential given of human existence is sociality, the condition that tends to bring individuals together. God's design

9. For further discussion, see Aimee Byrd, *Why Can't We Be Friends? Avoidance Is Not Purity* (Phillipsburg, NJ: P&R, 2018).
10. My appreciation to Gracilynn Hanson for providing the language of objectification, dehumanization, and assignment of sexual intent for this discussion.

for his image bearers is that we are social people who express our sociality in appropriate interpersonal relationships and, in the case of marriage, through sexual activity. Expressing our sociality according to its divine design enables us to live as whole people in a fractured world.

Application

The application question is, How are you expressing your sociality in God-honoring, self-valuing, and others-respecting ways?

To push in a bit more, how would you assess the relationships you currently enjoy? Are you developing strong friendships with men and women as brothers and sisters in Christ? If not, what is preventing you from these sibling relationships? If you struggle with lust, same-sex attraction, or homosexual activity, with whom can you talk so that you don't have to face your difficulties alone?

If you are an older woman, do you cultivate mentoring relationships with younger women in your church (Titus 3:2–5)? If you are petrified of doing one-on-one discipleship, could you ask another older woman to join you in mentoring three or four younger women? If you are a younger woman, do you seek out older women in your church so that you may glean from their wisdom and experience?[11]

If you are a man and not officially involved in any church ministry (e.g., as an elder or deacon), do you still view yourself as a servant who has much to contribute to others? The lack of a formal title or position shouldn't stop you from using your gift(s) in relationships with others and in engaging in ministries.

For both women and men, are you intentional about forming sibling relationships with brothers and sisters of different ethnicities, ages, socioeconomic status, background, and the like?

---

11. An example of these age-disparate relationships is the one that developed between seventy-something Clara and my teenage daughter Hanell. In addition to faithfully praying for her, Clara taught Hanell cake decorating and flower arranging. And Hanell brought a youthful joy and eagerness for companionship to Clara.

For the Curious

The discussion about sociality and siblingship isn't a call to be naïve or careless in cross-gendered relationships, but it does address the need to consider how we live out those relationships. According to Scripture, purity is of the highest value and therefore must be promoted. But purity isn't a matter of avoidance or abstention. It's not isolation or escape from others. Rather, it's a wholeness or integrity expressed in relationships that develop for the good of those involved and for the advancement of the kingdom of God. When we regard purity and reputation individualistically—being holy is only about *me*; it is *my* reputation that is always at stake—we may (inadvertently) communicate to others that *they* are dangerous/carnal/sinful and that *their* reputation is suspect. Thus we need to be attentive to how our posture toward others, and the rules we impose in consequence of that attitude, reflects on them.

Practically speaking, this idea prompts reflection on the advisability of the so-called Billy Graham rule or its counterpart, the Mike Pence rule. The rule is that a Christian should never be alone with someone of the other gender who is not their spouse. Examples of application include driving in a car, meeting together (even in a public place), and riding in an elevator. If a woman requests to meet with a man to discuss a possible ministry direction, the rule says that the man (in most cases the rule seems to be invoked by male believers) must arrange for a (male) chaperone to be present, even when the meeting takes place in a public venue. At first, the rule may seem like a good idea, at least from the man's perspective.[12] But on further reflection, it makes the woman feel

---

12. But it also raises questions about the man's own hope in the Lord's redemptive work in his life. If he doesn't trust himself to meet with a Christian woman in a public place and engage in a pure conversation with her, what does this imply about his progress in sanctification, his reliance on the Holy Spirit to overcome his sinful nature, and his confidence in the Lord's gift of holiness? My thanks to Torey Teer for his thoughts on this matter.

mistrusted, treats her like a seductress, and implies she has a poor reputation. The man's appearance of purity raises questions about the woman's propriety.[13]

Personally, how do you live out such other-gendered relationships? What benefits may accrue to you and to your other-gendered siblings in Christ? What particular pitfalls loom large in your mind? What structures have you or can you put into place to promote the advantages and minimize the dangers of such relationships? If you are married, have you discussed your perspective with your spouse? If so, is he or she in agreement with you, or are there reservations? What can you do to bring clarity into this situation?

To conclude, perhaps you've noted throughout this book that I acknowledge the contributions of a number of women. Some are students. All are friends. Through their conversations with me and interactions with a draft of this book, they have enriched me and contributed to my understanding of human embodiment. I highly value them as sisters in Christ, appreciate their friendship, and assure you that this theology book is much stronger because of their insights.

---

13. For further discussion, see Karen Swallow Prior, "The Problem with 'Don't Eat Alone with Women': Good Character Is Better Than Strict Rules," *Vox*, April 1, 2017, https://www.vox.com/first-person/2017/4/1/15142744/mike -pence-billy-graham-rule. A response to that article is Mike Hutchinson, "Virtue Ethics, the Billy Graham Rule, and Mike Pence: A Response to Karen Swallow Prior," *Reformed Book Reviews*, April 6, 2017, https://re4ormedreviews.word press.com/2017/04/06/virtue-ethics-the-billy-graham-rule-and-mike-pence-a-re sponse-to-karen-swallow-prior/.

CHAPTER 5

THE SEXUAL BODY

Consider

"The overall biblical framework of human sexuality and sexual activity is . . ." How would you complete this statement, and why?

Big Idea

The big idea addresses one particular aspect of sociality (the topic of the previous chapter), which is the condition that tends to bring individuals together. God's design for his image bearers is that, as social people, we express our sociality in the case of marriage through sexual activity.

Application Question

How are you expressing your sexuality in God-honoring, self-valuing, and spouse-respecting ways?

Definition and General Framework

As one type of expression of human sociality, sexual activity refers to any physical event or movement between people that is intended to arouse erotic desires and sensations for various purposes. According to Scripture, the general framework for human sexuality includes several elements. First, as designed by God, sexual activity is to be between a husband and wife who have covenanted together to be in a monogamous, unbreakable relationship. Thus when it's an activity between a married couple, sex is divinely approved, good, and right. Second, the purposes for sexual activity are several. It joins the two into a "one flesh" unity. It may result in procreation, bringing into existence a new life or lives. It's intended for the couple's pleasure and sense of fulfillment, leading to their flourishing. It may provide comfort through physical closeness.

While there's no section in Scripture that spells out this framework for sexual activity, several passages support it. Within the narrative of God forming Eve and bringing her to Adam, the author provides this principle for marriage for all time: "This is why a man leaves his father and mother and bonds with his wife, and they become one flesh" (Gen. 2:24).[1] The post-fall narrative about Adam and Eve underscores the procreative aspect of sexual activity: "The man was intimate with his wife Eve, and she conceived and gave birth to Cain" (Gen. 4:1). The Song of Songs and Proverbs 5 affirm the pleasurable nature of sexual intercourse,[2] which is to

1. In Jesus's reference to this instruction, he adds an additional comment about the husband and wife: "So they are no longer two, but one flesh. Therefore, what God has joined together, let no one separate" (Matt. 19:6).
2. Physiologically, men and women experience pleasure by means of their sexual organs. For men, sexual pleasure is centered on the penis and scrotum. Due to a dense network of nerve fibers in these structures, when men are touched or rubbed there, they become sexually aroused. The increased pleasure may result in ejaculation. Women experience sexual pleasure through the clitoris, the inner labia, and the vaginal opening, as these structures have many nerve fibers. When those areas are stimulated, feelings of pleasure increase and may result in an orgasm. Up to a few years ago, the clitoris was considered to consist only of the clitoral gland covered by the clitoral hood and located near the opening of the urethra. Recent discoveries, however, now understand the organ to consist not only of the clitoral gland but the vaginal wall as well: two crura extending down from the clitoris gland, deep within the tissue of the vulva on either side, and two bulbs on both sides of the vaginal opening. Apparently, this extensive clitoral system serves only one purpose, and that is to produce pleasure.

be reserved for a husband and wife. Following the death of their infant son, David extended comfort to Bathsheba through sexual activity (2 Sam. 12:24).

This general biblical framework for sexual activity holds out the ideals of living as whole people. Tragically, due to sin, we are sexually broken people living in a fractured world.

Our Contemporary Context and Problems with Sexuality

While human sexuality has always been plagued with problems, it seems that such difficulties have increased exponentially in most Western countries since the beginning of the sexual revolution in the 1960s.[3] Chipping away at the expression of sexuality within biblical guidelines are the following: a relaxing of national and ecclesial laws, as well as the social stigma, against divorce; the widespread use of birth control; unrestricted access to, and normalization of, abortion; the disappearance of social taboos against pregnancy outside of marriage; the development of a macho culture in which women are viewed as sexual objects for men to possess and so prove their masculinity; the rise of artistic media—movies, books, television—that promote sexual liberation; unrestricted access to pornography through always-available internet. The list could go on.

Add to this unprecedented transformation the reluctance or embarrassment of the church to talk about human sexuality. As difficult as these matters are, if we don't address sexuality and sexual activity, the culture and its perverse notions and practices will dominate the church's viewpoint. We must also avoid addressing the topic wrongly; for example, by portraying sex to be evil,

3. For further discussion, see Pope Benedict XVI, "The Church and the Scandal of Sexual Abuse," Catholic News Agency, April 10, 2019, https://www.catholic newsagency.com/news/full-text-of-benedict-xvi-the-church-and-the-scandal -of-sexual-abuse-59639.

shameful, and dirty instead of highlighting its beauty, wonder, and divine design.

As for this last point, we've already presented the general biblical framework for human sexuality. We now turn to specific passages that address notable problems that the church encounters in this area. While the tenor of these texts is largely negative, we may also draw positive lessons from them regarding the right attitudes and practices for God-honoring, self-valuing, and spouse-respecting sexual activity. Our goal is to learn how to live as whole people in a fractured world.

Biblical Affirmations

The Intimacy of the Sexual Bond (1 Cor. 6:12–20)

In 1 Corinthians 6 Paul denounces sexual immorality, placing it into a category by itself. He explains, "Every other sin a person commits is outside the body, but the sexually immoral person sins against his own body" (v. 18 ESV). This heinous sin is twofold. It wrenches away one's body—which "is not meant for sexual immorality but for the Lord, and the Lord for the body" (v. 13)—from its rightful membership with Christ and, if married, with one's spouse. And it unites one's body with the body of someone other than Christ and, if married, one's spouse. The result is that "the two [engaged in sexual activity] will become one flesh" (v. 16), which is a tragic disorientation of the body.

When it comes to sexuality, there are two possible "memberships" for the body: the body is a member of Christ or the body is a member of immorality (v. 15). Importantly, these two memberships are mutually exclusive. People can hold either one or the other, but not both. It's like the situation for Chicago baseball fans: Chicagoans are for either the Cubs or the White Sox, but they can't be for both teams. So being a Christian, and thus having one's body joined in membership to Christ, means that engaging in illicit sexual activity is prohibited, wrong, and sinful. When you use your body, which properly belongs to Christ, and you engage in improper intercourse, you wrench your body from its rightful membership and join it to a wrongful membership in immorality.

An objection is raised to Paul's use of a case of sexual activity with a prostitute (vv. 15–16). We're not talking about two lives becoming intimately intertwined on many fronts. This sexual act can't possibly involve a bonding between a believer and a prostitute! As Paul underscores, this objection manifests a misunderstanding of the intimacy of the physical bond created through sexual intercourse. Paul cites Genesis 2:24 to support his case: "Don't you know that anyone joined to a prostitute is one body with her? For Scripture says, 'The two will become one flesh'" (v. 16). Again, isn't this passage about marriage, the sexual intimacy between husband and wife? It certainly is. But the focus of Genesis 2:24 is on the intimacy of the physical bond that is created when a husband and wife—or any man and any woman—engage in sexual intercourse: the two become one flesh. Engaging in sexual intercourse with a prostitute, thinking it's fine because it is just a normal human activity like eating food to fill one's stomach, is mistaken. Paul offers this correction: sex isn't like that. It's profound—and profoundly different—because an intimate union is forged between the man and the woman. Sexual intercourse is in a class by itself.

Another objection is raised. What about alcoholism, drug abuse, and gluttony? Aren't these also sins against the body? They may be abuses of the body, but they are introduced from the outside. Whiskey, heroin, and excessive food are external substances that are ingested or injected into the body and wreak havoc with it. Sexual immorality is profoundly different because it engages (parts of) the body itself in an illicit activity. It contradicts the truth, purpose, and destiny of the body. Because of the intimacy of the sexual bond forged in intercourse, sexual immorality is a devastatingly evil sin.

The solution is an imperative: "Flee sexual immorality!" (v. 18). Christians who are engaged in illicit sexual intercourse must drop their immoral membership and stop engaging in such activity. To clinch this point, Paul emphasizes that the body is a temple of the Holy Spirit (v. 19). As the dwelling place of the Spirit, the body can't be engaged in such defiling matters. Our body doesn't belong to us, for we were purchased (redeemed) by the precious blood of Christ. Therefore, we must glorify God—honor him, exalt him—in our body (v. 20). No sexual immorality is permitted.

There are several implications of this passage. Sexual intercourse is proper and permitted *only* in a marriage relationship. Paul deals with illicit sexual relationships between a believer and someone who isn't their spouse. He makes no mention of sexual intercourse between a believer and their spouse, because such activity is completely legitimate, in accordance with God's design.[4] Sexual activity is intended for the flourishing of the couple.

This provision that restricts sexual activity to marriage isn't just another rule similar to prohibitions against drunkenness, illegal drug use, and cheating on one's income taxes. Because of the intimacy of the sexual bond, the rule that restricts it to marriage is in a category by itself.

A common question may be raised: What is it that Paul is prohibiting? Certainly, sexual intercourse between nonmarried people is the specific matter that he addresses. By extension, it isn't a stretch to include any physical activity that arouses sexual desire and is intended to lead to intercourse. Oral and anal sex would

---

4. "Divine love—*agape*—and human love are intrinsically linked. [Pope] Benedict decried *eros* in the sense of sinful erotic love that dehumanizes and is exclusively physical. Still, he skillfully explained that Christianity is not anti-body; after all, it is a human person—body and soul—who loves. Accordingly, when *eros* is about concrete matters of human existence, *eros* and *agape* are not antithetical but belong together. It is only when *eros* is sinfully reduced to physicality, leading to a debasement of the body, that it is no longer compatible with divine love." Gregg R. Allison, "The Virtues of a Theologian: Faith, Hope, and Love," in *The Theology of Benedict XVI: A Protestant Appreciation*, ed. Tim Perry (Bellingham, WA: Lexham Press, 2019), 60.

be included as well. Also prohibited are noncontact activities such as sexting—posting, receiving, and forwarding sexually explicit photos, messages, or images—and meeting in online chat rooms for sexual exchanges.

Another important question: What if you are currently practicing this immoral behavior, or have fallen in this area in the past? Have you lost your salvation? Paul doesn't indicate this in any way. But steps must be taken to rectify the matter. First, confess this as sin (1 John 1:9). Second, repent by quitting the relationship(s). Turning away means cessation, not moderation.[5] Third, seek counseling for several purposes: to work through the deficits in your life that led to such activity, to address the problem of seeking satisfaction in the wrong places, to deal with lasting fantasy issues, and to reset the course of your life. Fourth, receive teaching to live morally empowered with the Holy Spirit (Gal. 5:16).

The sexual bond established through sexual activity between people is a uniquely intimate event. It is to take place according to God's will and purpose and not out of one's sinful nature.

Sanctified Sexuality (1 Thess. 4:3–8)

In 1 Thessalonians 4, once again Paul denounces sexual immorality, calling Christians to know and do God's will in both a general sense—that they become mature disciples—and a specific sense—that they avoid illicit sexual activity (v. 3). On the contrary, married people are to express their sexuality in a God-honoring and spouse-respecting manner (v. 4).[6] They should be able to exercise control of their sexual desire so that it is expressed "in holiness

---

5. In the case of engaged couples who are already sexually active, they can take several steps. They should stop having sex. If they are living together, they should separate. Churches can help with this step by providing alternative living arrangements for the couple. And they should move ahead quickly toward marriage. At this point, postponing the wedding will probably occasion slips back into sexual activity.

6. In the words of Kramer from the TV show *Seinfeld*, both the husband and the wife must be "masters of their own domain."

and honor, not with lustful passions" (vv. 4–5). Sexual activity in marriage is right and good, but a husband and wife must be able to control the expression and character of that sexual activity. Their physical desire can't be followed wherever it leads.

Paul then turns to a tragic situation: Christian men were committing adultery with the wives of other Christians. Accordingly, he warns the church "that no one transgress and wrong his brother in this matter" (v. 6 ESV). Such sexual activity is considered trespassing; it is illegally crossing a boundary into forbidden sexual territory. Moreover, such sexual activity is defrauding, which means possessing something or someone that isn't one's own. No one is to "enrich" himself in this area of sexuality at his brother's expense by engaging in sexual intercourse with that brother's wife. The close relationships that church members enjoy with one another should never be allowed to cross these lines of sexual morality. Paul's instruction applies for both men and women.

Paul's emphatic conclusion warns violators that God will take revenge and that they must give close attention to his instructions (vv. 6–8). Because Christians have the presence of the Holy Spirit dwelling in and empowering them, they must—and are enabled to—live in holiness.

The implications of this passage include the following: Sexual activity between husband and wife must bear all the marks of mature holiness. Forced sexual intercourse is precluded. There is such a thing as marital rape, and it is repugnant.[7] Additionally, forms of sexual activity to which one's spouse objects are precluded. If your spouse objects to some activity you find appealing, then your spouse's preference not to engage in that activity must be respected. On the contrary, sexual expression must be set in an atmosphere of love, companionship, tenderness, respect, honor,

---

7. For further discussion, see Sheila Wray Gregoire, "Reader Question: Can There Be Rape in Marriage?" To Love, Honor, and Vacuum, February 5, 2018, https://tolovehonorandvacuum.com/2018/02/christian-take-on-marital-rape/.

and nurture. Sexual activity is to be expressed in a God-honoring and spouse-respecting way.[8]

As for the church in general, we must not let the extended contact and close relationship between ourselves become the occasion for adultery or other kinds of sexual immorality. Reprehensibly, the church is notorious for affairs between male pastors and their female executive assistants. Other-gender counseling also has this bad reputation. At the same time (as seen in the previous chapter), these pitfalls must not have a chilling effect on our relationships as siblings. But the dangers do call for us to be wise, discerning, and prudent in this matter.

Sexuality is to be sanctified. Sexually holy Christians live as whole people in a fractured world.

The Gifts of Marriage and Singleness (1 Cor. 7:1–9, 25–40)

In the back of some people's mind is the idea that marriage with its sexual activity is somehow dirty, wrong, or maybe even sinful. Thus, in their view, it's not God's best for Christians.[9] In 1 Corinthians 7 Paul dispels any such incorrect assumption as he issues instructions to ascetically minded Christians:[10] they shouldn't avoid getting married or prevent single believers from getting married because—they (wrongly) believe—sexual intercourse is evil.

---

8. Reprehensibly, authoritarian and patriarchal individuals and churches that cower behind an alleged biblical warrant for husbands to sexually disrespect and abuse their wives bring shame on the name of Christ, dishonor his body, and contaminate the temple of the Holy Spirit. Moreover, when they violate the covenant in which they've entered with their wife, do they not break the marriage bond?

9. In some cases, the Roman Catholic rule of celibacy for its priests and religious orders, and its elevation of Mary as "Ever-virgin," contributes to this suspicion about the married state and intercourse. So too do evangelical churches that struggle to broach the topic of sexual activity without a sense of shame and embarrassment.

10. Ascetic Christians insist on the goodness of spiritual activities but disregard physical activities. They eat sparingly, sleep little, and fast often. We addressed this Gnosticism/neo-Gnosticism in our opening chapter.

Moreover, married people can't pursue holiness before God by refusing to engage in sexual intercourse.

The ascetic's motto in verse 1 can be understood in two different ways. First, "It is good for a man not to touch a woman"[11] is a prohibition of any physical contact between men and women. Second, "It is good for a man not to have sexual relations with a woman"[12] is a prohibition of sexual intercourse. In either case, the motto must be nuanced. In general, it should be followed as a basic principle of Christian conduct. But when it comes to the husband and wife relationship, it is to be soundly rejected.

The ascetic slogan can't be used to prohibit Christians who don't have the gift of celibacy from getting married. Tragically, if they don't marry, they will end up burning with passion—being obsessed with and dominated by sexual urges that go unfulfilled (v. 9). Furthermore, it can't be used to encourage married Christians to refrain from sexual activity on the grounds that it is (wrongly believed to be) inherently evil and must be avoided. On the contrary, Paul sanctions sexual intercourse between a husband and a wife (vv. 2–4). Among other purposes (e.g., pleasure and procreation), sexual intercourse acts as a protection against sexual immorality. The physical expression of sexual desires within marriage renders the couple less likely to express those desires in immoral ways. Specifically, Paul sets forth the conjugal rights of husbands and wives: the spouse has a claim to the partner's body for sexual fulfillment.[13]

In this discussion of marriage, Paul also addresses singleness (vv. 8–9). This state, like that of marriage, is a gift of God. There may be a seasonal nature to this "gift," in that God grants grace,

11. NASB, CSB literal translation.
12. ESV, NIV.
13. Paul concedes—not commands—that regular sexual activity may be interrupted for a time if the two mutually agree, if there is a good purpose, and if they reengage after the period is complete (vv. 5–6). This abstinence, however, doesn't make them more holy. On the contrary, it can even lead to disastrous results if not treated properly.

patience, and ability to attend to one's studies, work, and other responsibilities for a time. Faithfulness to those callings takes precedence over the pursuit of marriage, with a general contentment with one's singleness for that season. When that time extends beyond a season and becomes a permanent state, the following considerations are key.

Paul's preference is that "the unmarried and the widows . . . remain single" (v. 8 ESV) as he is, for celibacy offers many advantages.[14] These include avoidance of worldly troubles, freedom from anxieties, and undivided devotion to the Lord (vv. 29–35). The advantages of singleness are many, yet only those to whom this gift is given should remain single. Those with the gift of celibacy aren't asexual beings who lack sexual desire, but they are able to control those urges by channeling them in God-honoring ways. Lacking such self-control, people should pursue marriage so they aren't overwhelmed by sexual desire and thus fall into immorality.

Several implications arise from this passage. The first is for married people. Husbands and wives should develop an enjoyable, satisfying sexual relationship. This includes communicating their needs, desires, what feels good, what doesn't feel good, and the like. They should maintain physical excitement and not let their relationship become boring or mundane, and they must remember the mutuality of their sexual relationship. The husband isn't

14. Paul doesn't contradict himself in his first letter to Timothy when he instructs younger women who are widows to marry (1 Tim. 5:11, 14). In that pastoral letter, Paul differentiates between older women whom the church should enroll on its list of widows to support (vv. 3–6, 9) and younger women whose widowhood doesn't qualify them to be put on the list. It is the viability of one's financial status that is under discussion. Older widows who are without any financial support are to be cared for by the church. Younger widows should get married and have children, and their husband and sons will financially support them. In his letter to the Corinthians, Paul encourages "the unmarried and the widows" to remain single with the assumption that in some way they will be provided for financially. An unmarried woman may be cared for by her father and extended family members. A widow may qualify for financial assistance by the church (as Paul explains in his letter to Timothy) unless her late husband left her in a good financial situation.

necessarily the sole initiator, with sex being for him. The wife is also the initiator, not just the passive responder, with sex being for her.

Moreover, one spouse should never use sex as a tool to manipulate the other spouse. The proposed deal—"I'll have sex with you if you do such and such for me"—isn't the right approach. Sexual intercourse isn't so much "You owe me!" but "I owe you!" The husband is to render his duty: he is to fulfill his wife's sexual needs. The wife is to render her duty: she is to fulfill her husband's sexual needs. In certain circles, the latter is often emphasized and the former is rarely, even embarrassingly, noted. But this passage highlights a strong dose of equality and mutuality. Far from the husband being the only one to initiate and the wife being the one to respond, the wife may similarly initiate and the husband respond. Paul endorses both rhythms.[15] In our hypersexualized society, with so much pressure to do the wrong thing, couples should build up a strong defense against immorality by finding sexual fulfillment with their spouse.

The second implication is for single people. Admittedly, I write this from the perspective of a married person, with help from my single friends. As a single person, you may have a sense of incompleteness, and this sense may be reinforced and augmented by our culture in general and the church culture in particular. The basic church sentiment is that everyone should be (happily) married and should have (lots of) kids. Given that dominating opinion, you as a single person may question what is wrong with you, feel pressure to get married at all costs, and sense that you are a second-class citizen. But the church's sentiment is off target,

15. It is beyond doubt that perverse people can and do abuse this biblical instruction. They quote Scripture and insist that their spouse, who is the object of their derision and contempt, concede to meet their sexual demands. In such loveless marriages, blind obedience to wrongly invoked Scripture does nothing to resolve the problems and conflicts. On the contrary, it merely reinforces the evil status quo. Christian counselors must be alert to this far too common situation, and they should never direct couples to engage in sex to bring the two closer together.

and I'm sorry you've experienced such mistreatment. As my own church's statement of faith affirms, your singleness by no means entails a "loss or diminution of personhood, dignity, or contributive capability." On the contrary, you are a holy and whole image bearer whom the church is to love and respect.[16]

Community should be a relational place that encourages singles to enjoy life-giving friendships with others—both married and single. Married couples should befriend single men and women and incorporate them into their family, community group, circle of friends, activities, and hobbies. Such friendships value single people as divine image bearers to love and from whom to receive love. Drawing near is not about trying to "fix" them or "fix them up" for the purpose of getting them married.

In terms of its leadership, the church must not be driven by fear and suspicion of its staff members who are single. Sadly, several broad, poisonous attitudes have taken root in the church. One fear is that a single man on staff will have sex with girls in the youth group. Alternatively, if a man is getting older and is

16. When reflecting on your state of singleness, consider the best way of talking about it: a "season" of singleness, the "gift" of singleness, or something else. Live your singleness moment by moment. Don't worry about the past; don't feel disappointed that your life hasn't been what you dreamed it would be and is now gone forever. At the same time, don't fixate on the future, pining with the wish/dream for a perfect mate to bring completeness and satisfaction. If that time of singleness extends beyond a season and becomes a permanent state, you may respond in different ways. Longsuffering in the face of unmet desires properly leads to lament before God. If grumbling and complaining arise from distrust of God, work to transform those feelings to mourning and grief that flow from disappointed but not abandoned hope in him.

Don't dismiss or denigrate the fact that you as a single person are a social being with sexual feelings and drives. With the call to glorify God and to express that calling with sexual integrity, as a single person you are to enjoy relationships with others—both married and single. Engage in this world while guarding your heart, rejecting instant gratification, and fleeing temptation. Set your thoughts and affections on honorable and pure things, making the right choices so that you don't have to learn the difficult way from hindsight, even taking extreme measures when being bested by temptation and sin. Avoid sexually tempting situations, limit the intake of sexually stimulating media, and evade sexually compromising places and circumstances. My thanks to Kelly Nall and Lainey Greer for pushing me to develop these thoughts.

not yet married, the suspicion is that he must be homosexual. These attitudes are manifested in the heightened difficulty that single men encounter when trying to find a church staff position. Another attitude is that a single woman on staff must be one of the "three ghosts": a usurper, a temptress, and/or a child.[17] She has designs on claiming authority and taking over the leadership of the church. Or she is a seductress, plotting how to get men to have sex with her. Or she is weak, incompetent, and needs to be coddled. These ghosts also come in combination. Treating single men and women in the church on the basis of these attitudes is both wrong and disastrous.

The gifts of marriage and singleness are to be received thankfully and lived joyfully.

In summary, God's design for his image bearers is that, as social people, we express our sociality in the case of marriage through sexual activity that is God-honoring, self-valuing, and spouse-respecting.

Application

How are you expressing your sexuality in God-honoring, self-respecting, and others-respecting ways?

Specifically, are you satisfied with your progress toward holiness and sanctification before God and others in the matter of your sexuality? What do you find most helpful in this regard? How can you strengthen weaknesses in this area?

For the Curious

Certainly, much more can and needs to be said about sexuality expressed in uprightness. Given the hypersexualization of our

---

17. Jen Wilkin, "3 Female Ghosts That Haunt the Church," The Gospel Coalition, February 12, 2015, https://www.thegospelcoalition.org/article/3-female-ghosts-that-haunt-the-church/.

culture and the prevalence of wrong expressions, however, we give further consideration to sexual sins. Beyond what we've discussed already—adultery, immorality among Christians, withholding of sexual intercourse within marriage, and the struggles of singleness—we address five other areas: lust, pornography, masturbation, same-sex attraction and homosexuality, and polyamory and polygamy.

Lust

Before discussing lust, we need to define it in relation to both sociality and sexuality. Recall that sociality, as presented in the previous chapter, is the basic human orientation toward other people for friendship and community. It can be expressed positively and according to divine design through relationships that are life-promoting. Alternatively, sociality can be expressed negatively through destructive relationships.

Second, as we've just discussed, sexual activity refers to any physical event or movement between people that is intended to arouse erotic desires and sensations for various purposes. When placed in the right context of a covenant marriage relationship, sexual activity is right and good (assuming it is expressed in proper ways, as noted above). When pursued outside marriage, sexual activity is ruled out by Scripture.

Lust then falls under the first category of sociality expressed in a negative manner. It arises from a divinely designed social desire for companionship and bonding, but lust expresses that good gift in a sinful way. Lust can be defined as the practice of objectifying other people for satisfying one's personal sexual desire.[18] Examples are many and include fantasizing about engaging in sexual activity, gazing inappropriately at others with wrong intentions, evaluating others only in terms of sexual attractiveness, devaluing others by viewing them as a means for satisfying sexual desire, and thinking

18. My thanks to Gracilynn Hanson for suggesting this definition of lust.

about abusing or violating others. In all cases, lust is sinful and is ruled out by Scripture.

What can we do to avoid lust?[19] How can we express our God-given desires in God-honoring and others-respecting ways so as to overcome the rampant, tragic sins in this area? These suggestions aren't exhaustive but represent possible approaches. First and foremost, we need to develop a vision of Jesus and his many saving benefits that so enthralls us that lustful enticements fade in comparison. Second, we must work hard to cultivate appropriately close friendships with those of the other sex. Third, we should give thanks for the wonders of both sociality and sexual activity while living within biblically prescribed boundaries. Fourth, to combat the hypersexualized culture in which we live, we need to cultivate maturity, self-control, and discipline that postpones instant and momentary gratification in anticipation of something else: holiness and a clean conscience in our relationship with God and, in the case of marriage, a covenant relationship with our best friend. Fifth, and along those same lines, we must acknowledge that it's possible to control our sexual urges just like we can control our other desires. We should never dismiss sexual purity as being unrealistic to achieve. The notion that our mind possesses a life of its own and that lust is therefore normal is wrongheaded.

Given the widespread epidemic of lust, what do we do when we lust? Personally, we should repent and confess our lust. Such confession—agreeing with God that lust is wrong and displeasing to him—should be practiced regularly and with faith that God does indeed cleanse from all sexual failures (1 John 1:9). Such confession should be seen as more than a duty, because it offers the promise of restored intimacy with the Lord. Moreover, within the church we should act graciously and relentlessly to rescue those who struggle with persistent lust. Interventions such as pastoral

19. For further discussion, see Gregg R. Allison, "Am I Lustful, Gluttonous, or Slothful?," *Christianity Today*, March 29, 2011, http://www.christianitytoday.com/biblestudies/articles/spiritualformation/lustfulgluttonousslothful.html.

counseling, redemption groups for sexual addiction, and accountability for internet usage when someone struggles with pornography should be commonplace in the church.

Pornography

Because of its extensive and constantly increasing use, pornography warrants discussion in between the topics of lust and masturbation. The statistics are staggering. A high percentage of men and women, as well as adolescent boys and girls, regularly consume some form of pornography. Many young people first learn about sexual activity through visiting pornographic websites. Married couples experiment with new forms of sexual activity by watching pornography, leading to a weakening of their relationship. At the heart of pornography usage is the objectification of men and women, the dehumanizing of people created in the image of God.

Consumption of pornography has led to a devastating increase in disrespect for the other gender, cyberbullying, victimization of adolescents, incidents of violence during sexual intercourse, acceptability of pornography usage, sex trafficking and other sex crimes, infidelity, and divorce.[20] Alteration of the brain's chemistry through persistent use of pornography means that its consumption becomes addictive, similar to alcoholism and drug dependency.[21] Deleterious effects of such addiction include an increasing need for greater and more explicit stimulation, unrelenting feelings of shame and guilt (or a searing of the conscience to muffle those feelings), a lessening of need for "actual" sexual intercourse, and more. While many people consider this to be primarily a male problem, an increasing number of women are engaging with pornography.

20. For a discussion of these and other statistics, see "Statistics by Category: Pornography," Enough Is Enough: Making the Internet Safe for Children and Families, https://enough.org/stats_porn_industry.
21. Gary Wilson, *Your Brain on Porn: Internet Pornography and the Emerging Science of Addiction* (Kent, UK: Commonwealth Publishing, 2014).

What is pornography's relationship to lust and masturbation? As discussed above, lust arises from a divinely designed social desire for companionship and bonding, but lust expresses that good gift in a sinful way. For example, a man who lusts objectifies a woman mentally and considers satisfying his personal desire in an illicit, sexual way. That lust may remain a mental and emotional event and not advance beyond the conceptual stage. When pornography is involved, the event takes on the added dimension of visual stimulation. The man's level of lust increases. Seeking physical satisfaction during this mental/emotional/visual event, he engages in masturbation. At this point, his entire embodied being is engaged sinfully. As his lust goes unchecked, and as his consumption of pornography becomes intensified, masturbation becomes a regular vice.

Conquering pornography usage involves many of the suggestions offered in our discussion of overcoming lust. Additional measures to counter pornography include use of internet filters; restriction of access to computers, tablets, and smart phones; participation in Sexual Addicts Anonymous or Sexaholics Anonymous; accountability to close friends; and pastoral care and professional counseling.

Masturbation

Often associated with lust is masturbation, one type of impure sexual activity. Masturbation is the act of stimulating one's own genital organ(s) for the purpose of achieving physical climax, carried out in isolation and exclusive of sexual intercourse. For our purposes, masturbation doesn't include erotic activity between husband and wife in which they stimulate one another's genitals. Nor does it include a husband stimulating himself or a wife stimulating herself in the presence and with the approval of their spouse.[22]

---

22. Helpful resources for this discussion, and from which some elements have been drawn, include Keith Sanford, "Toward a Masturbation Ethic," *Journal of*

Curiously, no biblical passage directly addresses masturbation. Some people consider the sin of Onan to be a case of masturbation, with the conclusion that it is a deadly sin (Gen. 38:6–10). However, Onan's sin was *coitus interruptus*—withdrawing his penis before ejaculation—as a means of avoiding his covenantal responsibilities to impregnate his dead brother's widow. Other people point to 1 Corinthians 6:9 in the King James Version: "abusers of themselves with mankind." They understand this verse to refer to masturbation, with the conclusion that those who masturbate are excluded from salvation (1 Cor. 6:10). But the proper translation is "males who have sex with males" (CSB). Thus it is homosexuality, not masturbation, that is condemned as a deadly sin. Still others cite the description of rebellious people as those "who burn with lust among the oaks, under every green tree" (Isa. 57:5) as standing against masturbation. But the reference there is to idolatrous worship (with green trees symbolizing idols) and the associated practice of orgies. Leviticus 15:16–18 (par. Deut. 23:9–11) seems to include a situation in which masturbation takes place during consciousness, yet the act wasn't considered sinful because the uncleanness was ceremonial, not moral.[23]

Psychology and Theology 22, no. 1 (1994): 21–28; James R. Johnson, "Toward a Biblical Approach to Masturbation," *Journal of Psychology and Theology* 10, no. 2 (Summer 1982): 137–46; Alex W. Kwee and David C. Hoover, "Theologically-Informed Education about Masturbation: A Male Sexual Health Perspective," *Journal of Psychology and Theology* 26, no. 4 (2008): 258–69; Mark Driscoll, *Porn-again Christian: A Frank Discussion on Pornography and Masturbation*, available at https://archive.org/details/Porn-againChristian/mode/2up; and "Flesh Series: What's Up with Masturbation?," Cru, https://www.cru.org/us/en/train-and-grow/life-and-relationships/men/flesh/whats-up-with-masturbation.html.

23. "When a man has an emission of semen, he is to bathe himself completely with water, and he will remain unclean until evening. Any clothing or leather on which there is an emission of semen is to be washed with water, and it will remain unclean until evening. If a man sleeps with a woman and has an emission of semen, both of them are to bathe with water, and they will remain unclean until evening" (Lev. 15:16–18). A parallel passage is Deut. 23:9–11: "When you are encamped against your enemies, be careful to avoid anything offensive. If there is a man among you who is unclean because of a bodily emission during the night, he must go outside the camp; he may not come anywhere inside the camp. When

The conclusion then is that no biblical passage specifically condemns masturbation.

Historical considerations are different, as masturbation was consistently and roundly condemned in the past.[24] Augustine viewed masturbation as unnatural because it doesn't lead to procreation.[25] Medieval Judaism, based on the Talmud, condemned masturbation because it was identified as the sin of Onan. Thomas Aquinas believed that rape, incest, and adultery are natural sins in contrast with masturbation, which is an unnatural sin. He considered them to be "natural" in the sense that they involve actual sexual intercourse with another person.[26] But he viewed masturbation as "unnatural" because it is self-sex, done apart from another person. During the Renaissance, masturbation was denounced because it was believed that all elements of human life are present in semen. Thus to spill semen was to destroy human persons therein contained. Even the modern medical profession of the time warned that masturbation produces severe physical and emotional damage.[27]

___

evening approaches, he is to wash with water, and when the sun sets he may come inside the camp." The first scenario (Lev. 15:16–17; par. Deut. 23:9–11) is one of involuntary emission of semen: a nocturnal emission, "wet" dream, or spontaneous orgasm that includes ejaculation of semen. These biblical instructions don't include a similar experience for females of spontaneous vaginal wetness or orgasm. The second scenario (Lev. 15:18) is probably not one of involuntary emission, because that case has just been addressed. Rather, it is a man engaging in masturbation while with a woman. It isn't sexual intercourse because, in that case, his emission would be internal to her, not external. Rather, it is masturbation, as his emission is external to her. It renders both of them ceremonially unclean and requires both of them to bathe to remove the spilled semen.

24. As will be apparent, these historical discussions of masturbation were almost exclusively male-focused.

25. Still today, the Roman Catholic Church, because of its procreative position, condemns masturbation.

26. Note: Aquinas still considered rape, incest, and adultery to be sins.

27. In 1758 Samuel Tissot published *Onania* in which he asserted that masturbation causes excessive blood flow to the brain and leads to insanity. Even into the nineteenth century, doctors affirmed that the loss of sperm in masturbation reduces precious health-preserving fluids. To counteract this loss, special whole grain foods, which were presumed to reduce the urge to masturbate, were

To update this position, there is no scientific evidence that masturbation in and of itself causes any physical harm or any form of psychological maladjustment or social deficiency.

In our contemporary context, compulsive masturbation may be a symptom of underlying psychological problems such as anxiety, insecurity, interpersonal conflict, guilt, and loneliness. It also reflects a physiological reality that frequent masturbation leads to even more frequent masturbation as the body (here, we address the male body) produces more semen after ejaculation, resulting in stronger biological urges for more ejaculations. Additionally, masturbation may contribute to a pattern of (again, focusing on men) male laziness. Rather than working hard to develop a relationship with a woman leading to marriage, and rather than working hard to love and romance his wife, the man prefers to take a shortcut. Masturbation becomes an easy substitute for the development of an interpersonal relationship as it mimics the physical (for many, the easier) part of that relationship while neglecting the emotional, vulnerable, and conversational (for many, the more difficult) parts. It may interfere with cultivating maturity and self-discipline when it comes to postponing gratification in anticipation of something right and good: sexual intercourse with one's spouse.

Where does this leave us? Numerous views on masturbation circulate among people, even among church members.[28] In my

---

developed. This view led to two foods we still enjoy today: Kellogg's Corn Flakes and graham crackers.

28. For example, some believe it isn't reasonable or beneficial to expect people to refrain from masturbating. Others maintain that masturbation isn't a biological necessity and therefore people should not do it. Some point to the fact that masturbation is very prevalent and is able to bring about an unfailing sensation of delight or at least relief (for some women, masturbation provides some reprieve from menstrual cramps). Thus they claim that some important human need is being met by it, and they warn that those who unconditionally condemn masturbation must be prepared to face the dilemma that could result from making such a prohibition. Others hold that masturbation in and of itself isn't sinful, but being unable to control masturbation or being enslaved by it is sinful. Thus because masturbation can so easily become a controlling power in a person's life, Christians should abstain from it. Still others assert that masturbation is sinful

view, because no biblical passage specifically condemns masturbation, we should be cautious about carelessly calling it a sin, especially a principal sin. Our approach should be to draw implications for masturbation from biblical principles and models and from its connection to other matters. In light of these considerations, I regard it as a low-grade sin.[29] That is, on a spectrum running from abominations—heinous crimes—to minor sins, masturbation is closer to the latter category than the former category. Don't misunderstand. I'm not saying it's not a sin. Masturbation is a self-pacifying action that relies on a human solution (ejaculation, orgasm, and the feelings of well-being they prompt) instead of on God and the resources that he provides for calmness, tranquility, solace, and stability. Moreover, we still need to reject the immediate gratification that prompts it, exercise self-control, work hard to resist temptation, and ruthlessly engage in bodily discipline.[30]

Though in and of itself masturbation isn't a serious sin, its connection with other matters renders it very problematic. These related matters include lust, anxiety, frustration, use of pornography, unbelief in God's provision, escape from boredom, unclean conscience, laziness to cultivate a strong personal relationship leading to marriage or within an established marriage, and more. Frequently, the stimulus for masturbation is the objectification

---

because it is solo sex or because it always involves lust or because it destroys one's relationship with God.

29. When considering the degrees of sin, we must distinguish between sin in relationship to guilt and sin in relationship to its impact on God and people. In terms of guilt, all sin is equally sin and brings guilt before God and leads to condemnation (Gal. 3:10; James 2:10–11). In terms of sin's impact on one's relationship with God and with people, some sins are more severe than others. For example, idolatry (Exod. 20:3–6), sexual immorality (as we've seen in 1 Cor. 6:12–20), and murder (Gen. 9:6) are serious sins in that they produce a greater disturbance in one's relationship with others. It is in this second sense that I evaluate the degree of sinfulness of masturbation.

30. For further discussion, see "Questions and Concerns about Masturbation," Focus on the Family, https://www.focusonthefamily.com/family-qa/questions-and -concerns-about-masturbation/.

of others, reducing other people to sexual targets by means of fantasy, imagination, or pornographic images.[31] Its association with these other matters renders masturbation dangerous, as does the fact that it may lead to greater sins. Under these conditions, masturbation rises to the level of a very serious sin.

Helping ourselves and others to understand masturbation at a personal level may best be accomplished by engaging in a series of questions that reflect biblical principles on this matter:

- Does this activity enslave me? If so, why engage in it?
- Does this activity involve lust? If so, it is precluded.
- Is this activity beneficial? If not, why waste time doing it?
- Can I give thanks to God as I engage in this activity? If not, it is precluded.
- Does this activity create a barrier in my relationship with God? For example, does it hinder my prayers? If so, it is precluded.
- Does this activity hinder or distort my relationship with others? If so, it is precluded.

Because masturbation isn't directly addressed in Scripture, we are called upon to consider those other areas connected to it. Specifically, we must help ourselves and others to develop a strong relationship with God, to develop strong relationships with others, to resist temptation of all kinds, and to replace lust with pure thoughts. We must also emphasize the gospel of the forgiveness of sins.

Same-Sex Attraction (SSA) and Homosexuality

Reflective of our discussion of lust, our treatment of same-sex attraction (SSA) falls under the category of sociality expressed in

---

31. My thanks to Gracilynn Hanson for her perceptive thoughts on this issue.

a negative manner.[32] Moreover, our treatment of homosexuality falls under the category of illicit sexual activity.

SSA arises from a divinely designed desire for social companionship and bonding, but it expresses that good gift in sinful ways that include fantasizing about engaging in sexual activity with someone of the same gender, gazing inappropriately at others of the same gender with wrong intentions, evaluating others of the same gender only in terms of sexual attractiveness, devaluing others of the same gender by viewing them as a means for satisfying sexual desire, and thinking about abusing or violating others of the same gender. In all such cases, SSA is sinful and is ruled out by Scripture.

SSA isn't the same as homosexual activity, though it may lie at the root of such activity. Nor should we confuse SSA with the divinely given social desire for relationships with those of our same gender. We are called to love and bond with others, and fear and misunderstanding of SSA can't be permitted to put a chill on our relationships with those of the same gender.

SSA that expresses itself in actual sexual activity with someone of the same gender is also sinful and ruled out by Scripture. First and foremost, homosexuality contradicts the divinely established expression of sexual intercourse, which is to be between a man/husband and a woman/wife in a covenant marriage. Genesis 1–2 fixes that pattern from the outset of human creation, and Jesus affirms that pattern in his discussion of marriage between a man and a woman (Matt. 19:4–6, citing Gen. 2:24).[33]

Second, homosexuality is denounced in Scripture, as the following demonstrates. The narrative of God's destruction of Sodom

32. I'm not going to enter the debate on whether one's attraction to a member of the same gender—same-sex *desire*—is in and of itself sinful. I will only treat *activity* arising from same-sex attraction, which is indeed sinful.
33. The argument for the legitimacy of homosexuality because Jesus himself never condemned it fails. Jesus was a Jew who abided by Torah and thus would have affirmed the biblical pattern of sexual activity between a husband and a wife.

and Gomorrah underscores the sinfulness of homosexuality (Gen. 19:1–11).[34] Two Old Testament passages clearly prohibit homosexual intercourse and label it as an abomination before God (Lev. 18:22; 20:13).[35] In the New Testament, Paul considers the human drift from "natural" (hetero)sexual activity to "unnatural" (homo)sexual activity to be an aspect of divine deliverance to disgraceful and shameful acts that merit his wrath (Rom. 1:18–27).[36] Additionally, in two of his lists of sins that exclude people from the kingdom of God, Paul includes homosexual activity (1 Cor. 6:9–11; 1 Tim. 1:8–11).[37] Finally, Jude uses "sexual immorality and perversions" committed by the men of Sodom and Gomorrah to "serve as an example by undergoing the punishment of eternal fire" (Jude 6–7).[38] According to Scripture, homosexuality is a deadly sin deserving of divine condemnation.

As with all sins, the gospel provides hope for forgiveness, justification, cleansing, and transformation for people wrestling with SSA or/and who are engaged in homosexual activity. While the church does not affirm SSA and homosexuality, it must be a

34. Some people object that the sin of Sodom and Gomorrah wasn't homosexuality but a violation of the hospitality code, or idolatry, or homosexual gang rape, or the desire to engage in unnatural sexual activity with angels.

35. Those who object to these prohibitions argue that homosexuality isn't wrong in and of itself but because it was practiced by the pagan nations surrounding Israel, which was to distinguish itself from them by not engaging in their practices. They say the prohibition against homosexuality is part of the ceremonial elements, not the moral elements, of the holiness code of Leviticus, and therefore it isn't binding on the church today.

36. While there are several objections to this traditional understanding, we focus on two: (1) what Paul condemns is "unnatural homosexual activity" but not sexual activity between consenting adults who are constitutionally homosexual; and (2) what Paul condemns is pederasty (sexual activity between an older man with a young boy) and promiscuity like prostitution, but not homosexuality per se.

37. Objections focus on the obscurity of the terms that Paul uses in relation to this activity and the nature of the sins that Paul actually condemns.

38. Similar to the objection to the traditional understanding of Gen. 19:1–11, the objection to the traditional interpretation of Jude 6 is that the sin of Sodom and Gomorrah was actually the failure to show proper hospitality to strangers or the desire to engage in unnatural sexual activity with angels.

welcoming community for those who struggle. We are called to befriend them, invite them in, listen to them, and be steadfastly gospel-centered in our walk with them.[39] Our aim is to be, and help others to be, whole people living in a fractured world.

Polyamory and Polygamy

Disturbingly, the incidence of polyamory and polygamy is on the rise in the United States and has the potential of becoming the next trend in sociality and sexuality that the church will face. Thus a brief treatment is needed.

Some definitions are in order. "Polyamory—from the Greek *poly*, meaning 'many,' and the Latin *amor*, meaning 'love'—refers to 'the practice of, or desire for, intimate relationships with more than one partner, with the consent of all partners involved.' While these intimate relationships between three or more people are typically sexual, they don't need to be."[40] Polygamy—from the Greek *poly*, meaning "many" (at least more than one), and *gamos*, meaning "marriage"—refers to marriage in which either the husband (in most cases) or the wife has more than one spouse at the same time.[41]

39. For further discussion, see Rachel Gilson, *Born Again This Way: Coming Out, Coming to Faith, and What Comes Next* (Charlotte, NC: The Good Book Company, 2020); Rachel Gilson, "How to Be a Safe Space for the Same-Sex Attracted," The Gospel Coalition, January 30, 2018, https://www.thegospelcoalition.org/article/safe-space-for-ssa/.

40. Preston Sprinkle and Branson Parler, "Polyamory: Pastors' Next Sexual Frontier," *Christianity Today*, September 25, 2019, https://www.christianitytoday.com/pastors/2019/fall/polyamory-next-sexual-frontier.html. The article doesn't indicate the source of the citation. One expression of polyamory is a "thruple," that is, a three-way relationship between homosexual men or bisexuals. Another type is a "throuple," that is, a three-way relationship between people, either two men and a woman or two women and a man. For the latter relationship see Aryelle Siclait, "Why Being in a Throuple Could Be Your Best Relationship Ever," *Women's Health*, May 10, 2019, https://www.womenshealthmag.com/relationships/a27346835/what-is-a-throuple-relationship/.

41. Polygamy was popularized by the HBO series *Big Love* and two TLC series, *Sister Wives* and *My Five Wives*. Though illegal, it is practiced in the state of Utah among some Mormons. There is a growing movement to decriminalize polygamy in Utah. Andrea Smardon, "Polygamy Is about to Be Decriminalised in Utah. Is It

Both polyamory and polygamy are wrong. To be clear, the desire for close relationships at the heart of polyamory, as our chapter on sociality underscores, is divinely given and thus to be embraced and actualized. Polyamory then arises from a divinely designed social desire for companionship and bonding, but it expresses that good gift in a sinful way. The desire becomes a craving for overly intimate relationships with various people. The longing goes beyond the bounds that are inherent in siblingship. Though that line may be difficult to draw, it does exist. Even if the bonding doesn't express itself in sexual activity, the depth of polyamorous intimacy goes beyond the love that is rightly shared between brothers and sisters.

As for polygamy, yes, Scripture does tell about the polygamous customs of the patriarchs, of Gideon, of kings such as David and Solomon (though Israel's kings were prohibited from having multiple wives; Deut. 17:17), and of others. The law of Moses even accommodated polygamy (Deut. 21:15–17) and made it mandatory in the case of a man marrying his brother's widow (Deut. 25:5–6). But we must not overlook the fact that in all of these stories polygamy did not turn out well for those who engaged in it.

Despite these Old Testament narratives and regulations, polygamy should be viewed as a divine accommodation in particular circumstances while still being against God's clear pattern of marriage between one man and one woman (Gen. 2:18–25; Matt. 19:4–6). Polygamy creates a situation of adultery, which is clearly sinful. So while polygamy isn't as directly denounced and explicitly prohibited as homosexuality is, Scripture's less direct approach shouldn't be interpreted to mean that God approves of polygamy.

Our God-given sociality, which propels us toward relationships with others, may be rightly expressed as sexual activity in only one

Good News for Women?," *The Guardian*, March 5, 2020, https://www.theguardian .com/lifeandstyle/2020/mar/05/polygamy-is-about-to-be-decriminalised-in-utah -is-it-good-news-for-women. In certain countries, Muslim men are permitted to have multiple wives. In the Qur'an, Sura 4:3 allows men to have up to four wives.

case: a monogamous marriage. Certainly we may, and should, have close friendships with our siblings in Christ. However, we must not allow these relationships to overstep the bounds of proper intimacy as in the case of polyamory. And we must not express that companionship in more than one marriage as in the case of polygamy.

CHAPTER 6

THE SON'S BODY

Consider

 Think carefully about the following question: What does it mean that, in the incarnation two thousand years ago, the eternal Son of God became embodied?

Big Idea

 The incarnation is about God the Son becoming embodied. The triune God's design was for the eternal Son of the Father to become the God-man by virtue of the Holy Spirit's uniting him to a human nature just like ours. In keeping with our first five chapters, this incarnation means that God the Son took on a created, gendered, particular, social, and sexual body. The purpose of this embodiment was so the Son, without spot or blemish and perfectly prepared for his mission, would be the once-and-for-all embodied sacrifice for sin. Through him, we may live as whole people in a fractured world.

wow

Application Question

How does the embodiment of the Son of God instruct you about your existence as an embodied person?

113

The Son's Body and Our Body

In recent years, Christian scholars have increasingly recognized the importance of understanding the humanity of God the Son incarnate for understanding our humanity. Some go so far as to believe that "Christology is absolutely central to any adequate knowledge of the human person."[1] Without entering into that debate, it makes sense that if the Son is the perfect image of God (John 14:8–9; 2 Cor. 4:4; Heb. 1:3), if we Christ followers are being transformed into his image (Rom. 8:29; 2 Cor. 3:18), and if we will be fully conformed into his image when we experience the resurrection of our body (1 Cor. 15:47–49), then we should pay attention to the Son "in the flesh" (John 1:14; Rom. 8:3). And while the incarnation is certainly about more than his taking on a human body, it surely includes that aspect. So we will seek to learn about our embodiment from the Son's embodiment.

The Affirmation of the Son's Embodiment

In an intriguing passage in which he addresses how the church is to conduct itself, Paul underscores that "most certainly, the mystery of godliness is great: 'He was manifested in the flesh'" (1 Tim. 3:16). Apparently, while godliness is surely about behavior, its central focus isn't on *what* but on *whom*: he—the eternally existing, divine Son of God—was revealed "in the flesh." Immediately our minds go to the same idea expressed in John's Gospel: "In the beginning was the Word . . . and the Word became flesh" (John 1:1, 14). We see again that the preexisting Word of God, who was always with God and was himself fully God, "became flesh." For our purposes, we will render this phrase as "the Word became embodied." In so doing, we don't mean that, in the incarnation, the eternal Son of God

---

1. Marc Cortez, *ReSourcing Theological Anthropology: A Constructive Account of Humanity in the Light of Christ* (Grand Rapids: Zondervan, 2017), 19.

only took to himself a human body. That is the ancient error of Apollinarianism, which the church has denounced—and so do we.[2] Rather, while affirming that the Son took on the fullness of human nature—a human mind, human emotions, a human will, human motivations, and human purposing—our rendering underscores the topic of this book: Jesus became an embodied human being.

The Nature of the Son's Embodiment

Following the big ideas of the first five chapters, Jesus's embodiment means, first, that he took on a *created* body. In the incarnation, the eternal, divine Son didn't join with an already existing embodied person—Jesus son of Mary. To affirm that is to commit the error of Nestorianism.[3] Rather, God the Son was united to an embodied human nature that was miraculously created through the powerful work of the Holy Spirit in the virgin Mary. So his embodiment is the same as our embodiment: both his body and our bodies are created.

2. Apollinarianism is "the denial of the full humanity of the incarnate Son. Major tenets: (1) In taking on human nature, the Word of God only became united with 'flesh' (John 1:14). (2) Christ's human nature consisted of only a human body but not a human soul, which was replaced by the divine Word. The church objected that if Jesus was not a fully human being, then he could not save ordinary human beings. The Council of Constantinople (381), in its Nicene-Constantinopolitan Creed, and the Council of Chalcedon (451), in its Chalcedonian Creed, condemned Apollinarianism as heresy." Gregg R. Allison, *The Baker Compact Dictionary of Theological Terms* (Grand Rapids: Baker Books, 2016), s.v. "Apollinarianism."

3. Nestorianism is "the denial of the hypostatic union, that the incarnate Christ had two natures—one divine, one human—united in one person. Major tenets: (1) In the incarnation, two distinct persons—one divine, one human—worked in conjunction with each other. (2) This is true because a union of divine and human would have involved God in change, which is impossible. Though Nestorius denied that he held this position, the Councils of Ephesus (431) and Chalcedon (451), in the Chalcedonian Creed, condemned Nestorianism: Christ was not divided into two persons, but two natures united in one person." Allison, *Baker Compact Dictionary of Theological Terms*, s.v. "Nestorianism."

Second, the divine Son took on a *gendered* body—Jesus of Nazareth is male. He is the God-*man*. It is important to remember that God isn't gendered. The eternal triune God is neither male nor female.[4] Thus the incarnation isn't about the male Second Person of the Trinity becoming what he eternally is: a man. Rather, given the possibility of the Second Person becoming either a man or a woman (remember our earlier discussion of binarity), there is a fittingness to the Second Person becoming a man. One reason is the *eternal relation* existing between the First Person and Second Person: the latter is the *Son* of the Father. As the only begotten Son, he became embodied as a man. A second reason is the *role* of the Second Person in becoming incarnate: he came to be the second Adam, sent to undo the disobedience of the first Adam (Rom. 5:12–21). As the first Adam was a man, so too the second Adam was a man. A third reason is the biblical structure of *sonship*: sons are the heirs, the offspring who inherit the family blessing. As the incarnate Son who accomplished redemption, he inherits the divine blessings and shares them with all those who become sons of God through faith in him: brothers and sisters in Christ (Gal. 3:26–28).

Third, the Son of God became a *particular* gendered embodied person. His individuality is characterized by a specific ethnicity,

4. The use of gendered pronouns for God—referring to God as "he" and "him" rather than "she" and "her" or "it"—is another matter.

When my wife and I learned Italian living overseas, we had to learn the (sometimes seemingly random) gender of lots of words. *Tavolo*, for example, is a masculine word that refers to a table, the piece of furniture in the dining room. *Tavola* is a feminine word that refers to a set table, the cloth-covered, fork/spoon/knife holding, plates-of-food sustaining surface-with-legs where meals are eaten. The words are gendered, but the tables they refer to are not. Likewise, when we read the Bible and come across an expression like "*God* demonstrates *his* love," we should not jump to the conclusion that the divine being whom we worship and serve is masculine. The use of masculine words for God should not be confused with the gender of God. (Gregg Allison, "What's the Difference between a Pansexual Miley Cyrus and a Non-Gendered God?," Gospel Taboo, September 8, 2015, http://gospeltaboo.com/home/pansexual-miley-cyrus-and-non-gendered-god.)

family, temporality, spatiality, context, and story. In terms of his *ethnicity*, his lineage was Jewish, as traced in the New Testament genealogies (Matt. 1:1–17; Luke 3:23–38). In fulfillment of prophecy, Jesus was "a descendent from David according to the flesh" (Rom. 1:3 ESV). As such, he came to save his own people (John 1:11), as vividly displayed in his near-exclusive ministry to the people of Israel (Matt. 10:5–6). Jesus was a Jew. As for *family*, his mother was Mary, his father by way of adoption was Joseph, his siblings were both brothers and sisters, his cousin was John the Baptist, and his extended family included Zechariah and Elizabeth.

In regard to *temporality*, Jesus came in the fullness of time (Gal. 4:4), that is, at just the right moment two thousand years ago. He was a first-century Jew. As for his *spatiality*, Jesus was born in Bethlehem, spent his earliest years in Egypt, and came back to live in Nazareth. His extensive ministry—some estimates calculate that Jesus traveled about fifteen thousand miles over the three years— took him to places such as Galilee, Capernaum, Cana, Bethany, Jericho, Jerusalem, and Samaria. Still, he never traveled outside a hundred-mile radius.

In terms of his *context*, Jesus's adopted father was a carpenter, a trade that Jesus learned. As such, he was on the lower end of the socioeconomic scale. Politically, Jesus lived under the Roman oppression of his Jewish people. He gave honor to the system, insisting that taxes be paid to Caesar, and he rejected the popular desire that he be a political messiah. Educationally, Jesus probably never attended a formal school. Still, through his regular attendance in the synagogue and temple, he learned and practiced his Jewish faith. His Jewish cultural context in the backwaters of Nazareth meant that, until he launched his ministry, Jesus was a relative unknown. His rather obscure ethnic, familial, temporal, spatial, and contextual background makes it even more surprising that his story—which he never shared, but which is narrated in four Gospels—is the greatest story ever told.

Fourth, the *sociality* of Jesus underscores the reality of his incarnation. The entirety of his three-year ministry was spent in the company of the twelve disciples, three of whom formed an inner circle and one of whom was known as "the one Jesus loved" (John 13:23). This itinerant group was supported by several well-to-do women who traveled with them (Luke 8:1–3). Jesus had a special relationship with Mary, Martha, and Lazarus (John 11). Beyond these specific people, Jesus reached out to the innumerable crowds of people to whom he restored sight, speech, hearing, mobility, wholeness, freedom from demonic oppression—even life itself. As he came "eating and drinking," he was known as "a glutton and a drunkard, a friend of tax collectors and sinners" (Matt. 11:19). Jesus was a social person.

Fifth and finally, Jesus expressed his *sexuality* in God-honoring, self-valuing, and others-respecting ways. He lived a pure, celibate life, not marrying and not engaging in sexual intercourse. Moreover, he didn't commit the sin of lust. Rather, he channeled the sexual desires typical of him as a man in an appropriate manner. In one sense, Jesus experienced the many advantages of being single that Paul highlighted: Jesus was unconcerned "about the things of the world—how he may please his wife" (1 Cor. 7:33) and was able to "be devoted to the Lord without distraction" (1 Cor. 7:35). Jesus's mission demanded that he be unmarried.

In the incarnation, God the Son became a human being united to a created, gendered, particular, social, and sexual body. To summarize, the many aspects of Jesus's embodiment included "conception, birth, growth, fasting in the desert, immersion in the River Jordan, treks to the mountain or walks along the water's edge, meals, festivals, the laying-on of hands, the draining of physical strength after healing, transfiguration, trials, suffering, death, resurrection, ascension."[5] Certainly, Jesus's embodied experiences

5. Ola Sigurdson, *Heavenly Bodies: Incarnation, the Gaze, and Embodiment in Christian Theology* (Grand Rapids: Eerdmans, 2016), 67.

were unique to him as the God-man. The same may be said for each of us particular individuals. Yet the array of his embodied experiences rendered Jesus just like the rest of us.

The Purpose of the Son's Embodiment

As Scripture underscores, Jesus had to become embodied if he was to free us from sin, Satan, suffering, and death:

> Now since the children have flesh and blood in common, Jesus also shared in these, so that through his death he might destroy the one holding the power of death—that is, the devil—and free those who were held in slavery all their lives by the fear of death. For it is clear that he does not reach out to help angels, but to help Abraham's offspring. Therefore, he had to be like his brothers and sisters in every way, so that he could become a merciful and faithful high priest in matters pertaining to God, to make atonement for the sins of the people. For since he himself has suffered when he was tempted, he is able to help those who are tempted. (Heb. 2:14–18)

We human beings are "flesh and blood"—embodied people—who are enslaved not by our bodies (an error of Gnosticism) but by Satan. To save us human beings—not nonembodied angelic beings—God the Son had to become an embodied person just like us.

Replacing the shadows of sacrifices before his coming, the incarnate Son became the definitive embodied atoning sacrifice:

> For it is impossible for the blood of bulls and goats to take away sins. Therefore, as he was coming into the world, he said:
>
> > You did not desire sacrifice and offering,
> > but you prepared a body for me.
> > You did not delight
> > in whole burnt offerings and sin offerings.
> > Then I said, "See—

it is written about me
in the scroll—
I have come to do your will, O God." . . .

By this will, we have been sanctified through the offering of the body of Jesus Christ once for all time. (Heb. 10:4–7, 10)

Incarnated, without spot or blemish, and perfectly prepared to be the once-and-for-all embodied sacrifice for sin (Heb. 5:7–10), God the Son died on the cross to accomplish salvation. God (the Father) "condemned sin in the flesh by sending his own Son in the likeness of sinful flesh as a sin offering" (Rom. 8:3).

Only God the Son incarnate can rescue his people from their sins. God couldn't merely forgive sin without meeting his own demands for its punishment. It wouldn't be just for him to do so, thus contradicting Scripture's affirmation that God is "just and the justifier of the one who has faith in Jesus" (Rom. 3:26 ESV). Additionally, God could not save human beings in a nonembodied way, because we are embodied people. To paraphrase one theologian, "What is not taken on in the incarnation is not saved."[6] If salvation were somehow accomplished apart from embodiment, then our bodies would not be redeemed and we could not be whole people living in a fractured world. Thankfully then, in the incarnation God the Son took on a whole human nature, including a body, to rescue us embodied people from our sins.

No wonder the confession of Christ's incarnation—his embodiment—is essential to salvation: "Every spirit that confesses that Jesus Christ has come in the flesh is from God, but every spirit that does not confess Jesus is not from God. This is the spirit of the antichrist, which you have heard is coming; even now it is already in the world" (1 John 4:2–3). Accordingly, we reject all the denials

6. Gregory of Nazianzus, *Letter* 101, in vol. 7 of *The Nicene and Post-Nicene Fathers*, 2nd series, ed. Philip Schaff (1886–1889; repr., Peabody, MA: Hendrickson, 1994), 440.

of Jesus's embodied humanity. Docetism denies the incarnation, believing that it was impossible for the holy Son to take on an evil body.[7] Apollinarianism denies that the Son took on the whole of human nature; rather, it affirms that the only aspect the Son took to himself was a human body. Eutychianism denies that both natures in the incarnate Son retain their respective properties. Rather, it believes "(1) the divine nature nearly absorbed the human nature of Christ, meaning that his one nature is DIVINEhuman; (2) the divine and human natures fused, meaning that Christ's one nature is d^{h}i^{u}v^{m}i^{a}n^{n}e."[8] These errant views, which either deny the incarnation or seriously distort the kind of human nature that was united to the divine Son, are dangerous and should be denounced.[9]

7. Docetism is "the denial of the humanity of Christ. Docetism (from Gk. *dokeō*, 'to appear, seem') holds that Christ only seemed to be a man. He was, instead, a spirit being who only appeared as a human being. Scripture warns against this heresy: the refusal to acknowledge 'that Jesus Christ has come in the flesh' (1 John 4:1–3). Early church leaders demonstrated that Christ was truly human because he experienced the true activities of human beings: he was born, ate and drank, suffered, and died. Moreover, Christ's followers suffer in reality because Christ was human in reality." Allison, *Baker Compact Dictionary of Theological Terms*, s.v. "Docetism."

8. Allison, *Baker Compact Dictionary of Theological Terms*, s.v. "Eutychianism."

9. According to the Chalcedonian Creed (451), the church is united in its faith and taught

> to confess one and the same Son, our Lord Jesus Christ, the same perfect in Godhead and also perfect in manhood; truly God and truly man, of a reasonable [rational] soul and body; consubstantial [coessential] with the Father according to the Godhead, and consubstantial with us according to the manhood; in all things like unto us, without sin; begotten before all ages of the Father according to the Godhead, and in these latter days, for us and for our salvation, born of the Virgin Mary, the Mother of God, according to the manhood; one and the same Christ, Son, Lord, only begotten, to be acknowledged in two natures, without confusion, without change, without division, without separation; the distinction of [the divine and human] natures being by no means taken away by the union, but rather the property of each nature being preserved, and concurring in one Person and one Subsistence, not parted or divided into two persons, but one and the same Son, and only begotten, God the Word, the Lord Jesus Christ. ("The Symbol of Chalcedon," in Philip Schaff, *Creeds of Christendom*, 3

In summary, the incarnation is about God the Son becoming embodied. The triune God's design was for the eternal Son of the Father to become the God-man by virtue of the Holy Spirit's uniting him to a human nature just like ours. The purpose of this embodiment was so the incarnate Son would be the once-and-for-all embodied sacrifice for sin. He saves us so that we may live as whole people in a fractured world.

Application

The question for application is, How does the embodiment of the Son of God instruct you about your existence as an embodied person?

To start off, perhaps it is difficult for you to think in these terms: in the incarnation, "the Word of God took on a particular kind of human flesh—the kind that goes through puberty, grows armpit hair, has a ring finger longer than his index finger, a deeper voice than most women, and a penis."[10] If you struggle with these particularities of Jesus's human nature, why do you wrestle so? If not, what helps you to consider the incarnation in such concrete ways?

Personally, what are the connection points between the Son incarnate and you in terms of the created body, gendered body, particular body, social body, and sexual body? What does growing into fuller conformity to Christ's image look like concretely for you in terms of your embodiment?

For the Curious

An important consideration of the Son's embodiment is the fact that he is gendered as a male. Questions arise: If he is the true

vols [New York, 1877–1905], 2:62, https://www.ccel.org/ccel/schaff/creeds2.iv.i.iii.html. The text has been rendered clearer.)

10. Todd Wilson, *Mere Sexuality: Rediscovering the Christian Vision of Sexuality* (Grand Rapids: Zondervan, 2017), 45.

image of God and that image is male, does that mean that women are somehow not image bearers or bear God's image in some lesser, inferior way? How can he as a male High Priest sympathize with his women followers?

Regarding the first question, our first two chapters set forth the biblical affirmation that all human beings—male and female—are created in the image of God. We don't say that bearing God's image is a status conferred regardless of gender. Rather, we insist that all men and all women bear the divine image, and they do so as either male or female. There are no such things as agendered image bearers. Yes, the perfect image bearer, Jesus, is male. But this truth doesn't render men superior to women in the sense of being created more in the image of God. Nor does it render women inferior to men in the sense of being created less in the divine image.

As for the other objection, our discussion of genderedness underscores that there are no particular capacities and properties (obviously, outside of reproductive capabilities) that belong exclusively to women or that belong exclusively to men. There are, instead, common human capacities and properties that are—indeed, given gendered embodiment, will be naturally—expressed by women in ways that are fitting to women and that are expressed by men in ways that are fitting to men. Cognition, emotion, will, and purposing aren't gender-specific but common human capacities that are and will be innately expressed by women and men in ways that reflect their femaleness and maleness. Gentleness, courage, initiative, nurturing, patience, and protectiveness aren't gender-specific but common human properties that are and will be naturally expressed by women and men in ways that reflect their femaleness and maleness. In becoming incarnate, God the Son took on the fullness of human nature, that is, all common human capacities and properties. As fully human, he possesses the common capacities of cognition, sentiment, will, and purposing. And he possesses the common properties of gentleness, courage, initiative, nurturing, patience, and protectiveness. Therefore, the incarnate Son is able to sympathize as High Priest with all people who share those common capacities and properties. All men. And all women.

In order to save human beings, the Son had to become fully human, including becoming embodied. As embodiment maps onto genderedness, Jesus had to be gendered as either male or female. As we noted above, there are good and fitting reasons why he became a man: his eternal relation as the Son of the Father, his role as the second Adam, and the biblical privilege of sonship for the purpose of inheritance. But his being male does not interfere with or diminish his capacity to be our High Priest, the one who shares all the common human capacities and properties we do. And in so doing, his saving work enables us to live as whole people in a fractured world.

CHAPTER 7

THE SANCTIFIED BODY

Consider

When was the last time you heard a sermon on physical discipline? When was the last time you participated in a Sunday school class that broached the topics of gluttony and sloth? Why do you think this is?

Big Idea

Maturing as Christ's followers is not only about spiritual and moral/ethical progress but physical development as well. God's design for his embodied image bearers is that we are holistically sanctified, which includes growing in holiness in our body. Such progressive embodied sanctification fights against "deadly" sins of the body—lust, gluttony, and sloth. It also pursues physical wellness through sleep and rest.

Application Question

How should you progress in sanctification as an embodied believer?

Definition and General Framework

Broadly speaking, sanctification is defined as follows:

> The cooperative work of God and Christians (Phil. 2:12–13) by which ongoing transformation into greater Christlikeness occurs. Such maturing transpires particularly through the Holy Spirit (2 Cor. 3:18; Gal. 5:16–23) and the Word of God (John 17:17). Unlike other divine works, which are monergistic (God alone works), sanctification is synergistic. God operates in ways that are proper to his divine agency (e.g., convicting of sin, empowering by the Spirit, willing and working to accomplish his good pleasure), and Christians work in ways that are proper to their human agency (e.g., reading Scripture, praying, mortifying sin, yielding to the Spirit).[1]

As might be expected, Scripture emphasizes sanctification in terms of our spiritual and moral/ethical progress: growing in our love for God and for others (Matt. 22:34–40), imitating Christ (Phil. 2:5–11), expressing the fruit of the Spirit (Gal. 5:22–23), excelling in humble service (Matt. 23:11–12), repudiating sin (1 Pet. 2:11–12), increasing in Christian qualities (2 Pet. 1:3–11), and much more. Such progressive sanctification is the focus of sermons, Bible studies, community groups, discipling relationships, and the like—as it should be! We rightly orient ourselves toward the renewal of our mind, emotions, will, motivations, purposing, and relationships.

What is indeed a proper emphasis is sadly accompanied by a regrettable oversight: the sanctification of our body. To drive this point home, let's echo the questions at the start of this chapter. When was the last time you heard a sermon on physical discipline? When was the last time you participated in a Sunday school class that broached the topics of gluttony and sloth?

Three years ago? A decade? Never?

I thought so.

---

1. Gregg R. Allison, *The Baker Compact Dictionary of Theological Terms* (Grand Rapids: Baker Books, 2016), s.v. "Sanctification."

*and
Platonism*

To return to our earlier discussion, the church has been infected with the disease of Gnosticism and neo-Gnosticism. The church elevates spiritual and immaterial matters and minimizes or even denigrates physical and material matters. The church is held captive to anti-body sentiments. As a result, a holistic sanctification—a full-orbed process of maturing as wholly developed Christians that includes making progress as embodied believers—is rarely envisioned and pursued.

Biblical Affirmations

Paul concludes his first letter to the church of Thessalonica with an apostolic blessing: "Now may the God of peace himself sanctify you completely. And may your whole spirit, soul, and body be kept sound and blameless at the coming of our Lord Jesus Christ. He who calls you is faithful; he will do it" (1 Thess. 5:23–24). This benediction acknowledges that the one who is ultimately responsible for our growth in holiness is God himself. He personally undertakes to sanctify us. And we will be sanctified indeed because of the faithfulness of God, who is always true to his covenant and therefore to render his covenant people holy.

The hope for this progressive work—the goal for which this apostolic prayer is offered—is complete sanctification. No aspect of our being is excluded from Paul's all-encompassing list of spirit, soul, and body. We will make progress, kept sound and blameless by divine power, all the way until our death (not mentioned in the passage, but an actual termination point) or until Christ's second coming. This sanctifying action affects (1) our mind, reasoning, thinking, imagination, intellect; (2) our emotions, feelings, sentiments; (3) our will, decision-making capacity, volition; (4) our motivations, incentives, drives, passions; (5) our purposing, resolving, goal setting; and (6) our bodies.

In what ways do we experience the sanctification of our body? Before getting into specifics, there are several general considerations. As we progress in greater Christlikeness, we employ our tongues, which we once used to curse God and to tear down others, to bless God and to build others up (James 3:1–12). We employ our hands, which we formerly used by clenching our fists to protest against God and to steal from others, to praise God and to work hard so we can support others out of our well-earned resources (Eph. 4:28). We employ our feet, which we previously used to run from God and toward trouble, to do God's will and to bring the gospel to others (Rom. 10:1–15). We employ our sexual organs, which we once used to rebel against God and to exploit others immorally, to glorify God, to enjoy the gift of physical intimacy that he gives us within marriage, and (when possible) to contribute with our spouse to the multiplication of the human race (Gen. 1:28; 1 Cor. 6:12–20). Because we are embodied image bearers, our sanctification must extend to our physicality.

What then does embodied sanctification involve? We begin with some negative considerations.[2]

Embodied Sanctification: Avoiding the Abuse of Our Body

Progress in sanctification of our embodied self involves wrestling with and overcoming three sins of the body: lust, gluttony, and sloth.[3] Traditionally, these three sins are included in the list of seven deadly sins: pride, covetousness, gluttony, lust, sloth, envy, and

2. Much of the following is adapted from Gregg Allison, "Spiritual and Embodied Disciplines," in *Biblical Spirituality*, ed. Christopher W. Morgan (Wheaton: Crossway, 2019), 239–66.

3. Some of the following is adapted from Gregg R. Allison, "Toward a Theology of Human Embodiment," *Southern Baptist Journal of Theology* 13, no. 2 (Summer 2009): 4–17 (used with permission); also Gregg R. Allison, "Am I Lustful, Gluttonous, or Slothful?," *Christianity Today*, March 29, 2011, http://www.christianitytoday.com/biblestudies/articles/spiritualformation/lustfulgluttonousslothful.html.

anger.[4] As we have already treated the sin of lust in the chapter on the sexual body, our attention turns to the sins of gluttony and sloth.

so good

The Properly Nourished Body and Overcoming Gluttony

Embodied sanctification demands physical discipline and wrestling to overcome the deadly sin of gluttony. But what is this sin, and what Scripture supports it being considered as such a serious failure?

"Gluttony is the immoderate consumption of food arising from the unchecked appetite for something more than, or other than, what the Lord has provided and is therefore judged a sin by God."[5] Gluttony is often associated with drunkenness: "Do not be with heavy drinkers of wine, or with gluttonous eaters of meat; for the heavy drinker and the glutton will come to poverty, and drowsiness will clothe one with rags" (Prov. 23:20–21 NASB). So drunkenness is to the overconsumption of alcohol as gluttony is to the overconsumption of food.

Biblical portrayals of gluttonous people help us understand various aspects of this sin. Esau came in from the field and saw his brother Jacob cooking stew (Gen. 25:29–34). Esau claimed to be exhausted, famished to the point of exaggeration: "I am about to die!" Accordingly, he demanded to devour the red stew being prepared by his brother. Colloquially, he insisted that Jacob let him stuff his mouth with that red stuff. Esau's profane appetite

---

4. John Cassian developed a list of eight *principal* sins; as principal sins, they lead to all other sins. John Cassian, *Third Conference of Abbot Theonas*, chaps. 11, 16, in *A Select Library of Nicene and Post-Nicene Fathers of the Christian Church*, 2nd series, ed. Philip Schaff and Henry Wace, vol. 11, *Sulpitius Severus, Vincent of Lerins, John Cassian* (1886–1889; repr., Grand Rapids: Eerdmans, 1983), 525, 528. Thomas Aquinas enumerated seven *capital* sins, from the Latin *caput*, or head; as capital sins, they direct to other sins. Thomas Aquinas, *Summa Theologica* 1.2.84.

5. Jeff Olson, "Once a Deadly Sin: A Contemporary Assessment of the Sin of Gluttony" (ThM thesis, Western Seminary, Portland, OR, 2000).

was so out of control that it resulted in him engaging in a stupid, immoral act: the selling of his birthright. By being a slave to his appetite in the moment, he forfeited his birthright and lost the opportunity to play a crucial role in Israel's election. Gluttony so consumed him that he couldn't even repent of the evil he had committed (Heb. 12:16–17). Though not a commentary on this particular incident, Paul's warning is appropriate here: "their god is their belly" (Phil. 3:19 ESV).

King Eglon of Moab (Judg. 3:12–30) is described as "an extremely fat man" (v. 17). By means of a devious tribute paid to Moab, Ehud, Israel's left-handed judge, got alone with the king and delivered a divine "message" to him: "Ehud reached with his left hand, took the sword from his right thigh, and plunged it into Eglon's belly. Even the handle went in after the blade, and Eglon's fat closed in over it, so that Ehud did not withdraw the sword from his belly. And the waste came out" (vv. 21–22). This portrait of the obese king of Moab underscores the pathetic nature of this enemy of Israel and the shamefulness of his gluttony.

The sons of Eli, characterized as "worthless men . . . [who] did not know the Lord" (ESV), further illustrate the sin of gluttony (1 Sam. 2:12–17). It was the custom in Israel that when a person came to a priest to offer a sacrificial animal, the priest's servant would take some of the meat while it was boiling and reserve it for the priest. By this means, the priests were well provided for in terms of nourishment. Eli's sons, however, weren't content with this kind of priestly provision. They demanded raw meat, not boiled, because they preferred to roast it. If their immediate demand was refused, they threatened violence: "No, I insist that you hand it over right now. If you don't, I'll take it by force!" (v. 16). Their insistence on raw meat rather than boiled meat underscores an important aspect of gluttony: the unchecked appetite for something more than, or other than, what the Lord has provided.

As the people of Israel journeyed through the wilderness, the conspicuous lack of food prompted them to complain and crave (Num. 11:4–10; Ps. 78:18). Their complaint focused on the abundance and variety of food they had eaten in Egypt, a lavishness they lacked in the wilderness. Consequently, they pined for "the good old days" when they ate fish, cucumbers, melons, leeks, onions, and garlic in Egypt—despite the fact that they were slaves in that land. Their craving focused on their rejection of God's good provision for their nourishment—manna—and their wish for another type of provision: "Oh that we had meat to eat!" (v. 4 ESV). Their intemperate appetite, an aspect of gluttony, led to them lusting for something more than, or other than, what the Lord had provided. Rejecting God's provision, which was designed to develop their daily trust in him, they sought to be satisfied by something—really, someone—other than God. Gluttony led the people to put God to the test and to speak against him, prompting God's furious anger to blaze against them.

Gluttony is a deadly sin.

These biblical narratives emphasize that gluttony consists of several interrelated elements. Being the overconsumption of food, at the heart of gluttony is an unchecked appetite, the absence or loss of self-control. Moderation in one's appetite for food is forfeited. Then it becomes a matter of eating to excess. As Frederica Mathewes-Green explains, "Gluttony is not wrong because it makes you fat; it's wrong because it is the fruit of self-indulgence."[6] Manifestations of gluttony as the fruit of intemperance are many:

> Finicky eating; for example, demanding that food be cooked in a certain way and served piping hot.
>
> Restricting one's eating to sumptuous foods; for example, steak, lobster, caviar, and other costly food.

6. Frederica Mathewes-Green, "To Hell on a Cream Puff," *Christianity Today*, November 13, 1995, 45. Available at http://frederica.com/writings/to-hell-on-a-cream-puff.html.

Speedy eating; for example, gulping down food without en-joying its taste and without consideration for the pace of others who are also eating.

Being obsessed with food; for example, planning one's day so that it revolves around meals and snacks.[7]

Gluttony is a serious problem for believers.[8] It isn't evidenced only by excessive weight. On the contrary, one may be pencil thin and yet gluttonous. Christians who can't pass a fast-food place without pulling into the drive-through and ordering a burger and fries, even though their nutritional needs are more than satisfied, commit the sin of gluttony. Some people turn to food as a reward, either to congratulate themselves or to incentivize others. Others eat to provide comfort as they go through emotionally distress-ing times. Many people are fascinated with competitions that award participants for eating the most hot dogs (seventy-four) in ten minutes.[9] While we may boast about the immense quantities of greasy food at church potlucks and joke about deacon Bob serving up his third heaping plate of it, gluttony isn't a laugh-ing matter.

What can we do to avoid gluttony, to express our God-given ap-petite in God-honoring ways, and to overcome the rampant, tragic sins in this area? Scripture encourages us to develop thankfulness

7. Thomas Aquinas, *Summa Theologica* 2.148.4. As William Backus described it, gluttony is eating "too soon, too expensively, too much, too eagerly, or with too much finicky fussing about your food." Backus, *What Your Counselor Never Told You* (Minneapolis: Bethany House, 2000), 191. Scripture also advises us that the manner in which we eat depends on the company in which we dine. Eating with the wealthy and eating with the poor demand different approaches (Prov. 23:1–3, 6–8).

8. Among all denominations, Southern Baptists have the highest incidence of obesity. The pioneering study of the relationship between religion, body mass index, and obesity was authored by Krista M. C. Cline and Kenneth F. Ferraro, "Does Religion Increase the Prevalence and Incidence of Obesity in Adulthood?," *Journal for the Scientific Study of Religion* 45, no. 2 (June 2006): 269–81. Available at https://www.ncbi.nlm.nih.gov/pmc/articles/PMC3358928/.

9. The current record holder is Joey Chestnut at the 2018 Nathan's Hot Dog Eating Contest.

for God's provision: food is one of his good gifts (1 Tim. 4:3–4).[10] Additionally, Scripture prescribes the development of self-control through the power of the Spirit (Gal. 5:22–23). This orientation means that proper eating isn't an end in itself but a means to flourishing for the sake of the Lord and his purposes in this world. Spirit-empowered self-control in this area is not, as is so commonly the case, to conform to the cultural idol of thinness. Moreover, Scripture calls us to be keenly aware of the unsatisfied nutritional needs of others throughout the world (Gal. 2:10).

Practical suggestions for avoiding or overcoming gluttony include eating at mealtimes and avoiding snacks when our appetite rages for satisfaction. At mealtimes we should eat with moderation, not hastily or impatiently, with the goal of providing the necessary nourishment for our physical wellness. (Nutrition will be covered in the next chapter.) Additionally, we should be aware of factors that can contribute to gluttony. These factors include a chemical imbalance that leads to craving food, a genetic propensity toward obesity, poor parental or family guidance in the area of nutrition, and compulsive eating triggered by forces beyond our knowledge or control. Awareness of these factors doesn't mean we use them as excuses but encourages us to take special precaution so as not to fall prey to them. Being accountable to others when gluttony is beyond our ability to control underscores that we don't have to wrestle alone.

Though a deadly sin, gluttony can be overcome.

The Productive Body and Overcoming Sloth

Another deadly sin of the body is sloth. Before addressing that problem, however, it's important to set our discussion in the broader context of a biblical theology of the productive body.

---

10. John Milton associated gluttony with thanklessness: "Swinish gluttony / Ne'er looks to heav'n amidst his gorgeous feast, / But with besotted base ingratitude / Crams, and blasphemes his feeder." *Comus*, lines 776–79.

Created in the divine image, all human beings have been charged with and equipped to carry out the mandate to exercise dominion over the rest of the created order (Gen. 1:28). As we have discussed, the initial fulfillment of this divine mandate is narrated in Genesis 4: Abel was a shepherd who tended sheep, and Cain was a farmer who worked the ground (v. 2). Cain was also an entrepreneur who built a city (v. 17). Jabal was a herdsman who tended livestock, Jubal was an artist who played musical instruments, and Tubal-cain was a builder who forged bronze and iron tools (vv. 20–22). To contemporize this point, we build civilization by employing our God-given abilities and skills to work in areas such as education, medicine, construction, government, agriculture, business, and the arts to promote human flourishing.

With this portrait as the divine design for human beings, failure to engage in work is another deadly sin: sloth. But what is this sin, and what Scripture supports it being considered as such a serious failure?

Sloth is psychological indifference and physical weariness toward the work that God has provided for us to accomplish.[11] It may involve and be masked by frantic yet misdirected activity. It is a conscious neglect of doing what is humanly possible and what one is required to do. We possess the necessary mental, emotional, and physical abilities. We've earned the right educational degree(s) or developed the necessary technical skill(s). Even more, we have a job or at least the opportunity for employment. But the sloth-ful person doesn't engage properly in the work. Mentally, sloth is characterized by affectlessness, the lack of any feeling about self, others, and God that gives rise to boredom, apathy, and inertia. Occasionally, sloth is due to Christians' overemphasizing God's providential care for them and his promise to meet all of their needs. Regretfully, then, they neglect the important element of

11. For further discussion, see Solomon Schimmel, *The Seven Deadly Sins: Jewish, Christian, and Classical Reflections on Human Psychology* (Oxford: Oxford University Press, 1997), 193.

their human responsibility to use their God-given abilities to engage in vocation for civilization building.

Sloth results in the lack of resources for living: "How long will you lie there, O sluggard? When will you arise from your sleep? A little sleep, a little slumber, a little folding of the hands to rest, and poverty will come upon you like a robber, and want like an armed man" (Prov. 6:9–11 ESV; cf. 13:4; 20:4). The slothful person refuses to work, even inventing the most absurd excuses for not doing so. They end up finding every endeavor wearisome while considering themselves wise: "The sluggard says, 'There is a lion in the road! A lion is in the open square!' As the door turns on its hinges, so does the sluggard on his bed. The sluggard buries his hand in the dish; he is weary of bringing it to his mouth again. The sluggard is wiser in his own eyes than seven men who can give a discreet answer" (Prov. 26:13–16 NASB). Contrast this portrait of the sluggard with the description of the diligent wife of Proverbs 31. Her husband has no lack of gain (v. 11) because she works with willing hands (v. 13). She rises early while it is yet night and works hard (vv. 15–19), avoiding idleness (v. 27). The slothful person is the polar opposite of this industrious woman.

Sloth is a serious problem for believers. Paul denounces idleness for Christians: "If anyone is not willing to work, let him not eat. For we hear that some among you walk in idleness, not busy at work, but busybodies. Now such persons we command and encourage in the Lord Jesus Christ to do their work quietly and to earn their own living" (2 Thess. 3:10–12 ESV). Furthermore, Christians are expected both to provide for their families and to give sacrificially to the church and to the poor (e.g., 2 Cor. 8–9). Failure to do so means that one "has denied the faith and is worse than an unbeliever" (1 Tim. 5:8).

Sloth is a deadly sin.

What can we do to avoid sloth, to express our God-given gifts and abilities in God-honoring ways, and to overcome the rampant, tragic sins in this area? To begin, we acknowledge that God's explicit will for people in general and for us in particular is to work to build society. This is the divine purpose for humanity. Then we affirm that God has equipped us to do some kind of work: "God has provided the necessary abilities for me to engage in work. I may not be as intelligent, social, technologically savvy, articulate, skilled, entrepreneurial, artistic, or strong as others. But God has created me with my particular abilities to do the work that he has for me to do." And we embrace the joy of obeying God through working hard so as to be able to provide for our own needs, the needs of our family, and the needs of our church and the poor.

As for practical suggestions: if our slothfulness is particularly tied to poor personal management skills, we should work in a field that is highly structured. In this way, our schedule is established by someone else and not left up to us. If our slothfulness is particularly due to meager relational skills, we should work in a field that doesn't demand a lot of interaction with others. Such interaction prompts us to avoid working or inhibits us from working hard and well, so it should be minimized. If our slothfulness is particularly attached to weak initiative-taking, we should work in a field in which our leaders are strong in directing our work.

We should identify the source(s) of our psychological indifference toward work. These can include the poor examples of slothful parents and growing up with belittling criticism that makes us feel incapable of achievement. Another major contributor is poor mental health. Depression can be a debilitating condition that compromises our ability to engage in meaningful work. Having identified an underlying cause, we can then seek the help of others to overcome it. Awareness of these factors doesn't mean we use them as excuses but encourages us to pay special attention to them in our battle. Pastoral care and professional counseling are sources of help. Being accountable to others when sloth is beyond our ability to bring under control underscores that we don't have to wrestle alone. Additionally, we should ensure that our physical weariness isn't due to some medical problem, psychological condition, lowered energy level, or lack of proper nutrition, exercise, and/or rest, which are often correctable.

Though a deadly sin, sloth can be overcome.

In summary, lust (covered in an earlier chapter), gluttony, and sloth are three deadly sins. Only through a holistic embodied sanctification can we live as whole people in a fractured world.

Embodied Sanctification: Providing for the Wellness of Our Body

Turning from negative considerations about embodied sanctification, we consider regular activities that will provide for bodily wellness: proper sleep and rest.[12]

Proper Sleep

Let's admit it: many people today have problems with sleep.

For centuries, we have regarded sleep as a simple suspension of activity, a passive state of consciousness, and for centuries we have been wrong. This failure to understand the active nature of sleep is perhaps one of the reasons why our 24/7 society has developed such little regard for it. At best, many of us tolerate the fact that we need to sleep, and at worst we think of sleep as an illness that needs a cure. This attitude, held by so many in business, politics, industry, and even the health profession, is not only unsustainable but potentially dangerous.[13]

The average amount of sleep that Americans get per night is less than seven hours (eight hours is the average need), with 40 percent getting less than six hours. Some call this sleep deprivation; others

---

12. In the next chapter, we will discuss regular exercise, good nutrition, fasting, and feasting.

13. Steven W. Lockley and Russel G. Foster, *Sleep: A Very Short Introduction* (Oxford: Oxford University Press, 2012), 1.

call it a sleep epidemic. No matter its name, the lack of proper sleep seems to be at the core of many problems.

From a scientific viewpoint, "Shortened or reduced sleep duration is associated with an increased risk of a number of serious diseases including cardiovascular disease, diabetes, and certain types of cancer. There also appears to be a close link between sleep and mental health."[14] We detail these increased risks:

Safety concerns. "The most immediate risk of poor sleep to our health is the risk of drowsiness-related accidents and injuries. Falling asleep while driving or working when very tired dramatically increases the risk of both fatal accidents and minor slips and lapses."[15]

Heart disease. "People who experience reduced sleep (usually 6 hours or less) are at a higher risk of having high blood pressure, stroke, and heart disease, and die more often from heart attacks, than people who report sleeping longer (usually 7–8 hours)."[16]

Metabolic disorders. "Short or disrupted sleep is associated with weight gain, increased fat mass deposition, obesity, and diabetes. . . . [R]estricting sleep alters our metabolism in ways that increase the risk factors for these metabolic disorders."[17]

Immune function. Studies seem to support the idea that reduced sleep affects our body's immune system, lowering its response to illnesses such as the common cold and flu.[18]

14. Lockley and Foster, *Sleep*, 89.
15. Lockley and Foster, *Sleep*, 91.
16. Lockley and Foster, *Sleep*, 91.
17. Lockley and Foster, *Sleep*, 93.
18. The results of a recent study are summarized in Bobbi Nodell, "Chronic Sleep Deprivation Suppresses Immune System," University of Washington Health Sciences/UW Medicine, January 27, 2017, https://www.sciencedaily.com/releases/2017/01/170127113010.htm. The full study is N. F. Watson et al., "Transcriptional

Cancer. The link between sleep and cancer hasn't yet been definitively established. Limited studies show that shift workers (think of a car assembly line) experience a disruption in their normal body rhythm and an abnormal pattern of sleep and thus "have around a 50% increased risk of breast and prostate cancer compared to women and men who have not worked shifts."[19]

Mental illness and neurological disease. A wide range of emerging studies appears to demonstrate that reduced sleep and other sleep abnormalities play a role in incidents of depression (e.g., postpartum depression), bipolar disorder (especially manic episodes), anxiety-related disorders, Alzheimer's disease, Parkinson's disease, Huntington's disease, and multiple sclerosis.[20]

Individuals and our society as a whole suffer from these results: "Sleepiness and sleep disorders cost the economy billions of dollars each year in days off, lost time, inefficient work, and accidents, yet the machismo associated with short sleep and long work hours is pervasive. Society glorifies 'driven' individuals who succeed on apparently little sleep, whereas those who prioritize sleep are viewed as weak and not having the 'right stuff.' Some professions even demand excessive sleep deprivation as part of the job or a 'rite of passage.'"[21] From a scientific viewpoint comes this warning: "These attitudes are outdated and ultimately counterproductive, however, both individually and across a profession, as failing to get sufficient sleep has major consequences for safety, productivity, and health."[22]

Signatures of Sleep Duration Discordance in Monozygotic Twins," *Sleep* 40, no. 1 (January 1, 2017), https://academic.oup.com/sleep/article/40/1/zsw019/2952682.

19. Lockley and Foster, *Sleep*, 96.

20. Lockley and Foster, *Sleep*, 97–101.

21. Lockley and Foster, *Sleep*, 103. The citation has been modified from a British context to an American context.

22. Lockley and Foster, *Sleep*, 103.

Scripture has little to say about sleep, which it treats in several ways.[23] When sleep refers to physical rest, Scripture underscores two things: the righteous and wise receive sleep from God (Ps. 127:2) and enjoy it (Prov. 3:21–26), because they know God watches over and protects them even when they are most vulnerable (Ps. 4:8). Oppositely, the wicked and foolish find no rest because they are always plotting their next evil deed (Job 7:3–5; Prov. 4:14–16). Accordingly, God has designed his faithful and obedient people to enjoy his gift of rest. For others, sleep is hard to come by.

Whether we consider the scientific evidence or the Bible, or if we heed both, we need to sleep, and to sleep well. Well-supported suggestions for sleep are quite numerous. In terms of what to avoid: eating and drinking—especially things that contain caffeine and nicotine—for several hours before going to bed; exercising, watching television, and engaging in emotionally charged issues for several hours before bedtime; being exposed to high intensity elements like lights, noise, and temperature changes; becoming reliant upon or addicted to sleep aids (alcohol, pills) to fall asleep; and getting worked up or anxious about not being able to fall asleep.

As for what to do: Go to sleep about the same time and wake up about the same time each day. Relax by taking a warm bath or shower before going to bed. Unclutter the bedroom so its primary purpose is sleeping. Ensure that it is quiet and dark in the bedroom. Keep a cool temperature in the bedroom. Seek out treatment for chronic insomnia.[24]

23. "Sleep" can be a euphemism for death. For example, Lazarus was said to be "asleep" (John 11:13–14). It can serve as a metaphor for carnality (Eph. 5:14), spiritual apathy (Rom. 13:11), slothfulness (Prov. 6:4–11; 19:15; 24:3–4), and unpreparedness for the future (Mark 13:35–36; 1 Thess. 5:3–6). With reference to God, the fact that he never sleeps (Ps. 121:3–4; Isa. 40:28) assures his people of his attentiveness and readiness to intervene on their behalf.
24. Some of these suggestions come from Lockley and Foster, *Sleep*, 75.

Proper Rest

Closely tied to sleep is rest, the "intentional suspension of ordinary work for the purpose of refreshment and relaxation. Such repose isn't the cessation of activity but the purposeful substitution of one activity for another."[25] Scripture has much to say about rest.[26]

By his work of creation, God established a structure of weekly rest for his image bearers. Following his pattern of six days of work and one day of rest, people are also to work and rest (Gen. 2:1–4). Accordingly, weekly rest is proper and right. Subsequent Scripture provides details concerning how rest should be observed (e.g., old covenant Sabbath regulations for the people of Israel: Exod. 20:1–17; Deut. 5:6–21). The New Testament changes those details while confirming rest as a creation ordinance to be observed by the new covenant church (e.g., Matt. 12:9–14; Mark 2:27; Acts 20:27; 1 Cor. 16:2).

A case can be made for—and I will adopt—the position that rest is a creation ordinance. In terms of a definition, a creation ordinance is "a normative, but not uniformly observed, universal pattern, exceptions to which must fulfill and contribute to the pattern's fulfillment; moreover, the pattern must be confirmed, not negated or abrogated, by later biblical revelation."[27] There are four specific aspects.

First, a creation ordinance is *a pattern that is normative*. All people are expected to follow it. For example, let's set up a parallel between the creation ordinance of marriage and the creation ordinance of rest. The normal pattern in the first case is that a man and a woman are united in a monogamous, heterosexual

25. Allison, *Baker Compact Dictionary of Theological Terms*, s.v. "rest."
26. John English Lee, "There Remains a Sabbath Rest for the People of God: A Biblical, Theological, and Historical Defense of Sabbath Rest as a Creation Ordinance" (PhD diss, The Southern Baptist Theological Seminary, 2018). See also D. A. Carson, ed., *From Sabbath to Lord's Day: A Biblical, Historical, and Theological Investigation* (Grand Rapids: Zondervan, 1982).
27. Lee, "There Remains a Sabbath Rest for the People of God," 3. The four aspects are developments of Lee's discussion of creation ordinance (pp. 3–5).

relationship that produces children. This pattern is true for the majority of men and women. Likewise, the normal pattern in the second case is for people to work for six days and rest for one day. This pattern is true for the vast majority of people.

Second, *the pattern isn't observed uniformly*. There are exceptions. Returning to our parallel, in the first case, while marriage is the norm for most people, and while the majority of people will be married, marriage isn't demanded of everyone. People are free to remain single. Likewise, the normal pattern in the second case is that people engage in a vocation. But people who are unable to work (due to a physical or mental disability) are free not to work, and those who have worked and arrived at the age of retirement are free to stop working.

Third, *exceptions to the pattern must fulfill and contribute to the fulfillment of the pattern*. People who don't personally follow the pattern should live in such a way as to promote its observance. Returning to our parallel, in the first case, people who choose to remain single are certainly free to do so. Still, they should live in such a way as to promote the normal pattern of healthy marriage and procreation. They shouldn't belittle marriage and family but encourage others to get married and have children. Likewise, the normal pattern in the second case is that people engage in a vocation. However, when they are unable to work or when they retire from working, they should live in such a way as to promote the normal pattern of work. They shouldn't belittle work or make fun of those who still work while they themselves have stopped working.

Fourth, *the pattern must be confirmed, not negated or abrogated, by later biblical revelation*. Certain rules or provisions have been done away with by later revelation. Two examples are the old covenant sacrificial system and dietary laws. But with the creation ordinances of marriage and work, Scripture doesn't dismiss their observance but encourages it. For example, the creation ordinance of marriage is confirmed by Jesus (Matt. 19:4–6), and the creation ordinance of work is confirmed by Paul (1 Thess. 4:11; 2 Thess. 3:10).

Rest is a creation ordinance, given as a blessing and obligation for all people created in the image of God. Certainly, the Mosaic law prescribed a certain way and highlighted certain reasons for its observance by the people of Israel. People in general, and Christians in particular, aren't bound to those prescriptions or reasons. Rather, we observe regular rest because rest is a creation ordinance for all people.[28]

Practically speaking, rest may take some or all of the following forms. In terms of what to avoid: activity that is similar to our usual work; activity that stimulates worry and anxiety, such as making major purchases, paying bills, filling out tax forms, planning our schedule for the coming week, and engaging with people who are likely to provoke anger and frustration; and activity that we should have completed during our "work" phase of the week but failed to finish because of hectic pace, laziness, poor planning, procrastination, and the like. Additionally, if our day of rest corresponds with Sunday, we should avoid filling Sunday afternoons with church committee meetings and other "religious" activity.

In terms of what to do: Spend time with loved ones and enjoy being together. Nap, read, listen to music, exercise, reflect, take a walk, paint, and so forth. Visit shut-ins, talk with people who are lonely, and extend mercy. Additionally, if our day of rest corresponds with Sunday, we should gather together with others for worship.

Rest requires developing new rhythms. If we aren't used to resting and regularly taking a day off, we need to establish a new habit, which will take several months to become ingrained. Old habits die hard, and new habits are hard to establish. Rather than aiming for too high of a goal—for example, taking an entire day

28. A. T. Lincoln, "From Sabbath to Lord's Day: A Biblical and Theological Perspective," in D. A. Carson, ed., *From Sabbath to Lord's Day*, 346.

off each week when we haven't done so for years—we should start with small steps. For two months, we take off three hours one day a week. After we've settled into that pattern, we increase the amount to three hours two days a week. Once that habit is well established, we increase to eight hours per week—a whole day, or four hours distributed over two days each week.

Breaking the old pattern also means fighting against the idol of workaholism. If the Lord is our God, and if he has created the world with rest as a creation ordinance, then we honor him by developing a pattern of rest. In some cases, this change may involve overcoming prideful feelings that we are indispensable to the accomplishment of God's work in this world. By resting regularly, we communicate to ourselves, others, and God our acknowledgment that his kingdom will come and his will certainly will be done, even when we aren't busy 24/7. Remember, engaging in rest is an activity that is different from our normal work. It isn't being stagnant or loafing around. Finally, pastors and church staff who do a significant part of their work on Sundays need help to take a day off other than Sunday.

Breaking the old pattern and establishing a new rhythm also means becoming aware of how many of our current activities rob us of rest. Heavy use of social media correlates with sleeplessness. Besides those virtual relationships, our social networks of family members, work colleagues, neighbors, and friends seem to be constantly expanding and thus demanding our time. Keeping up with our children's many school and sports activities is exhausting. Relocating frequently leads to restlessness and an agitated sense of rootlessness. To break this pattern and establish a new rhythm will require disengaging from much of what consumes our attention today. As limited creatures to whom God has given the creation ordinance of rest for our flourishing, at a certain point we need to cry, "Enough is enough."[29]

29. My thanks to Hanell Schuetz for her good thoughts about this area.

In summary, maturing as Christ's followers isn't only about spiritual and moral/ethical progress, but physical development as well. God's design for his embodied image bearers is that we are holistically sanctified, which includes growing in holiness in body. Such progressive embodied sanctification fights against "the deadly sins" of the body—lust, gluttony, and sloth. It also pursues physical wellness through sleep and rest. By practicing a holistic embodied sanctification, we can live as whole people in a fractured world.

Application

How should you progress in sanctification as an embodied believer?

Specifically, what concrete steps can you take to grow in physical holiness? As an embodied believer, are you physically capable of responding to God's will for you in terms of being fit for the marathon race toward Christlikeness, persevering through the suffering to which God is calling or might call you, and shouldering the burdens of others in the church? Or are you physically weary, worn down, burned out for life and ministry? In either case, how can you develop yourself physically for the race and task ahead of you?

Additionally, do you wrestle with gluttony and/or sloth? Looking back at the suggested steps for combating these deadly sins of the body, what practical action plan can you adopt to overcome these besetting sins?

Finally, if you're like most people, you find sleep and rest difficult to come by. Looking back at the practical suggestions for getting a good night's sleep, how can you pursue wellness in this area? And considering the proposals for developing regular rhythms of rest, how can you pursue wellness in this area?

For the Curious

As you consider holistic, embodied sanctification and develop concrete plans for pursuing it, make sure that you don't overlook this key passage about Christian maturity: "Therefore, my dear friends, just as you have always obeyed, so now, not only in my presence but even more in my absence, work out your own salvation with fear and trembling. For it is God who is working in you both to will and to work according to his good purpose" (Phil. 2:12–13). Working out your salvation—pursuing and actualizing sanctification—has two dimensions. The first is divine. The second is human. The first dimension is the foundation for the second dimension, not vice versa. God's good work in you prompts both your willingness and your work to accomplish his good pleasure. The second dimension is the fruit that flows from the first dimension. Your good work to fight against the deadly sins of the body and to pursue wellness through sleep and rest should be—needs to be—empowered by God's good work.

To make the good progress that God wills and that you desire, be sure that both of these dimensions are constantly working in tandem. And never lose sight of the purposefulness of sanctification. In connection with the next chapter, as embodied people we progress in sanctification to pursue the blessedness of embodiment through embodied discipline.[30]

---

30. My thanks to Gracilynn Hanson for making this connection.

CHAPTER 8

THE BLESSED AND DISCIPLINED BODY

Consider

Answer the following two questions: For what specific physical blessings—both personal and in the world surrounding you—are you thankful? How would you assess yourself in terms of physical discipline such as exercising, eating, fasting, and feasting?

Big Idea

Through the physical senses, human embodiment brings blessings that are too numerous to count. At the same time, it also demands bodily discipline. God's design for his embodied image bearers is that we live physically blessed and disciplined lives in areas such as regular exercise, good nutrition, fasting, and feasting.

Application

Design a personal program of bodily discipline that you consistently follow.

Good

Our Contemporary Context and Problems with Embodiment

In the opening story of our book, Drake approached me because of the many bodily ailments that were disturbing him. When I pursued a line of questioning that probed his eating and exercise habits, he tuned me out. He simply dismissed any importance for his body. All he cared about was spiritual matters. In the first chapter, we traced this neglect of, or disdain for, human embodiment to the old problem of Gnosticism and its new guise of neo-Gnosticism.

We return to this topic with a slight twist to emphasize human embodiment in terms of blessing and discipline.

In our contemporary society, we tend to go to extremes in this area. Either we make an idol out of our body, or we ignore our body. The overemphasis on embodiment is seen in people spending hours in the fitness center, sculpting their body in an attempt to build the perfect "temple" or object of their idolatry. Equal attention is paid to the fuel that people put into their body: nothing with additives such as MSG, artificial food coloring, sodium nitrate, high-fructose corn syrup, artificial sweeteners, and trans fats; no plant food that was grown using chemicals such as fungicides, herbicides, and insecticides; no animal food that was grown adding antibiotics and growth hormones. Organic food, and only organic food, is eaten.[1] The point here (as will become evident in this chapter) isn't to put down regular exercise and proper nutrition. Rather, it is to decry an unhealthy overemphasis that

---

1. If space permitted, I could explore important issues related to food consumption, issues such as how we treat the earth, what constitutes real food, and health conditions that require drastic diets to undo damage to our bodies through years of unhealthy eating, and similar topics. For further discussion, see Michael Pollan, *The Omnivore's Dilemma: A Natural History of Four Meals* (New York: Penguin, 2007); Wendell Berry, *The Unsettling of America: Culture and Agriculture*, rev. ed. (Berkeley: Counterpoint, 1996); and the popular documentary *Food, Inc.*, directed by Robert Kenner (Magnolia Pictures, 2008). My thanks to Hanell Schuetz for her insights in this area.

dominates some persons' lives and displaces their attention from other responsibilities.

The underemphasis on embodiment is evident when people dismiss physical fitness as having any importance. They reason in a way similar to Drake's pushback on my counsel: because their body is going to be sloughed off at death anyway, they don't need to be concerned about exercising regularly and eating properly. These bodily matters are irrelevant—and useless. So they don't run, lift weights, swim, do yoga, or even walk. And they balk or roll their eyes at choosing organic—or even nutritious— foods. They point to studies that show that the health benefits of eating organically aren't substantial, and they complain that the high cost of these foods puts them out of range for a limited budget.

Interestingly, within the church the issue of exercise and eating is causing a new division. Christians who exercise regularly and eat organic foods look down on their brothers and sisters who don't make those lifestyle choices. And those who don't follow such an exercise and eating regimen criticize Christians who waste time taking care of their body.

Before we jump into the fray and address these problematic issues, a good place to start is with some positive considerations.

The Blessings of Embodiment

The blessings of embodiment through the physical senses are too numerous to count but include the following: the taste of a mouth-watering steak at Ruth's Chris; the feel of eight-hundred-thread-count Egyptian cotton sheets on a king-sized bed at the end of a bone-weary day; the smell of freshly mowed grass or chocolate chip cookies hot out of the oven; the sound of a powerful Midwest thunderstorm; the sight of a full double rainbow across the vast sky at the end of that storm; the handsome features of a man and the stunning beauty of a woman. Only as embodied beings can we sense and enjoy these physical blessings.[2]

A good theology of creation helps us recognize the blessings of embodiment. As unfolded in the opening chapter of Genesis, God's creation of the earth counteracted the formless, empty, dark, and watery initial space. From it he fashioned a formed and filled, lit and grounded place that would be hospitable for his image bearers. At each step of the way as God brought this world into existence, he pronounced his assessment: good, good, good, good, good, good, and—when his creation project was complete—very good. This goodness wasn't about the earth's moral quality; after all, there was no evil in the first place. Rather, goodness applied to the correspondence between the divine design and the finished product. The earth corresponded perfectly to the sovereign Architect's blueprint for it. Additionally, goodness referred to the beauty of the created world. It was stunningly lovely, magnificently splendid.

At the center of this enchanted environment, God planted a garden. To nourish his human creatures, God embedded groves of trees with fruit that was both "pleasing in appearance and good for food" (Gen. 2:9). Beyond mere utilitarian purposes, the Creator designed the garden to be beautiful. The apples were bright red, sunny yellow, and brilliant green. The berries were ebony black, crimson red, and midnight blue. Into this beautiful garden God placed the first man and the first woman who, like the lush environment into which they were introduced, were the epitome of handsomeness and beauty. In a pre-fall world, colors didn't fade, textures didn't decay, and Adam's and Eve's physical senses weren't dulled or blurred. The world and all of its inhabitants, including the divine image bearers, were gloriously beautiful.

2. For further discussion, see Philip Shepherd, *Radical Wholeness: Embodied Present and the Ordinary Grace of Being* (Berkeley: North Atlantic Books, 2017).

As it was in the beginning, so it shall be in the end. Tragically, this idyllic world became spoiled and marred as a result of our first parents' sins and God's curse of judgment. Everywhere we look, we see evidence of decay, decline, and distortion. Yet great beauty still shines in the creation, tainted as it may be. And it is that defiled creation that yearns for its renewal in the new heaven and new earth.[3] As that future world is described, it will be beautiful once again. This is the vision of the new Jerusalem—as a walled city, it is "pure gold clear as glass" (Rev. 21:18) and decorated with magnificent jewels: jasper, sapphire, chalcedony, emerald, sardonyx, carnelian, chrysolite, beryl, topaz, chrysoprase, jacinth, and amethyst. The twelve gates are made of pearls, and the city's main street is "pure gold, transparent as glass" (v. 21). Moreover, there is no "temple in it, because the Lord God the Almighty and the Lamb are its temple. The city does not need the sun or the moon to shine on it, because the glory of God illuminates it, and its lamp is the Lamb" (vv. 22–23). With care for its apocalyptic genre, we don't want to read too much into this vision. But what certainly stands out is the magnificent beauty and brilliant glory of this future world.

It is in this world that Christians live. Aware of the debate about just how much we should allow ourselves to enjoy what God has created, we mention only two passages that grant us the privilege of finding pleasure in the creation. God has given us the good gift of marriage, with its accompanying sexual pleasures, and the good gift of eating food, with its satisfying smell and taste, yielding satisfaction. The proper posture toward such physical blessings is to receive them with gratitude (1 Tim. 4:1–10, the topic of our next section). Additionally, without chastising Christians for their wealth, Scripture instructs "those who are rich in the present age not to be arrogant or to set their hope on the

---

3. For further discussion, see Paul J. Griffiths, *Decreation: The Last Things of All Creatures* (Waco: Baylor University Press, 2014).

uncertainty of wealth, but on God, who richly provides us with all things to enjoy" (1 Tim. 6:17). Certainly, the rich are also to engage in good works and generously share with others (v. 18) so as to store up treasures for themselves in the age to come (v. 19). As they so live, they are to find pleasure in the untold number of physical blessings.

This is the blessed body.

Paired with it is the disciplined body.

The Disciplined Body: Biblical Affirmations

A key biblical text for bodily discipline is found in Paul's first letter to Timothy (4:1–10). The apostle issues a stern warning from the Holy Spirit for the church in "later times," the period between Christ's first and second comings: an evil, deceptive, even demonic teaching will lead some Christians astray. They will apostatize, fall away from the Christian faith, by paying allegiance to the maleficent stratagems of Satan (vv. 1–2).

One element of this false teaching is *asceticism*, the view of life that denies the goodness of material things and emphasizes spiritual matters. (Yes, asceticism is associated with Gnosticism.) Two specific prohibitions are insisted on by this false teaching (v. 3). The first is that marriage is forbidden. Why? Sexual intercourse involves the body and its physical desires; therefore, it is inherently evil and to be avoided. We've already seen this view in 1 Corinthians 7:1–7. Some Corinthians insisted that single people shouldn't marry and, if people are married, they shouldn't engage in sexual intercourse.

The second prohibition is abstinence from certain foods (for our purposes, let's pick steak and lobster). Why? Because these luxurious foods appeal to people's physical appetites, which should be denied and severely controlled. Christians shouldn't fuel their body's desire for fine foods. Rather, they should abstain from steak and lobster.

Paul condemns this teaching as wrong (1 Tim. 4:4–5). But what is incorrect about asceticism? (Our critique of Gnosticism helps answer this question.) It denies that God created material things—for example, our body with its sexual organs and food for our consumption. But because God created these material things, they are good. If a good God created these good material things, they can't be forbidden. Abstinence is wrong.

So what *should* our attitude and behavior be toward these things? First, we shouldn't reject them. They can't be prohibited. Second, we should share in them with gratefulness. They should be enjoyed with thanksgiving. Paul gives a fine way of exhibiting our gratitude for God's good material gifts. We offer a prayer of thanksgiving at meals, a blessing of the food we are about to eat, a dedication based on the Word of God. Such a conscious, verbal blessing sets our food in its proper framework: It is a good gift of God, part of his provision for us. And the prayer enables us to regard food as special.

Paul continues. Not only are we nourished by the food that comes from God; we are also nourished by good biblical instruction such as Paul has passed down to Timothy. We should pay attention to weightier matters and not give heed to pointless, silly things (1 Tim. 4:6–7a).

In contrast, we should train or discipline ourselves for the purpose of godliness (v. 7b).[4] Paul uses a metaphor from the athletic world. Like an athlete, Timothy must keep himself in rigorous training so as to grow in Christ and please God. Such discipline is purposeful. All discipline, of whatever variety (physical, spiritual, financial), is purposeful and never an end in itself. Discipline is always directed at some purpose, aim, or goal.[5]

---

4. The Greek word for "train" or "discipline" is the origin of our word "gymnasium."

5. I emphasize this point to challenge Christians who are rightly involved in discipline but engage in it as an end in itself or who have lost sight of the goal of their discipline. For example, we fast, but we don't fast for fasting's sake; that

What would this training for godliness include?[6] To put the list into three categories: *Inward disciplines* consist of meditation, prayer, fasting, and study. *Outward disciplines* consist of simplicity, solitude, submission, and service. *Corporate disciplines* consist of confession, worship, guidance, and celebration. Why should we engage in these rigorous spiritual disciplines? Because godliness is so valuable, both in our present walk with God—it pleases him and furthers his work in this world—as well as in our future life, when godliness will be rewarded (1 Tim. 4:8b).

One more matter (which we've purposefully moved to the end) is valuable. Still working with the metaphor of athletic training, Paul not only comments on religious training but also pauses to reflect on the actual bodily training that an athlete undertakes (1 Tim. 4:8a). What is true of this physical training? It's of some value. It's of limited benefit. Bodily discipline is restricted to our earthly life, but in this limited period it's still of value. Moreover, a disciplined body isn't reserved for Christian athletes. On the contrary, it's for all Christians. As embodied people, care for and training of our body is important for as long as we are in this earthly existence.

As we discussed in our opening chapter, this point is just what we would expect:

- if the proper state of human existence is embodiment, and
- if an essential given of human life is embodiment, and

would be nonsensical (though it may be very beneficial). Additionally, we don't fast because Scripture commands us to fast. Though it is indeed the case that Scripture commands fasting, the imperative to fast and the reason for fasting are two different matters. In obedience to God's will expressed in Scripture, we fast for the purpose of experiencing God's presence in a more intimate way, or to seek urgently his direction. Discipline is purposeful. For further discussion, see Gregg R. Allison, "Spiritual and Embodied Disciplines," in *Biblical Spirituality*, ed. Christopher W. Morgan (Wheaton: Crossway, 2019), 239–66.

6. This list is structured according to Richard J. Foster's *Celebration of Discipline: The Path to Spiritual Growth*, 20th anniversary ed. (San Francisco: HarperSanFrancisco, 1998). Another excellent treatment of spiritual disciplines is Dallas Willard, *The Spirit of the Disciplines: Understanding How God Changes Lives* (New York: HarperOne, 1999).

- if God designed us as his image bearers to be embodied, and
- if the triune God dwells in our embodied selves by means of the Holy Spirit, whose temple we are, and
- if, at the return of Christ, the Holy Spirit will re-embody us with our glorified, resurrected body,

then we would expect that it is proper for us to live as disciplined embodied Christians, caring for, treating rightly, our body.

Embodiment is a good gift of God, so we embrace a disciplined body.

Embodied Disciplines

What do these embodied disciplines include?[7] Remember, all discipline is purposeful, and the physical training presented is designed to keep us in good shape, cultivate good health, ward off many illnesses associated with poor physical care, and keep us responsive to God's will and able to carry it out. Elements of this training include regular exercise, good nutrition, fasting, and feasting.[8] Such training prepares us for living as whole people in a fractured world.

---

7. The following discussion is taken from Allison, "Spiritual and Embodied Disciplines." Also, we are called to exercise physical discipline in many areas of our life. These include abstinence instead of sexual activity, work rather than rest, rest rather than work, and pain rather than pleasure. We will look at several other areas that demand physical discipline: exercise, nutrition, and fasting and feasting.

8. To avoid misunderstanding, this section about physical well-being isn't intended to elevate health in an exaggerated way. Such inordinate attention to wellness is exemplified by René Descartes's supreme modern value, "the conservation of health, which is without doubt the primary good and the foundation of all other goods of this life." René Descartes, *Discourse on Method*, ed. Pamela Kraus and Fred Hunt, trans. Richard Kennington (Indianapolis: Focus, 2007), 49.

Regular Exercise

Anyone living in our contemporary American society is aware of the importance of regular exercise.[9] From walking and jogging around our neighborhood to swimming at our local pool, and from home exercise equipment to local fitness gyms, we are offered myriad choices for keeping in shape physically. One element of embodied discipline for Christians is regular exercise.[10]

As Christians we shouldn't regularly exercise because we have fallen prey to the cultural idols of thinness, feeling good, looking good, or feeling attractive. Those may be important yet are secondary outcomes. Rather, the goal of our regular exercise should be fitness, which can be defined in two ways: (1) our body's ability to utilize and facilitate the uptake of oxygen into our circulatory system, and (2) the absence of disease.[11] Exercise promotes the proper functioning of our cardiorespiratory system and strengthens our muscular system. Benefits of exercise leading to fitness can be broken down into two general categories: reduction of diseases leading to death and promotion of good health.

First, regular exercise reduces all causes of mortality, divided into several areas. The risk of cardiovascular disease mortality in

9. The following discussion incorporates material taught in my theology of human embodiment classes over many years by exercise physiologists such as Rebecca Adams, Renee Stubbs, Janet Spear, Roberto Pelayo, and Lainey Greer. Other exercise physiologists might make other suggestions for regular exercise.

10. Most of us engage in informal exercise. In terms of formal exercise, Ken Hutchins provides the following definition: "Exercise is a process whereby the body performs work of a demanding nature, in accordance with muscle and joint function, in a clinically-controlled environment, within the constructs of safety, meaningfully loading the muscular structures to inroad their strength levels to stimulate a growth mechanism within minimum time." Ken Hutchins, "The First Definition of Exercise," http://www.ren-ex.com/the-first-definition-of-exercise/.

11. Some people would expand the goal of exercise to include physical health. Due to other factors beyond the reach of regular exercise, however, it may be the case that such wellness isn't the outcome. Some chronic illnesses—e.g., endometriosis, lupus, rheumatoid arthritis, fibromyalgia, and cystic fibrosis—may be exacerbated by exercise. People who suffer from these illnesses can achieve fitness through exercise, but physical health is usually out of reach.

general, and coronary heart diseases in particular, is lowered. High blood pressure is prevented or lowered. Hypertension is prevented or lowered. Importantly, inactive people are at 35 to 52 percent greater risk for hypertension than those who exercise regularly. Exercise reduces blood pressure. The risk of disease associated with cholesterol is lowered. Specifically, exercise increases the "good" cholesterol (HDL) and reduces the "bad" cholesterol (LDL). The risk of non-insulin-dependent diabetes mellitus is lowered because exercise eases blood sugar regulation. The risk of cancer is lowered. Studies have demonstrated this lowered risk for colon cancer, and it may also apply to breast and prostate cancers. The symptoms of depression and anxiety are relieved as fitness can contribute to improved mood.

The second category of the benefits of exercise is the promotion of good health. The increase in wellness encompasses four areas: Muscle strength and endurance is increased. Bone strength is increased. The metabolic, endocrine, and immune systems are benefited. And one's overall good sense of health is raised.

Importantly, these many benefits aren't reserved for athletes or exercise fanatics but accrue to most people who engage in regular exercise.

As embodied human beings and bearers of the renewed image of God, you and I should aim at fitness through the physical discipline of regular exercise. Most exercise physiologists suggest some type of thirty-minute workout at least five days a week. If we haven't exercised regularly for a long time, we should begin slowly and increase our workout gradually. Those of us who do currently engage in exercise may increase the intensity and/or duration of our workout for greater health benefit. In either case, we should consult with a doctor before embarking on or increasing physical training.[12]

---

12. As I'm not an expert in this area, I offer only suggestions—not medical counsel—for how to exercise regularly. For further discussion, see Donna Shalala,

Good Nutrition

When Americans hear the expression "good nutrition," we often think of the "food pyramid" or its latest permutation, the "pyramid plus."[13] This pyramid-shaped guide illustrates how much food from five major food groups we should eat each day. Starting from the bottom and working to the top, the pyramid directs us to consume six to eleven servings of breads and cereals, three to five servings of vegetables, two to four servings of fruits, two to three servings of milk and milk products, and two to three servings of meat and meat alternatives.

Alternatively, given that most Americans don't follow the food pyramid/pyramid plus but eat unhealthily, we often associate "good nutrition" with dieting. Far more often than not, our attempts at dieting go through the following cycle. Perhaps as a result of a New Year's resolution or a health scare, we develop good intentions to lose weight. Watching the many convincing ads on TV, we make an initial expenditure of a significant amount of money to go on a crash-diet program. Just as the promos promise, we experience the initial and immediate success of weight loss. After a bit of time, we hit a plateau and become frustrated with the lack of ongoing success. Despite what the publicity promised, this dieting experience turns out to be hard work! Tired of trying so hard, we give up, binge on junk food, lose all discipline in eating properly, and gain back all the initial weight that we lost—and more beyond that.[14] Tragically, weight loss programs are notori-

"Physical Activity and Health: A Report of the Surgeon General," Centers for Disease Control and Prevention, 1994, https://www.cdc.gov/nccdphp/sgr/.

13. The following discussion incorporates material taught in my theology of human embodiment classes over many years by nutritionists such as Marsha Hilgeford, Julianna Crider, and Lainey Greer. Other nutritionists might make other suggestions for proper nutrition.

14. For further discussion of how (certain types of) diets may contribute to weight gain, see Evelyn Tribole, "Warning: Dieting Increases Your Risk of Gaining MORE Weight," The Original Intuitive Eating Pros, January 21, 2012, https://www.intuitiveeating.org/warning-dieting-increases-your-risk-of-gaining-more-weight-an-update/. For statistics on dieting in the United States, see M. Shahbandeh,

ously unsuccessful. But they are big business: the American diet industry earns about $20 billion annually.[15]

We seem to equate "good nutrition" with dieting. But such isn't the case, and dieting can be both a failure and dangerous.[16]

Briefly, nutrition is the act or process of providing or obtaining food and drink for the energy necessary for metabolism, health, growth, and repair. Nutrients come in six classes: carbohydrates, proteins, fats, vitamins, minerals, and water. The proper intake of these nutrients constitutes good nutrition.

The physical discipline of good nutrition includes the following elements, summarized in six categories.[17] First, eat smaller meals over the course of the day. Rather than three big meals, we should eat five small portions every three hours. Importantly, our daily food cycle should begin with breakfast, which shouldn't be skipped. Second, drink a significant amount of water throughout the day.[18] Despite the lure, we should avoid carbonated beverages

"U.S. Diets and Weight Loss—Statistics and Facts," January 14, 2019, https://www.statista.com/topics/4392/diets-and-weight-loss-in-the-us/.

15. "The U.S. Weight Loss and Diet Control Market," Research and Markets, February 2019, https://www.researchandmarkets.com/research/qm2gts/the_72_billion?w=4.

16. To be clear, I am aware of various food convictions such as the paleo diet, plant-based diets, and the keto diet. Additionally, different cultures employ many different approaches to food and good nutrition. My purpose isn't to defend any one food philosophy but to demonstrate the importance of good nutrition, as many of us can agree.

17. For further discussion, see Lainey Greer, "The Christian's Role in the Obesity Epidemic" (ThM thesis, Dallas Theological Seminary, 2014). Good resources include Susan Albers, *Eating Mindfully: How to End Mindless Eating and Enjoy a Balanced Relationship with Food*, 2nd ed. (Oakland, CA: New Harbinger Publications, 2012); Christy Harrison, *Anti-Diet: Reclaim Your Time, Money, Well-Being, and Happiness through Intuitive Eating* (New York: Little, Brown Spark, 2019).

18. The old rule of drinking eight eight-ounce glasses of water each day is outdated and surpassed by new research. The Institute of Medicine now recommends thirteen cups of water daily for men and nine cups of water daily for women. These numbers increase for women who are pregnant and/or breastfeeding, and for both men and women who live in a hot climate, exercise often, live at a high elevation, or are sick with a fever, diarrhea, and/or vomiting. Institute of Medicine, "Dietary Reference Intakes for Water, Potassium, Sodium, Chloride, and

like soda/pop and high-sugar fruit juices. Third, consume complex carbohydrates rather than simple carbohydrates. For example, we should choose to eat whole grain foods rather than refined grains. Fourth, develop the habit of eating at home rather than regularly eating out. This practice would help us avoid the large portions served at restaurants with their high number of calories. Fifth, increase the intake of fiber by eating whole grain foods, nuts, oats, beans, and many vegetables. Sixth and last, avoid foods with hydrogenated oil/trans fat, saturated fat, enriched wheat flour, sugar, and high-fructose corn syrup. When these items appear among the first five of the ingredient list, their quantity is too high, and they shouldn't be consumed.[19]

As embodied human beings and bearers of the renewed image of God, Christians should aim at good health through the physical discipline of eating properly. Most nutritionists suggest we begin slowly to adopt new eating patterns. They also underscore that it will take weeks if not months for us to establish good nutritional habits. Slowly reducing caloric intake, occasionally introducing new and more nutritional foods, and always avoiding frustration when progress seems fleeting or nonexistent are other good recommendations to follow.

Fasting

Christian fasting is the "voluntary abstinence from food for spiritual purposes."[20] To expand, "Christian fasting, at its root, is the hunger of a homesickness for God. . . . Christian fasting isn't only the spontaneous effect of superior satisfaction in God, it is

---

Sulfates" (Washington, DC: National Academic Press, 2005), chap. 4. Available at The National Academies Press, https://www.nap.edu/read/10925/chapter/6.

19. As I'm not an expert in this area, I offer only suggestions—not medical counsel—for how to eat properly.

20. Donald S. Whitney, *Spiritual Disciplines for the Christian Life* (Colorado Springs: NavPress, 1991), 152. It should be noted that many people fast for the health benefits it provides and not for any religious reason.

also a chosen weapon against every force in the world that would take that satisfaction away."[21]

Jesus assumes his disciples will fast by giving us instructions about fasting: "And when you fast, do not look gloomy like the hypocrites, for they disfigure their faces that their fasting may be seen by others. Truly, I say to you, they have received their reward. But when you fast, anoint your head and wash your face, that your fasting may not be seen by others but by your Father who is in secret. And your Father who sees in secret will reward you" (Matt. 6:16–18 ESV; cf. 9:14–15). The specific elements of fasting are important. We should not appear to be fasting so as to draw attention to ourselves and our (alleged) religious superiority. We should hide from others the fact of our fasting so that we have only one—and the proper—audience: God. We stop eating for a time, and this abstinence from food often results in intense hunger, stomach cramps, withdrawal symptoms, tiredness, dizziness and fainting, and more. Some or many of these negative symptoms may ease as the fast extends. Importantly, fasting results in a deepened dependence on God and a heightening of our spiritual senses. We embrace the promise that God will reward our fasting.[22]

In terms of this last aspect, God may give us this reward in terms of manifesting his presence in a deeper, more intimate way. He may answer our passionate and ongoing prayers in the case of particularly important matters. He may vividly guide us when we (or others for whom we are praying during our fast) urgently need his direction. God may restore us after deep confession and repentance of prevailing sins. He may protect us from brutal enemies and evil circumstances that threaten to undo us. He may raise us up after we have humbled ourselves and renounced our prideful

---

21. John Piper, *A Hunger for God: Desiring God through Fasting and Prayer*, redesign ed. (Wheaton: Crossway, 2013), 17–18.

22. For further discussion of the reasons or purposes for fasting, see Whitney, *Spiritual Disciplines for the Christian Life*, 157–70.

ways. God may answer our intercession on behalf of others who are desperately in need. He may supply the needs of the poor and marginalized when we give the money not spent on eating to those in need. He may renew and freshly empower us for a pioneering or heightened ministry. He may tangibly communicate his sense of pleasure for us being his children, his worshipers, his servants. These rewards correspond to the many reasons for fasting.[23] As explained earlier and included in the definition of fasting, this discipline, like all other disciplines, is purposeful.

How should we fast?[24] Develop a plan for what you are going to do during the time you don't eat meals and ensure that your fast is oriented for proper spiritual purposes. In the case of an extended fast, prepare for it by slowly diminishing your food intake. Drink plenty of liquids, get plenty of rest and sleep, and watch for alarming physical changes that may need medical attention. Break your fast slowly, easing back into your regular eating and drinking habits over the course of at least a week. For those with health concerns, fasting should be carried out with your doctor's approval and close monitoring. It may be the case that fasting is too dangerous and thus should be avoided.[25]

This chapter is about both bodily blessing and discipline. Having looked at fasting as a discipline, it's good to balance that emphasis with a blessing—feasting.

Feasting

In our fasting, we never want to deny the goodness of food as divinely given for our sustenance and enjoyment (1 Tim. 4:3–5;

---

23. For these reasons, and from its earliest days, the church has historically engaged in regular fasting. See for example the *Didache*: "Let not your fasts be with the hypocrites (Matt 6:16) for they fast on the second and fifth day of the week; but fast on the fourth day and the Preparation (Friday)." *Didache* 8.1.

24. Other regular practitioners may offer other suggestions for fasting.

25. As I'm not an expert in this area, I offer only suggestions—not medical counsel—for how to fast.

6:17). Though the New Testament doesn't call for feasting, Old Testament precedent provides support for Christians doing so.[26]

The Jews under the old covenant celebrated three great feasts. Passover memorialized God's mighty liberation from slavery in Egypt (Exod. 12:14). The Feast of Harvest (or Firstfruits) commenced the wheat harvest (Exod. 23:16). The Feast of Tabernacles (or Booths) commemorated Israel's wandering in the wilderness and God's goodness to them to provide for their needs (Lev. 23:34–43). Being the new covenant people of God, Christians aren't required to celebrate these Jewish feasts.

Outside these special religious events, God's people celebrated marriages through feasts. Examples include Jacob and Leah (Gen. 29:22), Samson and Delilah (Judg. 14:10), and the wedding at Cana (John 2:1–11). Moreover, the people of God celebrated the establishment of new relationships by feasting. Two examples are Jacob and Laban's territorial agreement and peace accord (Gen. 31:54) and Isaac and Abimelech's peace treaty (Gen. 26:26–30). Additionally, the hearing of good news prompted celebration with feasting. One example is Abner's good news to David (2 Sam. 3:17–21). The Jews under Ahasuerus celebrated his permission to defend themselves against Haman (Esther 9:18). The merciful father called for a feast at the return of his prodigal son (Luke 15:11–32).

Christians aren't under obligation to celebrate weddings, new relationships, and good news with feasting. However, these biblical precedents affirm the rightness of doing so.

Still, there is one obligatory feast for Christians. The Lord's Supper is a regular symbolic feast that church members celebrate together. At this feast, the church remembers the work of Christ on its behalf and looks forward to the fullness of salvation when he returns. It experiences the presence of Christ in its corporate gathering. The church celebrates its unity in the body of Christ. It

26. For further discussion, see Jeff Olson, "Once a Deadly Sin: A Contemporary Assessment of the Sin of Gluttony" (ThM thesis, Western Seminary, Portland, OR, 2000). Other proponents of feasting may offer other suggestions.

is nourished by the gospel.[27] Though many contemporary observances don't seem like feasts, it should be recalled that the early church observed the Lord's Supper in the context of an agape or love feast (1 Cor. 11:17–34; Jude 12).

Moreover, many churches, following a traditional liturgical calendar, celebrate the feast days of Easter, All Saints' Day, the Ascension, Christmas, Pentecost, Epiphany, and Trinity Sunday.[28]

All celebrations, particularly the Lord's Supper, point to a final celebration. At this ultimate feast, believers will experience and celebrate the fullness of salvation. It is first prophesied in the Old Testament:

> On this mountain,
> the LORD of Armies will prepare for all the peoples a feast
> of choice meat,
> a feast with aged wine, prime cuts of choice meat, fine
> vintage wine.
> On this mountain
> he will swallow up the burial shroud,
> the shroud over all the peoples,
> the sheet covering all the nations.
> When he has swallowed up death once and for all,
> the Lord GOD will wipe away the tears
> from every face
> and remove his people's disgrace
> from the whole earth,
> for the LORD has spoken. (Isa. 25:6–8)

Part of Jesus's ministry was the announcement of the coming of the kingdom of God/heaven, which has a future dimension—a hope for

---

27. For further discussion of the meanings of the Lord's Supper, see Gregg R. Allison, *Sojourners and Strangers: The Doctrine of the Church* (Wheaton: Crossway, 2014), 365–409.

28. "The Calendar of the Church Year: Principal Feasts," The Episcopal Church, *The Book of Common Prayer*, https://episcopalchurch.org/files/book_of_common_prayer.pdf.

all people: "Hearing this [the centurion's word], Jesus was amazed and said to those following him, 'Truly I tell you, I have not found anyone in Israel with so great a faith. I tell you that many will come from east and west to share the banquet with Abraham, Isaac, and Jacob in the kingdom of heaven'" (Matt. 8:10–11). At his inauguration of the Lord's Supper, Jesus underscored its future consummation: "But I tell you, I will not drink from this fruit of the vine from now on until that day when I drink it new with you in my Father's kingdom" (Matt. 26:29). That future consummation will be a glorious feast—the marriage supper of the Lamb with his bride:

> Then I heard something like the voice of a vast multitude, like the sound of cascading waters, and like the rumbling of loud thunder, saying,
>
> > Hallelujah, because our Lord God, the Almighty, reigns!
> > Let us be glad, rejoice, and give him glory,
> > because the marriage of the Lamb has come,
> > and his bride has prepared herself.
> > She was given fine linen to wear, bright and pure.
>
> For the fine linen represents the righteous acts of the saints. Then he said to me, "Write: Blessed are those invited to the marriage feast of the Lamb!" He also said to me, "These words of God are true." (Rev. 19:6–9)

In one sense, then, our present celebrations with feasting, especially the Lord's Supper, point forward to one last, ultimate feast.

Thus celebrating certain occasions with a sumptuous meal is right and proper. Though there's no explicit command to Christians to feast, Scripture presents feasting in a positive light, and we will experience feasting in the age to come.

How should we feast? Feasting should be characterized by great joy, celebration, and honor.[29] Still, excesses in food and drink that

---

29. Some people may find it helpful to approach feasting in terms of a liturgical practice. As an example of a protocol, see Douglas Kaine McKelvey, "A Liturgy

might lead to gluttony and debauchery, and overindulgences that may be accompanied by immorality, arrogance, silliness, and embarrassing words and actions, are to be avoided.[30] Examples of occasions of feasting include birthdays, graduations, weddings, reunions, births, anniversaries, retirements, religious holidays (Christmas, Easter, Pentecost), and civil holidays (Thanksgiving, Independence Day).

To conclude, our eating and drinking, our feasting (and fasting), are intended to be acts of worship of and honor to the triune God: "So, whether you eat or drink, or whatever you do, do everything for the glory of God" (1 Cor. 10:31). As we do, we live as whole people in a fractured world.

In summary, through the physical senses, human embodiment brings blessings that are too numerous to count. At the same time, it also demands bodily discipline. God's design for his embodied image bearers is that we live physically blessed and disciplined lives in areas such as proper nutrition, regular exercise, fasting, and feasting.

Application

The application is to design a personal program of bodily discipline that you consistently follow.

The first step is to do an evaluation of your current status. How would you assess yourself in terms of the consistent—that is, daily or weekly—practice of regular exercise and good nutrition? Then, in terms of more sporadic rhythms, how would you measure yourself in regard to fasting and feasting?

The second step is to develop a plan for the incorporation of these practices. How can you develop good nutrition and exercise

---

for Feasting with Friends," in *Every Moment Holy*, vol. 1 (Nashville: Rabbit Room Press, 2017), 112–16.

30. Given the abundance of food in our society, the average American Christian's simplest meal would be considered a feast elsewhere. This plenty may make it difficult for us to distinguish a special feast from a typical meal.

habits? And how can you incorporate fasting and feasting into your life?

Returning to the start of our chapter, for what specific physical blessings—both personal and those in the world surrounding you—are you thankful?

For the Curious

As you assess your progress in these areas of discipline, consider another biblical passage. In 1 Corinthians 9:24–27, by means of analogy to training for the ancient Isthmian games (which featured both running and boxing), Paul presents a strong contrast (vv. 24–25): The self-control exercised by an athlete in training and competing is in view of receiving a perishable reward. The self-control exercised by Christians in living and ministering is in view of receiving an imperishable reward. By way of application (vv. 26–27), Paul doesn't run without purpose, and he doesn't box without purpose. His self-control is aimed at moving him toward and preparing him for the goal.

Paul disciplines his body and keeps it under control lest, after preaching to others, he himself should be disqualified. His ministry has been to start off people on the race and to encourage Christians to run the race so as to receive the prize. His concern is that he himself might fail to exercise the proper self-control, break the rules of the game so as to be disqualified, and thus fail to obtain the prize at the end of the race. Discipline is purposeful, aimed at completing the marathon of the Christian ministry and reaping its promised rewards.[31]

Consider a few matters. First, to ensure that you're not engaging in bodily discipline just for discipline's sake, identify the purpose(s) for which you work hard at regular exercise, good nutrition, and the like. If you don't presently aim at something

31. Adapted from Allison, "Spiritual and Embodied Disciplines."

beyond the activity itself, how can you aim at a good target, and what would that be?

Second, Paul seems quite severe when he expresses his concern about disqualification. For those with sensitive consciences, I assume you are loving the Lord, serving Christ, and walking in the Spirit. If you share Paul's apprehension about becoming ineligible—a worry you may be experiencing right now as fear—how can you ensure this fear doesn't get the upper hand and destroy your rightful confidence in God's powerful and preserving work to hold you in salvation? Oppositely, for those who find themselves drifting off course, how can you take to heart Paul's warning? Having begun so well, and having labored fruitfully on behalf of others, please don't become shipwrecked in the faith. "Let us not get tired of doing good, for we will reap at the proper time if we don't give up" (Gal. 6:9).

CHAPTER 9

THE WORSHIPING BODY

Consider

Give thoughtful consideration to two questions: How would you define worship? Then, after you've answered that question: What is your assessment of this definition of worship?

> Worship is the submission of all our nature to God.
> It is the quickening of conscience by his holiness;
> the nourishing of mind with his truth;
> the purifying of imagination by his beauty;
> the opening of the heart to his love;
> the surrender of will to his purpose.[1]

Given our topic of embodiment, what, if anything, would you change, subtract, or add?

Big Idea

Embodied worshipers properly render worship to God through whole-body devotion to him, expressing praise, thanksgiving, confession, repentance, joy, obedience, faith, lament, and love. God's

---

1. William Temple, *Readings in St John's Gospel* (1939; repr., Wilton, CT: Morehouse Barlow, 1985), 67.

design for his people gathered to worship him is that we express bodily what is transpiring in our heart and mind.

Application Question

How can you ensure that your physical posture and bodily activity during worship expresses what is transpiring in your heart and mind?

Definitions

Our opening question presents a common definition of worship. Your assessment may include some or all of the following points: This definition focuses on the individual worshiper and, more specifically, the personal transformation that they experience when engaged in worship. It has nothing to say about what we generally call the "worship service," the gathering of church members, typically on Sunday mornings (though the transformation envisioned by this definition may take place in that context as well). Additionally, the definition highlights a particular notion of worship: not celebration, not devotion, but *submission*. Worship is whole-nature submission to God. Furthermore, specific areas of human nature—conscience, mind, imagination, heart, and will—are linked with certain divine attributes—holiness, truth, beauty, love, and purpose. Transformation—quickening, nourishing, purifying, openness, and submission—of the whole worshiper is effected by who God is. Finally, this definition overlooks or neglects the aspect of human nature that is the topic of this book: embodiment. It says nothing about worship and the body, or our transformation as embodied worshipers. Perhaps we could add a final line to the definition: the humbling of our body before God's majesty.

We begin with this definition because it underscores a key point of our book. Whether due to Gnosticism or neo-Gnosticism or some other reason, the church tends to overlook the fact that an essential given of human existence is embodiment. Importantly for this chapter, we worship God as embodied disciples, and we should worship him through whole-body devotion.

While such worship should be our daily practice as individual believers, we are also and primarily called to assemble together with other believers for corporate worship. In terms of a definition, worship is the act of corporate celebration by which the church acknowledges and acclaims the majestic greatness of the triune God.[2] This definition highlights a particular notion of worship: not submission, not devotion, but *celebration.* Some people may react negatively to this idea, as celebration brings to mind a raucous, disorderly, irreverent party. But there is another type of celebration that is a respectful, orderly, yet festive ceremony commemorating an important event—Memorial Day or Thanksgiving, for example. In a similar vein, a service of worship is a celebration—specifically, a community celebration of knowing God as his people, the body of Christ and the temple of the Holy Spirit.

This ceremony consists of three elements or movements. First, it "consists in ascribing honor to God through praise of his nature and mighty works by singing and praying."[3] As the psalmist urges, "Give thanks to the Lord, for he is good; his faithful love endures forever" (Ps. 118:1) and "Let them give thanks to the Lord for his faithful love and his wondrous works for all humanity" (Ps. 107:31). The second movement focuses on "reading, preaching, and hearing the Word of God, with responses of obedience and faithfulness to covenantal responsibilities (e.g., giving money, confessing sin, edifying one another, sending missionaries)."[4] Third,

---

2. For further discussion, see Allen P. Ross, *Recalling the Hope of Glory: Biblical Worship from the Garden to the New Creation* (Grand Rapids: Kregel, 2006), 67–68.

3. Gregg R. Allison, *The Baker Compact Dictionary of Theological Terms* (Grand Rapids: Baker, 2016), s.v. "worship."

4. Allison, *Baker Compact Dictionary of Theological Terms*, s.v. "worship."

the church performs two rites, that is, "the administration of the new covenant ordinances of baptism and the Lord's Supper."[5] Some people may dislike the term *rite* as it brings to mind formal, lifeless, religious observance—going through pious motions for the sake of duty and without heart. But there is another type of ritual that is a sincere and earnest ceremony structured according to a certain protocol—a liturgy.[6] Two rites that should be regular elements of a church's worship services are baptism and the Lord's Supper.

The church engages in these three movements in celebration of knowing the triune God. Still, as the church lives the reality of "already but not yet"—sanctified but still sinful, maturing but still muddled—its worship takes place in an atmosphere of expectancy. On any given Sunday, and incessantly, worshipers will be burdened with sin and suffering: economic collapse, sickness, marital difficulties, addictions, infertility, family tensions, mental illness, death of a loved one, and the like.[7] Moreover, the church exists in a world that is plagued by problems: political unrest, terrorist attacks, pandemic, racial inequity, natural disasters, and more. In the midst of tears and heartache, the church worships God even as it laments.[8] We worship in hope that God will fulfill

5. Allison, *Baker Compact Dictionary of Theological Terms*, s.v. "worship."

6. As we will see, all corporate worship services follow some kind of liturgy or ritual order, even if it is the insistence that there be no structure and that no order is followed!

7. Kevin Twit of Indelible Grace Music explained that, as a composer and pastor, he looks for worship songs that help people "prepare for their encounter with death." Mike Cosper, "Songs That Prepare Us for Death," The Gospel Coalition, February 3, 2011, https://www.thegospelcoalition.org/article/songs-that-prepare-us-for-death/.

8. Such lamentation may be intensified and last for an extended period of time when church members aren't able to gather for worship. Three examples suffice. First, there are periods of persecution during which church members would be imprisoned or killed if they gathered for worship. Second, sick and incarcerated members are physically prevented from gathering with others for worship. Third, during the early days of the global pandemic, church members morally and civilly purposed not to gather for worship. In these cases, they tearfully lamented the

his promises and fully redeem us, his people. Then, in the new heaven and new earth, we will worship God in glory and forever.

Bodily Posture and Physical Activity in Worship

Let's begin with a few questions.

In your church's worship service, what is the focus of attention?

What physical activity is involved in that focal point?

In the other elements of the worship service, what physical activity is involved?

Does the physical space in which the worship service is held contribute to or detract from the worship of God?

If your church is like many evangelical churches, the focus of attention in the worship service is preaching the Word of God. Seemingly all the events leading up to the sermon—the welcome, singing, praying, recitation of a creed, and more—are done in preparation for that climactic element. Once the preaching is over, the remaining events are like the falling action of a narrative—something like an exit strategy, definitely anticlimactic in nature.

As for the physical activity of the members of the congregation during the sermon, it is sitting without (much) moving, listening without talking (except for, perhaps, an occasional shout of "Amen!"), and ensuring that one's children sit quietly. Certainly, the one doing the preaching may be more or less animated, moving around the platform, gesturing with hands, speaking more loudly or softly, and perhaps acting out some important point. Besides the preacher's activity, the sermon is largely the time for inactivity.

---

loss of physically assembling to worship the Lord, to build up one another, and to enjoy fellowship.

During the other parts of the worship service, congregational activities may include some or all of the following: standing and sitting at the appropriate moments; voicing words of the hymns and songs, perhaps with clapping and swaying during the singing; shaking hands or hugging others during the welcome time or the "passing of the peace"; putting a check or cash into the offering plate; and participating in the Lord's Supper, either by going forward to the front of the auditorium to be served the elements or, as the plate and cups are passed, taking the bread and the wine or grape juice and eating and drinking at the indicated time. Some churches may permit less activity than those just mentioned, while others may encourage much more movement.

Interestingly, Scripture presents worship among the people of God as a very animated, physically engaging activity. Such bodily posture and physical expressions compose a lengthy list:

Bowing one's head or face toward the ground. "Ezra opened the book in the sight of all the people, for he was above all the people, and as he opened it all the people stood. And Ezra blessed the Lord, the great God, and all the people answered, 'Amen, Amen,' lifting up their hands. *And they bowed their heads and worshiped the* Lord *with their faces to the ground*" (Neh. 8:5–6 ESV; cf. 1 Sam. 24:7–8; Ps. 35:13–14). This bodily action of bowing before God communicates paying homage to him as the exalted king and/or grief for having rebelled against his majesty.

Raising hands for various reasons. First, as a petition for help: "Lord, I call to you; my rock, do not be deaf to me. If you remain silent to me, I will be like those going down to the Pit. Listen to the sound of my pleading when I cry to you for help, when *I lift up my hands toward your holy sanctuary*" (Ps. 28:1–2; cf. 88:6–10).[9] Second, as an offering to God from a sincere heart: "Lord, I call on you; hurry to help me. Listen to my voice when I call on you.

9. For an example of raising one's hands as a petition for help in the case of idolatry, see Ps. 44:20–21.

May my prayer be set before you as incense, *the raising of my hands* as the evening offering" (Ps. 141:1–2; cf. 1 Tim. 2:8). Third, as a blessing: "Now bless the Lord, all you servants of the Lord who stand in the Lord's house at night! *Lift up your hands in the holy place and bless the Lord!* May the Lord, Maker of heaven and earth, bless you from Zion" (Ps. 134:1–3; cf. Neh. 8:5–6). This bodily action of raising hands to God communicates desperation, dependence, surrender, invocation, and approbation.

Kneeling for various reasons. First, out of shame: "*I fell on my knees* and spread out my hands to the Lord my God. And I said: My God, I am ashamed and embarrassed to lift my face toward you, my God, because our iniquities are higher than our heads and our guilt is as high as the heavens" (Ezra 9:5b–6). Second, out of a sense of neediness. When Daniel responded to King Darius's edict to throw into the lion's den anyone who did not worship the king, "he went into his house. The windows in its upstairs room opened toward Jerusalem, and three times a day *he got down on his knees*, prayed, and gave thanks to his God, just as he had done before. Then these men went as a group and found Daniel petitioning and imploring his God" (Dan. 6:10–11). Third, as a blessing. At his dedication of the temple, Solomon "*knelt down in front of the entire congregation of Israel* and spread out his hands toward heaven. He said: Lord God of Israel, there is no God like you in heaven or on earth, who keeps his gracious covenant with your servants who walk before you with all their heart" (2 Chron. 6:13–14). This bodily action of kneeling communicates, in some situations, shame, humiliation, and embarrassment because of overwhelming sinfulness. In other cases, it communicates a desperate need for God to intervene. Still other times, kneeling communicates blessing God for his exalted majesty and covenant faithfulness toward his people.

Prostration. "Whenever the living creatures give glory, honor, and thanks to the one seated on the throne, the one who lives forever and ever, *the twenty-four elders fall down before the one seated on the throne* and worship the one who lives forever and ever. They cast their crowns before the throne and say, Our Lord and God, you are worthy to receive glory and honor and power, because you have created all things, and by your will they exist and were created" (Rev. 4:9–11; see also 5:8–14). This bodily action of prostration before God communicates honor and adoration. As it establishes the worshiper in a position of abasement, it magnifies the majesty of the Lord before whom the act of prostration is rendered.

Clapping. "*Clap your hands*, all you peoples; shout to God with a jubilant cry. For the LORD, the Most High, is awe-inspiring, a great King over the whole earth" (Ps. 47:1–2; cf. Isa. 55:12). The bodily action of clapping communicates enthusiastic approval and admiration.

Shouting. "*Let the whole earth shout joyfully to God!* Sing about the glory of his name; make his praise glorious. Say to God, 'How awe-inspiring are your works! Your enemies will cringe before you because of your great strength. The whole earth will worship you and sing praise to you. They will sing praise to your name.'" (Ps. 66:1–4; cf. 100:1–5). The voiced action of shouting communicates intense joy and deep thanksgiving for what the Lord has done. In the case of God defeating the enemies of his people, shouting expresses exultation in his glorious triumph (2 Chron. 20:20–23).

Dancing. "LORD, listen and be gracious to me; LORD, be my helper. *You turned my lament into dancing*; you removed my sackcloth and clothed me with gladness, so that I can sing to you and not be silent. LORD my God, I will praise you forever" (Ps. 30:10–12; cf. 149:1–5; 150:1–6; Jer. 31:2–4; exemplified by David, 2 Sam. 6:14–17). The bodily action of dancing communicates extreme pleasure and profound gladness in what the Lord has done. When he has transformed disaster into delight, his people rejoice with dancing.

Burning incense. One location for this was in the tabernacle and the temple:

[God speaking] "You are to place the altar in front of the curtain by the ark of the testimony—in front of the mercy seat that is over the testimony—where I will meet with you. Aaron must *burn fragrant incense* on it; he must burn it every morning when he tends the lamps. When Aaron sets up the lamps at twilight, he must *burn incense.* There is to be *an incense offering* before the Lord throughout your generations. You must not offer unauthorized incense on it, or a burnt or grain offering; you are not to pour a drink offering on it." (Exod. 30:6–9; cf. Ps. 141:2; Luke 1:9–10; exemplified on the Day of Atonement, Lev. 16:11–14)

Another location where incense is offered is in heaven:

When he [the Lamb] opened the seventh seal, there was silence in heaven for about half an hour. Then I saw the seven angels who stand in the presence of God; seven trumpets were given to them. Another angel, with *a golden incense burner,* came and stood at the altar. He was given *a large amount of incense to offer* with the prayers of all the saints on the golden altar in front of the throne. *The smoke of the incense,* with the prayers of the saints, went up in the presence of God from the angel's hand. (Rev. 8:1–4; cf. Mal. 1:11; exemplified in the altar of incense as described in Exodus)

The physical burning of incense is a symbolic action that communicates the unceasing prayers of the people of God. The framework for the offering of incense is the holiness of God and the sinfulness of his people. The smoke created by the burning incense is like a covering, and its smell is pleasing to the Lord.

Singing accompanied by musical instruments. The physical singing of songs and playing of musical instruments communicates full-orbed praise to God, who is worthy of proliferating, swelling adoration:

Hallelujah!
Praise God in his sanctuary.
Praise him in his mighty expanse.
Praise him for his powerful acts;
praise him for his abundant greatness.

> Praise him with the blast of a ram's horn [*trumpet*];
> praise him with *harp* and *lyre*.
> Praise him with *tambourine* and dance;
> praise him with *strings* and *flute*.
> Praise him with *resounding cymbals*;
> praise him with *clashing cymbals*.
> Let everything that breathes praise the LORD.
> Hallelujah! (Ps. 150:1–6; cf. 33:1–3; 81:2)

While one voice or one instrument alone may extol the Lord, the abundance of voices and instruments makes for successive, ceaseless waves of adoration.[10]

To sum up, Scripture envisions and commands significant bodily movement and physical expression as the people of God corporately worship him.

Theological Reflections

A unique expression of praise is offered by embodied beings, both nonhuman creation and human creatures made in the image of God. Both groups are designed and created to be material realities oriented toward the praise of the triune God. This physicality differs from the immaterial realm of angelic beings, who are also created and designed to worship their Creator: "Ascribe to the LORD, O heavenly beings, ascribe to the LORD glory and strength. Ascribe to the LORD the glory due his name; worship the LORD in the splendor of holiness" (Ps. 29:1–2 ESV; cf. 148:2).

As for the material, nonhuman realm, all creation is to worship the Lord:

> Praise him, sun and moon;
> praise him, all you shining stars.

---

10. A list of musical instruments noted in Scripture includes stringed instruments of lutes, harps, and ten-stringed lyres; wind and brass instruments of reed pipes, flutes, horns, and trumpets; and percussion instruments of cymbals, tambourines, and castanets.

> Praise him, highest heavens,
> and you waters above the heavens.
> Let them praise the name of the Lord,
> for he commanded, and they were created.
> He set them in position forever and ever;
> he gave an order that will never pass away.
> Praise the Lord from the earth,
> all sea monsters and ocean depths,
> lightning and hail, snow and cloud,
> stormy wind that executes his command,
> mountains and all hills,
> fruit trees and all cedars,
> wild animals and all cattle,
> creatures that crawl and flying birds. (Ps. 148:3–10; cf. 98:8)

All the material, nonhuman creation is commanded to worship God.

To this adoration given by the physical nonhuman creation is added the worship expressed by embodied human beings:

> Kings of the earth and all peoples,
> princes and all judges of the earth,
> young men as well as young women,
> old and young together.
> Let them praise the name of the Lord,
> for his name alone is exalted.
> His majesty covers heaven and earth. (Ps. 148:11–13)

Therefore, we human beings are to worship God with the whole of our (embodied) being. It is for embodied worship, with all our senses, that we are designed, created, and redeemed.

The Regulative and Normative Principles of Worship

The question still remains about the proper manner and form of worship as the church regularly gathers to engage in worship.

Historically, two major principles have sought to provide a framework for answering the question of what specific elements may be incorporated into the worship service: the regulative principle and the normative principle. Both principles agree that God is the one who determines how he is to be worshiped. Thus the answer to the question is ultimately not left up to church leaders and worship directors. Rather, the answer must be found by following the directives of Scripture for the proper manner and form of worship.

The regulative principle features three major tenets: "(1) the church must worship God according to the way he finds acceptable; (2) Scripture regulates specific elements of worship, insisting that it must be intelligible, purposeful, orderly, and proper (1 Cor. 11:2–16; 14:26–40); (3) thus, a biblical warrant (e.g., a command) is required for including an element in worship, and if no such warrant exists for it, that element must be excluded."[11] In applying the regulative principle, churches incorporate hymns of praise, songs of thanksgiving, prayers, confession of sin and assurance of forgiveness, reading of Scripture, a sermon, giving, administration of the ordinances, and a benediction.

The normative principle features four major tenets: "(1) the church must worship God according to his design; (2) while Scripture regulates certain elements of worship, it leaves other indifferent matters to the church's discretion; (3) the church has authority to decide these matters, yet it cannot decide contrary to Scripture; (4) thus, a biblical warrant isn't required for including an element in worship; rather, only if Scripture prohibits its incorporation may the church not include it in worship."[12] In applying the normative principle, churches incorporate all the elements approved by the regulative principle. Additional elements that churches may incorporate include dramatic reenactments of biblical stories or

11. Allison, *Baker Compact Dictionary of Theological Terms*, s.v. "regulative principle."
12. Allison, *Baker Compact Dictionary of Theological Terms*, s.v. "normative principle."

life lessons, a children's sermon, celebration of important events (e.g., Sanctity of Human Life Sunday and Mother's Day),[13] banner waving, and commemorations of national holidays (e.g., the Fourth of July and Memorial Day).[14]

How do we assess these two principles? It's important to note that invoking one or the other principle isn't a panacea for solving the issue of which bodily postures and physical activities should and should not, or may and may not, be incorporated into a church's worship service. For example, those who champion the regulative principle must also decide which Scriptures come into play when deciding whether a potential element has or does not have biblical warrant. Questions that help with this decision include the following: Does the church consider the New Testament only? Those who take this approach limit congregational singing, for example, to a cappella music. Alternatively, does the church consult the New Testament and the Psalms, or both the New Testament and the Old Testament? In this case, the application of the

13. On these special days, churches should remember that some of their members find themselves left out and needing special attention. For example, on child dedication Sundays, members who might feel alienated include those who are single and couples who face infertility, who have experienced a stillborn birth or loss of a child to illness or violence, or who are estranged from an adult son or daughter due, for instance, to rebellion or drugs. These members need to sense they aren't forgotten. For example, after a baby dedication with its prayer of thanksgiving for new life, the service's next movement may be a song of lament for brokenness and disappointment, e.g. Sandra McCracken, "Send Out Your Light (Psalm 43)," track 10 on *Psalms* (2015).

14. On these important days, some churches dedicate some or all of their worship services to commemorate the events. Those churches need to remember that if they include patriotic elements in the services, members who aren't citizens will feel excluded from the celebration and may even become confused about the gospel and its relationship to nationality and race/ethnicity. For example, on Veteran's Day, singing patriotic songs like "God Bless America" is problematic for non-Americans in the church. Additionally, American Christians may be troubled by such patriotic expressions during worship services because they believe that the kingdom of God is not of this world. Thus they believe that the church should not be associated with any particular country and its commemoration of national holidays and tributes. My thanks to Amy Nemecek for this point.

regulative principle includes all the bodily postures and physical activities presented above.

As for the normative principle, by what criteria do its advocates decide whether Scripture prohibits a certain element of worship? This question is particularly important when Scripture doesn't come close to addressing the matter. For example, incorporating an artistic painting of the main point of the sermon while it's being delivered is an element far removed from any kind of biblical instruction or pattern. How then is the church to decide whether this activity may be going on up front during the worship service?

Additionally, the use and application of these two principles varies significantly in different cultural contexts. First, how many churches are actually familiar with them? To hazard a guess, some (many? most?) churches decide which elements should or may be included in their worship service by considering their tradition, the latest fads, and what best works for them to accomplish their (vague) purposes.

Second, there are many cultural factors that strongly influence the manner and form of worship. For example, older generations tend to engage in more traditional worship, whereas younger generations prefer contemporary worship. Enter a church that is different from your own in terms of ethnicity, and the dissimilarity in worship expression is immediately noticeable. An hour-long, largely staid formal worship service in an ethnically White congregation differs from an ethnically Black congregation's exuberant, fluid worship service that lasts several hours. Geographical diversity is also evident, as worship services in an urban church diverge significantly from services in a rural community. Churches are stratified according to the socioeconomic status of their members, and their worship services reflect this variety. We also note divergent approaches to worship according to the different denominations with which churches are aligned. Typical worship services of churches in the Southern Baptist Convention, the Presbyterian

Church of America, the Lutheran Church Missouri Synod, and the Assemblies of God each have their own unique manner and form.

Worship from the Heart, Bodily Posture, and Physical Activity

Reading about bodily posture, physical activity, worship principles, and cultural influences may rightly prompt some people to object and draws our attention to an overlooked yet crucial matter: worship must flow from our relationship with God and come out of a heart that loves him. Jesus addressed such genuine worship when he highlighted the dispute between the Samaritans, who believed that God should be worshiped on Mount Gerazim, and the Jews, who maintained that God should be worshiped in Jerusalem. He corrected both wrong ideas: "But an hour is coming, and is now here, when the true worshipers will worship the Father in Spirit and in truth. Yes, the Father wants such people to worship him. God is spirit, and those who worship him must worship in Spirit and in truth" (John 4:23–24). Jesus condemned any and all false worship, citing the Lord's rebuke delivered to his people through the prophet Isaiah: "This people honors me with their lips, but their heart is far from me. They worship me in vain, teaching as doctrines human commands" (Matt. 15:8–9, referencing Isa. 29:13).

So true worship must flow from our wholehearted devotion to God. Additionally, God himself establishes the manner and form of worship that is acceptable to him. Nadab and Abihu stand out as a warning for those who might seek to worship God in an unauthorized way (Lev. 10:1–3).

Returning to our big idea, God's design for his people gathered to worship him is that we as embodied human beings express bodily what is going on in our heart and mind. Embodied worshipers properly render worship to God through whole-body devotion to him. Putting together the biblical affirmations and theological considerations, we support this idea with several steps.

First, God requires heartfelt worship from his people. Such genuine adoration includes praise, thanksgiving, confession, repentance, joy, obedience, faith, lament, and love.

Second, God requires that his people worship him in the manner and the form that he prescribes. Whether a church is governed by the regulative principle or the normative principle, it acknowledges that God demands that he be worshiped in certain ways.

Third, Scripture both commands and illustrates whole-body devotion to God. As we've seen, these bodily postures and physical activities include the following:

- Bowing one's head or face toward the ground to pay homage or express grief.
- Raising hands to petition for help, as an offering, or to bless God, thereby communicating desperation, dependence, surrender, invocation, or approbation.
- Kneeling out of a sense of neediness or as a blessing, conveying shame, humiliation, embarrassment, need, or blessing.
- Prostrating oneself to express honor and adoration.
- Clapping to exult with joy, thanksgiving, or triumph.
- Dancing to exhibit gladness and delight.
- Burning incense to symbolize the unceasing prayers of sinful people before the holy God.
- Singing accompanied with musical instruments to offer full-orbed, swelling praise to the Lord.

Fourth, and in summary, church members gathered together should express their wholehearted worship of God through their bodily posture and physical activities. When flowing from hearts that love God, these embodied realities express our praise, thanksgiving, confession, repentance, joy, obedience, faith, lament, and love. This perspective should lead to a lessening of negative attitudes toward bodily expressions in corporate worship services. Moreover, it should reduce any sense of embarrassment or self-consciousness about engaging in such physical activities. Furthermore, it should bring courage to overcome peer-induced avoidance of such expressions in corporate worship services.

Application

How can you ensure that your physical posture and bodily activity during worship express what's transpiring in your heart and mind?

Digging deeper, how can you avoid or minimize embarrassment or self-consciousness about—and peer-induced avoidance of—bodily expressions when you worship? Alternatively, how can you avoid putting on a show that expresses more about you than about God, the object of your worship, and/or that becomes a distraction to those worshiping around you?

Additionally, if you have responsibilities for your church's worship service, remember: any incorporation of change to the service—in this case, an encouragement for members to engage in new bodily postures and physical activities—is never easy. It should be preceded by preaching and teaching and conversations about the changes. When they are introduced, those who lead the changes should coach participants, rather than demanding they engage in such a manner and shaming those who resist. By introducing change slowly and progressively, the likelihood is greater that a deep shift will result in the church's culture, not just a temporary and superficial change.

For the Curious

The last part of our application moved to a broader consideration of the church's worship service in terms of its design. Assuming we have settled on the elements of our service, how do we order those elements, and why? This discussion turns our attention to the church's liturgy. This topic is certainly not new, but a new interest in liturgy as formative discipline and embodied practice has arisen and is important for human embodiment.

Liturgy can be defined as the structure or order of the elements of worship. It's the protocol according to which the church conducts its worship service. The order of some of these elements is evident. A worship service starts with a beginning movement—traditionally, the *call to worship*—and ends with a concluding activity—traditionally, the *benediction* or blessing of dismissal. Sandwiched between these initial and final events are songs, prayers, baptism, reading Scripture, giving, a sermon, the Lord's Supper, and more. Is there a proper flow to these elements, or can the liturgy be structured any which way? And how do we decide?

A point of caution is raised. In some churches, the word "liturgy" has a bad connotation of empty rituals and vacuous worship, the very things that God condemns as characterizing his wayward, heartless people of Israel. In what may be a reaction to this deformed view of liturgy, these churches denounce any sense of order and structure. Their worship service becomes something like a free-for-all. Reacting against this, still other churches deploy their worship service for the purpose of worldview and intellectual formation, with a liturgy that is highly formal and cognitive.

Contemporary proponents of a return to traditional liturgy offer it as a corrective to an overintellectualized faith. Though not an aim per se, another result of this retrieval is counteracting structureless, chaotic worship services. This neo-traditional liturgy counters both positions because of its imagination-forming practices: liturgy fuels worshipers' love for God. This approach, popularized by philosopher James K. A. Smith, underscores the fact that human beings are what they love. What people love is what they worship, and what they worship is what they love.[15] People are "ritual, liturgical creatures whose loves are shaped and aimed by the fundamentally forming practices" in which they are immersed.[16]

This formation is evident in the case of secular liturgies—those practices associated with sporting events, for example. Think of a college football game. The entire stadium knows the songs and the chants, which jerseys or colors to wear, and when to rise and when to sit. Or think of shopping. The shoppers formulate their strategy the night before, they choose the stores that offer the best deals, and—in the case of multiple shoppers—one heads to the children's department, a second goes to clothing, and the third splits off to furniture. Participants know the precise routine to follow. Importantly, these secular liturgies influence people to love other kingdoms (Alabama football) and other gods (the latest fashion). Whether for good or for bad, these liturgies shape and mold those who participate in them.

As with secular liturgies, so with religious liturgies. The church's worship service can form Christians intellectually, haphazardly, legalistically, moralistically, and so forth. Or it can form them into lovers of God and his kingdom.

Once again, this approach to liturgy isn't new. Historically, the church has structured its worship of God according to a common liturgy.[17] An example of a gospel liturgy might be as follows:

- call to worship
- songs and prayers of praise (including responsive readings)

---

15. James K. A. Smith, *Desiring the Kingdom: Worship, Worldview and Cultural Formation* (Grand Rapids: Baker Academic, 2009); Smith, *Imagining the Kingdom: How Worship Works* (Grand Rapids: Baker Academic, 2013).

16. David Neff, interview with James K. A. Smith, "You Can't Think Your Way to God," *Christianity Today*, May 24, 2013, https://www.christianitytoday.com/ct/2013/may/you-cant-think-your-way-to-god.html. Some people are critical of Smith, thinking that he denies the importance of intellectual formation. This is a misreading of his work, which takes an Augustinian approach to formation.

17. For further discussion, see Gregg R. Allison, *Historical Theology: An Introduction to Christian Doctrine* (Grand Rapids: Zondervan, 2011), chap. 30.

- confession of sin
- absolution: assurance of forgiveness
- song of thanksgiving
- sign of peace
- giving
- reading of Scripture (with the congregation standing)
- prayer
- sermon
- ordinances (weekly or monthly celebration of the Lord's Supper; baptism when needed)
- songs of celebration
- benediction: a blessing for the road

This liturgy, as well as others like it, intends to form the participants in a weekly rehearsal of the gospel. God takes the initiative to invite sinful people into his presence. As they engage in worshiping him for who he is and what he does, they become aware of their sinfulness. Confessing and repenting of their sins, they are given assurance of their cleansing by and right standing before God. Appropriately, they express their gratitude for salvation. They are reconciled not only to God but also to one another, and they gratefully acknowledge that truth by warmly welcoming others. They also thankfully give to the Lord to support their church and its ministries, aid for the poor, church planting efforts, and global mission endeavors.

These liturgical elements aren't merely warm-ups to what is rightly considered to be the first mark of Protestant churches: the preaching of the Word of God. Neither is worship to be identified with congregational singing. Rather, all the elements are crucial movements of gospel-centered worship. In the reading of Scripture, prayer, and the sermon, the congregation hears from God through his designated servants. Given the transformative power of the Word of God and the Spirit of God, the expectation is that participants will respond with obedience, faith, praise, repentance, lament, thanksgiving, or whatever attitude or action is appropriate.

Given the centrality of the gospel, the church celebrates the two gospel ordinances/sacraments, baptism and the Lord's Supper, which constitute the second mark of Protestant churches. Pedobaptist churches baptize the infant children of believing parents (as well as new converts). Credobaptist churches baptize people who can offer a credible profession of faith. And the Lord's Supper, which proclaims Christ's death until he comes, reinforces the gospel message that has permeated the entire service. At its conclusion, the congregation is launched back into its mission field through a final benediction.

While this liturgy is only a sample, it reflects many elements that the church has historically incorporated into its worship service. Those elements, and the order in which they are enacted, play an important role in forming church members in the faith. This gospel liturgy goes beyond mere intellectual preparation while rejecting willy-nilly fluidity and counteracting other structures. Rather, it prompts Christians to love God—that is, to worship God—and to worship God—that is, to love God. When Christians are well formed by gospel liturgy, they are helped to live as whole people in a fractured world.

To conclude: worship services are physical events, so their order and structure can either help or hurt a church's ability to physically embed the gospel message and a love for God among its members.

CHAPTER 10

THE CLOTHED BODY

Consider

 Thoughtfully answer this question: Why are you wearing the clothes you have on today?

Big Idea

Clothed embodiment is the proper state of human existence after the fall. God's design for his embodied image bearers after sin entered the world is that we are clothed for the purpose of covering the shame of nakedness. The only exception is nakedness between husband and wife.[1] Moreover, clothing expresses something important about human beings.

Application

Be thoughtful regarding the clothes that you choose to wear.

---

1. There are other occasions—e.g., during a physical exam by a doctor—when nakedness is permitted. These other occasions will be addressed later in this chapter.

Definition and General Framework

Clothes are garments worn to cover the body. The types of clothing people wear reflect and are influenced by their body type, gender, ethnicity/race, family background, age, geographical location, socioeconomic status, culture, and the like. One of the most evident differences between cultures is clothing expectations.

Some people may wonder why, in a theology of human embodiment, the matter of clothes is addressed. Awhile back I was leading a Bible study about Paul's instructions that "women are to dress themselves in modest clothing, with decency and good sense, not with elaborate hairstyles, gold, pearls, or expensive apparel, but with good works, as is proper for women who profess to worship God" (1 Tim. 2:9–10). One participant insisted that the passage is NOT about clothing! So some people may consider clothes to be unimportant and thus of questionable value in a theology book. However, this chapter will show that the purpose for clothes, biblical instructions about clothes, the vast amount of money and time people spend on clothes, and what is communicated by clothes, all tie in well with the subject of embodiment.

Before exploring why we wear clothes in the first place, we'll raise another question: Why do people wear the clothes they wear?[2] The list is long because the reasons are many and quite diverse.

Comfort. In a relaxed environment and when they feel at ease, people choose comfortable clothes.

Style. People are significantly influenced by the latest fashion trends, so they choose to wear stylish clothes in keeping with those fads. Examples of fashion trends over the course of the past few decades include jumpsuits, leisure suits, rolled jeans, flannel shirts, shoulder pads, velour tracksuits, tie-dyed T-shirts, saggy pants,

---

2. Thus we move from observation—what clothes people actually wear—to foundation—the purpose for wearing clothes.

and yoga pants.[3] Obsession with style may reach unprecedented heights, as seen in the forty-four-page manual of style instructions for the bankers of an international bank.[4]

Identification. Sociality prompts us to be in community and identify with others. To be part of a community, people desire and feel peer pressure to conform to the expectations and demands of others in the group. Part of community identity is wearing similar clothes. Some groups foster community around brand names like Nike, Forever 21, Levi's, Under Armour, and Aeropostale. Others identify by a certain type of clothing they wear, like the black dresses, black pants, black T-shirts, and black boots of goths and punks. Some people seek to present themselves as a gender other than their biological sex, dressing in ways to contradict gender expectations. Still others identify themselves with a particular culture or worldview; for example, the Amish commitment to simplicity is expressed in their refusal of adornment.

Uniformity. People wear standardized sets of clothes for various reasons. Uniforms may be worn for safety purposes, as exemplified by firefighters wearing suits to protect them from flames and intense heat. Uniforms also serve to inform customers that one is performing a legitimate service in their home as a representative of a certain company. Examples include termite inspectors and delivery personnel. Requiring uniforms may minimize expenses and remove advantages that could accrue because of clothes. This is the reason that some schools expect their students to wear standardized clothes. Uniforms such as nursing scrubs may be necessary to maintain a clean environment. Sports teams wear uniforms to distinguish between the home and visiting teams.

---

3. The fashion industry generates annually an enormous amount of money, with the American clothing market worth over $50 billion and the global market worth over $325 billion.

4. The bank is UBS in Switzerland. Katya Wachtel, "La DressCode: The Banker's Guide to Dressing and Smelling Like a Winner," Business Insider, December 15, 2010, https://www.businessinsider.com/ubs-dresscode-clothes-bank-2010-12.

Productivity. Recent studies suggest that certain types of clothes may influence the way people think. For example, formal apparel seems to increase people's ability to engage in abstract thinking. However, such findings don't lead to the conclusion that wearing comfortable clothes detracts from such thought.[5]

Marking. Certain clothes may be worn for a particular situation as an expression of a personal (internal) situation. Scripture presents the wearing of sackcloth and ashes as a sign of repentance. At the death of a loved one, people in the West may wear black as a sign of mourning. Certain apparel may mark a rite of passage, such as academic regalia for graduation and the formal dress of a bride and groom. Adolescents passing through a period of rebelliousness may dress to violate social norms.

Status. Clothes may signal class, position, rank, and prestige. For example, in describing the American workforce, we distinguish people as either white-collar or blue-collar workers. Though a person may enjoy a certain status, they may seek to identify with people of another status by the way they wear their clothes. A CEO of a manufacturing company, for example, removes his coat and tie and rolls up his sleeves when talking with his assembly-line workers. This is his attempt to show that he's a hard worker just like them. In different situations, the same person may select other apparel to promote an image of power and privilege.

Intimacy. As genuine relationships deteriorate and a hookup culture ascends, people may dress to advertise their sexual availability or their desire to be known intimately. An example of the first is dressing provocatively to attract partners. An example of the second is the breaking down of the distinction between outerwear

5. "When Clothing Style Influences Cognitive Style," Association for Psychological Science, May 8, 2015, https://www.psychologicalscience.org/news/minds-business/when-clothing-style-influences-cognitive-style.html#.WTmBucaZNBw. For the study itself see Michael L. Slepian et al., "The Cognitive Consequences of Formal Clothing," *Social Psychological and Personality Science* 6, no. 6 (2015): 661–68. Available at http://www.columbia.edu/~ms4992/Publications/2015_Slepian-Ferber-Gold-Rutchick_Clothing-Formality_SPPS.pdf.

and underwear and exposing the latter. Some people may fail to recognize that their clothing choice advertises something they don't desire.[6]

Pragmatism. People may choose their clothes because they are the only clean outfit available or they are the only affordable choice. In the latter case, the lack of accessibility to clothes may limit what people can opt to wear.[7]

Comfort, style, identification, uniformity, productivity, marking, status, intimacy, pragmatism—these are the various reasons why people choose to wear the clothes they wear. Put them all together and a key principle emerges: clothes communicate. Our selection of the clothes we wear says something about us, and our clothes convey messages to those around us: We are trend setters. We represent a company. We are in mourning. We are powerful, prestigious people. We are available. In almost every situation, clothes communicate something about us, our heart, our life situation.[8] For this reason, choosing what clothes to wear becomes an important matter.

But why do people wear clothes in the first place? To answer this question, we turn to some biblical and theological considerations.

Biblical and Theological Considerations

The narrative of God's creation of the first man and the first woman concludes with details about the couple's newly established relationship: "Both the man and his wife were naked, yet felt no shame" (Gen. 2:25). The next story of the couple's fall into sin

6. Any attempt to blame the clothes wearer for (falsely) inviting sexual assault against themselves is despicable and to be rejected. My thanks to Morgan DeLisle for her insights on this matter.

7. My thanks to Torey Teer for his observation about accessibility.

8. "Clothes as text, clothes as narration, clothes as a story. Clothes as the story of our lives. And if you were to gather all the clothes you have ever owned in all your life, each baby shoe and winter coat and wedding dress, you would have your autobiography." Linda Grant, *The Thoughtful Dresser* (London: Virago, 2009), 48.

concludes with a tragic reversal of their original state of transparency: "Then the eyes of both of them were opened, and they knew they were naked; so they sewed fig leaves together and made coverings for themselves" (Gen. 3:7). Though the fallen pair tried to hide themselves from God's presence, "the LORD God called out to the man and said to him, 'Where are you?' And he said, 'I heard you in the garden, and I was afraid because I was naked, so I hid.' Then he asked, 'Who told you that you were naked? Did you eat from the tree that I commanded you not to eat from?'" (Gen. 3:9–11). Finally, following the articulation of the divine judgments against them, "The LORD God made clothing from skins for the man and his wife, and he clothed them" (Gen. 3:21).

Because we are used to wearing clothes, it is hard for us to imagine Adam and Eve's nakedness without shame.[9] From our perspective, their nakedness contradicts social norms, which exist in every culture in the world. Their shamelessness contradicts expectations, namely, that their nakedness would result in them feeling ashamed in a public setting. In their pre-fall state, Adam and Eve were naked not because they removed their clothes, but because they had never been clothed. Startlingly, this absence of clothing is joined with an absence of shame. They hadn't failed to obey or meet expectations, so they sensed no humiliation or regret. They had no inner feeling of being out of sorts as being bad or evil people, and there was no sense of inferiority or belittlement between the two. Rather, they were people of integrity who experienced an intimate transparency in their relationship.

Why did Adam and Eve have no shame? They were ignorant of evil, so no shame could exist. But they weren't ignorant of their sexuality and sexual organs, which were visible and active, and properly so because of the mandate to "be fruitful and multiply and fill the earth" (Gen. 1:28 ESV). The fall into sin first resulted

---

9. Much of the following discussion is influenced by Ryan Hanley, "Nakedness Imagery as Theological Language in the Old Testament" (PhD diss., The Southern Baptist Theological Seminary, 2019).

in shame, not in guilt. Adam hides not because he fears God's judgment (guilt leads to condemnation) but because he is naked (Gen 3:10). Still, sin's disruption isn't merely a sense of shame; sin brings pervasive and long-lasting consequences (Gen. 3:14–19). From "naked and not ashamed" to "naked and ashamed" indicates a cataclysmic shift from ideal to fallen, portrayed as innocence and intimacy lost. To rectify the abysmal situation, God provides clothes for Adam and Eve. Clothes ameliorate their shameful nakedness. And only God can rescue them.[10]

The first couple's nudity underscores original purity, not in a moral sense (Adam and Eve are good, know only good, and do only good) but in terms of lacking an accidental human feature: they are morally naïve or innocent.[11] This pre-fall condition contrasts with the post-fall existence in which public nudity is inherently shameful. To expose one's own nakedness, or to be stripped of clothes by another so one's nakedness is exposed, leads to shame. This *is* a moral category. Throughout Scripture, nakedness is associated with destitution (the poor are portrayed as naked, i.e., without resources; Isa. 58:6–7), military defeat (an act of abasement of conquered soldiers is to strip them of their clothes; Ezek. 16:36–39), and divine cursing to humiliate the sinful people of God (Deut. 28:45–48; Nah. 3:5).

Scripture approves of nakedness in only one context: between a husband and wife. Proverbs 5 and the Song of Songs make this divine approbation explicit. Because sexual intercourse in a marital relationship is good, nakedness is good as well. In all other

10. For a proper interpretation of this narrative, we should be careful of focusing on the skins as indicative of an animal sacrifice to address the couple's guilt and condemnation. The focus of the text is on covering for shameful nakedness.

11. An accidental human property is one that isn't essential to what makes a human being. Naïveté, innocence, and sinfulness, to take a few examples, are accidental properties because one can still be a human being without being naïve, innocent, or sinful. In the latter case, while it is a common human property—all human beings are sinful—it isn't an essential human property. Adam and Eve were fully human before the fall.

contexts, nakedness is precluded.[12] For example, throughout the book of Leviticus, God prohibits uncovering the nakedness of— that is, having sexual intercourse with—a member of one's own household or family (incest) and a wife during her menstruation. The latter prohibition is due to ritual uncleanness, not because of her being an illicit sexual partner. Additionally, covering the nakedness of another person is a righteous deed. For example, Shem and Japheth, in distinction from Ham, covered their father Noah's nakedness (Gen 9:20–23).

Thus clothing is a divine provision that serves as a remedy for the shame associated with nakedness. We speculate that had Adam and Eve never sinned, there would have been no need for clothes. Their nakedness signaled the unblemished relationship between themselves as a couple and between them and God. Tragically, their fall into sin permanently fractured both the human-to-human relationship and the human-to-God relationship. By his provision of clothes, God in his mercy relieves human shame due to nakedness and makes a way for sinful people to stand before him once again.

Regarding this restoration to fellowship with God, the early church's practice of nude baptism is illuminating.[13] According to an early church theologian, this practice of nude baptism was important for three reasons. First, it symbolized the new convert's putting off their old self. Second, it identified the new convert with Christ, who was stripped naked before he was crucified. And third, it paralleled Adam and Eve before sin, so the newly baptized convert would bear a likeness to the original pair in their innocence and uprightness. This parallel underscores the fact that salvation

12. In several other common situations, nakedness is permitted. A patient with their doctor shouldn't have reservations about undressing for annual checkups, preparation for surgeries, and the like. An elderly person needing assistance shouldn't be concerned about being undressed, taken to the bathroom, bathed or showered, and similar acts of assistance by their caregiver.
13. It should be recalled that deaconesses in the early church helped prepare women for baptism, which involved them removing their clothes and being immersed in water.

restores sinful people to a position of integrity before God, as was symbolized by Adam and Eve being naked and unashamed.[14]

This matter of clothing raises the question of the apparel of believers in the new heaven and new earth. Scripture doesn't present those who have been redeemed as reverting to the pre-fall state of nudity. Rather, they appear clothed in white garments:

> Then I heard something like the voice of a vast multitude, like the sound of cascading waters, and like the rumbling of loud thunder, saying,
>
>> Hallelujah, because our Lord God, the Almighty, reigns!
>> Let us be glad, rejoice, and give him glory,
>> because the marriage of the Lamb has come,
>> and his bride has prepared herself.
>> She was given fine linen to wear, bright and pure.
>
> For the fine linen represents the righteous acts of the saints. (Rev. 19:6–8)[15]

Aware of the symbolic nature of this passage, we cautiously speculate: the white garments symbolize salvation completed, purity actualized, and holiness perfected in the age to come. It thus leaves open the question of how believers in the new heaven and new earth will be clothed.

---

14. Cyril of Jerusalem, "On Baptism," *Catechetical Lecture* 20.2, in *The Works of St. Cyril of Jerusalem*, ed. L. P. McCauley and A. A. Stephenson (Washington, DC: Catholic University Press, 1969–70), 1:80.

15. This notion may have come from the extracanonical book of 1 Enoch:
    And the righteous and the chosen will be saved on that Day and they will never see the faces of the sinners and the lawless from then on. And the Lord of Spirits will remain over them and with that Son of Man they will dwell, and eat, and lie down, and rise up, forever and ever. And the righteous and chosen will have risen from the earth, and will have ceased to cast down their faces, and will have put on the Garment of Life. And this will be a Garment of Life from the Lord of Spirits; and your garments will not wear out, and your glory will not fail, in front of the Lord of Spirits. (1 Enoch 62:13–16)

Between the opening and closing chapters of the Bible that deal with nakedness, shame, earthly clothing for covering, and heavenly clothing of salvation, other passages give specific instructions about wearing clothes. One Old Testament text addresses cross-gendered clothing: "A woman is not to wear male clothing, and a man is not to put on a woman's garment, for everyone who does these things is detestable to the LORD your God" (Deut. 22:5). Two passages in the New Testament address the clothing of women. Paul gives instructions: "The women are to dress themselves in modest clothing, with decency and good sense, not with elaborate hairstyles, gold, pearls, or expensive apparel, but with good works, as is proper for women who profess to worship God" (1 Tim. 2:9–10). Peter offers similar directives: "Don't let your beauty consist of outward things like elaborate hairstyles and wearing gold jewelry or fine clothes, but rather what is inside the heart—the imperishable quality of a gentle and quiet spirit, which is of great worth in God's sight" (1 Pet. 3:3–4). Scripture doesn't prohibit the wearing of clothes and accessories. As we've seen, clothes are the divine design for covering our shame and making ourselves socially presentable. But Scripture does give principles that regulate the wearing of clothes.

Principles for Clothing the Body

One key principle is that the clothes we wear should communicate our gender. Women are to wear clothes that underscore and enhance their female embodiment. Men are to wear clothes that underscore and enhance their male embodiment. Thus Deuteronomy 22:5 is far more than a fashion statement regulating clothes, evidenced by the perhaps surprising assessment of cross-gendered dressing as being detestable to God. Rather, the passage reflects the big idea of our chapter on the gendered body: God's design for his embodied image bearers is that we are gendered human beings. Because an essential given of human existence is maleness or femaleness, even our clothes must bear witness to our embodied genderedness.

In terms of clothing selection, the biblical framework is one of contrast: *not* this, *but* that.

Not	But
what society values	what God values
elaborate, ostentatious, expensive dress	modest, decent, sensible dress
outward beauty that perishes	inward, imperishable beauty of the heart
obsession with clothing	a gentle and quiet spirit, and good works

Scripture doesn't address the clothes that men should wear, but by extrapolation from the texts in 1 Timothy and 1 Peter we can draw principles for male clothes as well as female clothes.

As a general principle, "With our clothing we acknowledge our sin, make ourselves presentable to society without seeking undue attention, and affirm our gendered nature."[16] In accord with our earlier discussion of gender, this last directive doesn't intend to absolutize a cultural stereotype like men wearing blue and women wearing pink. In a different culture, men could wear pink and women could wear blue. So the general principle is a normative one that must be applied contextually.[17]

As for detailed principles, we are to dress *modestly*, not sensually to draw attention to our sexual organs and/or signal our availability for sexual activity. This principle applies to both men and women in different ways.[18]

16. Aaron O'Kelley, final paper, "Theology of the Body" PhD seminar, Southern Baptist Theological Seminary.

17. My thanks to Mike Schuetz for helping to clarify this principle.

18. In concert with this principle for dressing modestly, we echo our earlier point that we must work hard to overcome the cultural hypersexualization that conditions us to view others as little more than sexual objects. Specifically, "We do well to encourage one another by not assuming sexual intentions of one another based on our own reactions or feelings toward their outfits." Morgan DeLisle, personal correspondence.

We are to dress *sensibly*, engaging in conscious thought in our selection of clothes. Questions to ask ourselves include: What does this outfit communicate? How does it affect others?

We are to dress *properly*, using good judgment. The application of this principle isn't that clothes function as mere utilitarian covering but that they communicate an appropriate message in different contexts. Questions to ask ourselves are: Do I dress in ways that appropriately convey my gender in my context? Am I properly dressed for the occasion?

We are to avoid dressing *ostentatiously*, donning gaudy or elaborate clothes to draw attention to our status or wealth or privilege. The application doesn't mean that people can't wear expensive, well-tailored suits and dresses when the context dictates that these are appropriate. The opposite of ostentatious isn't dowdy, old-fashioned, or inexpensive. Rather, it is a creative and joyful expression of our particularity with a context-sensitive freedom in our clothing choice. And that selection tends toward understatement rather than grandiosity.

We are to avoid *breaking the budget* on clothing purchases. To apply this principle, we may ask ourselves questions such as: What is appropriate in light of personal, family, church, and world needs? Did the manufacturing of the clothes exploit those who made them? Do I spend an inordinate amount of money on clothes, and why?

In applying these principles, we need to remember the ethnic, generational, geographical, socioeconomic, cultural, and vocational factors that influence clothing selection and regulation. In a globalized world, appreciation of and respect for other people's clothes should be expressed in refusing to judge clothing differences as wrong and declining to evaluate people as inferior because of their different apparel. It further means adapting our clothing choices out of respect for contexts that are different from our own.

In summary, clothed embodiment is the proper state of human existence after the fall. God's design for his embodied image bearers after sin entered the world is that we are clothed for the purpose of covering the shame of nakedness. The only exception is nakedness between husband and wife. Moreover, clothing expresses something important about human beings.

Application

The application is a call to thoughtfulness with respect to the clothes that you choose to wear.

Relate your clothing practices to this general principle: With our clothing we acknowledge our sin, make ourselves presentable to society without seeking undue attention, and affirm our gendered nature. How are you doing with respect to this notion?

Specifically, assess your clothing habits according to the principles of dressing modestly, sensibly, and properly, not ostentatiously or extravagantly so as to break your budget.

For the Curious

Discussions of the clothed body often lead to questions about the tattooed and pierced body. Why do people get tattoos and piercings? Is it okay for Christians to be tattooed and/or pierced? And how are we to decide the matter?[19]

We begin our discussion by placing the issue in the broader context of body modifications (bod-mod for short) and its reasons. For some people, self-mutilation—the intense physical sensation of burning or piercing—is seen as leading to enlightenment: "If I could bottle this feeling up, I would give it away." Other people view their body as a text or as their personal canvas on which to write or paint their life story. Theirs is a "body project" requiring tattoos and piercings that express the narrative of their life.

---

19. Some of the following takes inspiration from Edward Barnes, "Brand New Bodies," *Time*, September 13, 1999, 52.

Furthermore, some people get bod-mod as memorable symbols of life passages, with the tattoos and piercings possessing a kind of ritualistic power. Other people use markings to produce an effect that is intended to shock (though it is a fad in and of itself, with a consequent loss of shock value). Abuse survivors may get tattoos and piercings for therapeutic purposes, to reclaim control over their bodies that has been violently stolen from them. For some people, this practice is a type of branding that creates a sense of community, fraternity, or ancestral/tribal identity. For example, eight of the nine actors who composed the Fellowship of the Ring in the *Lord of the Rings* movie trilogy have matching tattoos of the word "nine" in Elvish. Being tattooed and pierced is also a religious act common in non-Christian religions.

Whereas few people are disturbed by the tattoos on soldiers who survive a war and mark that life event with an American flag or a naval insignia inked into their arm, bod-mod can be extreme. Examples abound, including the Lizardman, Erik Sprague, whose total transformation of himself into a fork-tongued, green scaly reptile is a complete rejection of his humanness. Stalking Cat resembled a tiger, having had his nasal septum surgically altered, his lip clefted, his ears given feline-like points, his brow and cheeks enhanced with implants, and his teeth removed and replaced with fangs. Iguana Mike has transdermal implants of metal spikes. Klingon wannabees have their tongue split to resemble the Star Trek characters.

Techniques of extreme body modification are also common and include neo-primitive skin stretching, as historically practiced in South America, Africa, and Southeast Asia. Body suspension involves inserting hooks into piercings in the back of a person, who is then hung from a beam by means of ropes or chains. Scarification is intentional disfiguration caused by placing hot metal on the skin or by scraping the skin. Corset piercing features piercings on both sides of the spine that are laced with ribbons and pulled taut. Eye tattooing is achieved by coloring the sclera, the white part of the eye. For example, Amber Luke had her eyeballs tattooed, which caused her to be blind for three weeks. She now goes by the name Blue Eyes White Dragon.

Perhaps the most tragic of these practices is elective amputation for people suffering from body integrity identity disorder (BIID), or apotemnophilia, literally, "a love of cutting."[20] This yearning to reshape their body to a desired form may be due to a person's thinking of themselves as incomplete with all the parts of their body. Three types of apotemnophilia are *wannabes*, those who desire an unnecessary amputation; *pretenders*, those who fake having an amputation by binding their limbs under clothes; and *devotees*, those who are attracted to amputees.

The one biblical instruction for tattooing and piercing is found in the Old Testament holiness code:[21] "You are not to eat anything with blood in it. You are not to practice divination or witchcraft. You are not to cut off the hair at the sides of your head or mar the edge of your beard. *You are not to make gashes on your bodies for the dead or put tattoo marks on yourselves*; I am the LORD" (Lev. 19:26–28). One biblical narrative, the battle between Elijah and the prophets of Baal on Mount Carmel, notes that the prophets, to get the attention of Baal, "shouted loudly, and *cut themselves with knives and spears, according to their custom, until blood gushed over them.* All afternoon they kept on raving until the offering of the evening sacrifice, but there was no sound; no one answered, no one paid attention" (1 Kings 18:28–29).

---

20. This mental disorder isn't included in the DSM-5.

21. The issue of the application of Old Testament laws for Christians today is a complex and hotly debated matter. One principle (among many) that people use is whether a law is general or specific. In the former case, it may still be applicable for us today. For example, the instruction about punishment in the case of children born prematurely due to violence seems to be a general law that addresses the issue of abortion even today. In the latter case, a specific law was for the people of Israel only and thus not applicable for us today. Many other principles enter into the discussion as well.

Two interpretations of the Leviticus passage are common. The first involves a creational perspective. The body is a marvelous creation of God, and its wholeness represents the beauty and perfection of holiness. Thus the body is to be kept whole. The biblical prohibitions against marking, cutting, and tattooing the body are to uphold the natural order of creation and preserve it from corruption. The external appearance of the faithful should reflect their internal status as the elect and holy people of God. According to this first interpretation, tattoos and piercings are precluded.

The second interpretation involves a ritual perspective. Pagan customs and rites are prohibited, and Leviticus addresses the importance of Israel distinguishing itself from the pagan nations surrounding it. In instructions that immediately follow the prohibition against tattooing and piercing, the Lord directs his people: "You must not follow the statutes of the nations I am driving out before you, for they did all these things, and I abhorred them" (Lev. 20:23).

In the passage under discussion (19:26–28), the pagan rites to be rejected include a mourning practice that involved shaping one's hair and beard and incising patterns on one's skin. This incision may have included the emblems of pagan deities, perhaps in an attempt to pacify the deceased person or placate the demons that caused their death. These passionate outbursts of mourning may have led to cutting oneself, a practice that was typical of the Babylonians, Armenians, Scythians, and others. Sadly, the Israelites seemed to have engaged in these practices as well: "'For this is what the LORD says: *Don't enter a house where a mourning feast is taking place.* Don't go to lament or sympathize with them, for I have removed my peace from these people as well as my faithful love and compassion.' This is the LORD's declaration. 'Both great and small will die in this land without burial. No lament will be made for them, *nor will anyone cut himself or shave his head for them*'" (Jer. 16:5–6; cf. 41:4–5; 47:4–5).

According to this second interpretation then, tattooing and piercing are prohibited because of their association with pagan customs and rites.

So the issue has two positions. If tattooing and piercing are prohibited merely because of their association with the cultic rituals of non-Israelite nations, their prohibition is more easily dismissed as irrelevant today. Because our context has changed, the rules against bodily markings are no longer binding. If, however, the prohibition is tied to the first interpretation—the human body is to be kept intact because its wholeness represents the beauty and perfection of holiness—it may be seen as a general rule to direct the church even today. If this is the case, then what is its application today? Specifically, what would be prohibited? Cosmetic piercings such as earrings? A nose stud? Piercings of the eyelids, nostril, nipples, and belly button? All tattoos? Certain tattoos? How about a tattoo of the cross, or Jesus's crown of thorns, or the crucifixion, or a favorite Bible verse?[22]

What is your position on this discussion? Is it permissible for Christians to have tattoos and piercings, or are such markings prohibited? If you have a tattoo or piercing, what is it and why do you have it? What practical factors should be considered when it comes to this decision?[23]

One further consideration: in many cases, clothing selection and tattoo preference aren't sinful matters. In most cases, then, how should believers decide about tattoos and piercings? If these

22. Does the following metaphorical description of the divine redemption of Israel have anything to offer our discussion? "I adorned you with jewelry, putting bracelets on your wrists and a necklace around your neck. *I put a ring in your nose, earrings on your ears*, and a beautiful crown on your head. . . . Your fame spread among the nations because of your beauty, for it was perfect through my splendor, which I had bestowed on you" (Ezek. 16:11–12, 14).

23. Among many sources that offer practical advice, see Will Honeycutt, "Should Christians Get Tattoos? 7 Points to Consider First," Crosswalk.com, August 27, 2019, https://www.crosswalk.com/family/singles/is-it-biblical-for-christians-to-get-tattoos.html; "Tattoos and Christians," *Doctrine and Devotion* (blog), December 11, 2018, http://www.doctrineanddevotion.com/blog/tattoos.

areas fall under the category of *adiaphora*, or indifferent matters, then people who get them should be convinced in their own mind of their legitimacy.[24] Moreover, they shouldn't flaunt their markings if by such disrespectful behavior they cause their weaker brothers and sisters to stumble. At the same time, these weaker believers aren't to judge and despise their tattooed and pierced siblings. With or without tattoos and piercings, we may live as whole people in a fractured world.

24. Adiaphora, or indifferent matters, are "activities that are neither moral nor immoral. Moral activities (e.g., loving one's neighbor) are in accordance with God's law. Immoral activities (e.g., murder) violate it. Activities that fall in neither category are adiaphora or indifferent before God; people may choose to engage in or abstain from them. Examples include eating meat sacrificed to idols and celebrating special days like Christmas and Easter. Christian conduct in these matters is ruled by two considerations: stronger Christians should not cause their weaker counterparts to stumble, and weaker Christians are not to condemn their stronger counterparts for engaging in them." Gregg R. Allison, *The Baker Compact Dictionary of Theological Terms* (Grand Rapids: Baker Books, 2016), s.v. "*adiaphora.*"

CHAPTER 11

THE SUFFERING AND HEALED BODY

Consider

Thoughtfully answer this question: In what way(s) has God been with you in your suffering?

Big Idea

Suffering is part and parcel of embodied existence, and suffering may persist, worsen, or improve, perhaps even be healed. God's design for his embodied image bearers after the fall is to permit us to suffer the physical consequences of living in a fallen world. Moreover, he calls Christians to suffer for the sake of Christ, even to the point of martyrdom. At all times, God's grace is sufficient to sustain his people, and sometimes he will rescue them from persecution or physically heal them.

Application Question

How should you face suffering and how should you seek healing as an embodied Christian?

The Reality of and Reason for Suffering

According to one very unscientific poll—my own interviews with people on the street—people are deeply vexed by two questions: What is my purpose in life? and Why is there so much suffering and evil in the world? The second question captures our attention in this chapter.

Even though some people deny the reality of suffering (a topic we will discuss in the next chapter), the vast majority acknowledge and are perplexed by the problem. Briefly, we can address the matter with three considerations, using examples from the physical realm in keeping with our theme of embodiment.[1]

First, all suffering can ultimately be traced back to the fall. As a consequence of the rebellion of Adam and Eve, sin and its accompanying problem of suffering were introduced into the world. Prior to this tragic and world-altering event, creation was characterized by light, peace, joy, goodness, harmony, flourishing, and life. All of this was shattered by Adam and Eve's rebellion and was replaced with darkness, anxiety, sadness, evil, conflict, failure, and death. Accordingly, whether the suffering takes place in the physical realm through natural disasters (e.g., pandemics, earthquakes, tsunamis, and droughts) or in the moral realm through self-inflicted pain (e.g., risky behavior and addictions) or abuse at the hands of others (e.g., rape and child molestation), all suffering is ultimately the result of the fall. Though not the way it's supposed to be, suffering is part and parcel of living in a fallen world.

Importantly then, much of our suffering as embodied people is due to factors out of our control. For example, our genetic makeup and biological vulnerabilities are determinative for much of our life, whether a propensity to physical ailments like obesity, Huntington's chorea, and heart disease, or mental health issues such as depression, bipolar disorder, and schizophrenia.

1. My thanks to Luke Allison for formulating these three categories of suffering.

Our family of origin or nurture exerts a significant influence on our embodied habits, leading to suffering caused by carelessness about our general health or a lack of physical flourishing due to a deficit of familial love. Miscarriages, experienced by upward of 50 percent of pregnant women, are outside our control, and only a few steps can be taken to prevent subsequent losses. Living in the path of a tornado that threatens physical harm to ourselves and our community is a source of intense suffering. Well-intentioned yet incorrect medical advice and procedures—for example, unnecessarily removing a person's gallbladder or prescribing sleeping pills for insomnia—may have negative effects over the long haul. By definition, we aren't responsible for these factors. They are fundamental givens of our life or are imposed on us by others or by external realities. Nevertheless, they are a significant cause of suffering.

Second, some suffering is self-inflicted. Assuming we're talking about responsible adults who are generally aware of good and bad, right and wrong, people sometimes make choices that bring suffering upon themselves. For example, if a person knows that diabetes runs in their family, their decision to consume certain foods and forego regular exercise may result in physical complications. And once diagnosed with the disease, failure to follow the prescribed medical treatment compounds the problem. As another example, a person who is caught up in an addictive cycle—alcohol, sex, drugs—scales increasingly downward on the spiral of suffering until they either get the necessary help or hit rock bottom. The contemporary tendency to consider addiction as a disease, while perhaps helpful in some sense, fails to acknowledge the self-imposed suffering at the start of the out-of-control cycle of increasing suffering. By definition, we are responsible for self-inflicted suffering.

Third, people-to-people suffering is common. We cause others to suffer by our selfishness, lack of love, inability to empathize, exaggerated push to get ahead, failure to trust God, sense of entitlement, racism, sexism, classism, ageism, and much more.[2] This other-oriented suffering may flow from our passive indifference toward others. We don't lift a finger to right the wrong of the status quo by correcting redlining (discrimination by withholding home mortgages in certain neighborhoods) or by providing accessible medical assistance for the poor. Or this other-oriented suffering may arise from our active sin against others. We target those who pose a threat to us by causing them bodily harm. In many cases, these actions are cruel in and of themselves. Still, some may be actions that are intended to be helpful but go awry, thus causing harm. By definition, we are responsible for the suffering we inflict on other people.[3]

Suffering may also be due to a combination of these three: factors beyond our control, poor choices on our part, and the actions of others. For example, the COVID-19 pandemic was caused by a virus carried in respiratory droplets. As an environmental factor, it has wreaked havoc for millions of suffering people. At the same time, when warned about the dangers of the disease and told to implement certain precautionary steps to mitigate its impact, some individuals paid no heed to those directives. Their particular infection was in part self-inflicted. Additional suffering was provoked by governments that reacted nonchalantly to the threat of the pandemic. Their inactivity compounded its potential deadly effect. Moreover, irresponsible healthy individuals who disregarded quarantine advisories and became infected with the virus may have experienced little or no suffering. As carriers of the disease, however, they infected the elderly and others with compromised immune systems. The result of this people-to-people selfishness

2. For further discussion of the trauma unleashed by suffering, see Bessel van der Kolk, *The Body Keeps the Score: Brain, Mind, and Body in the Healing of Trauma* (New York: Penguin, 2014).

3. In the case of well-intentioned actions that go amiss and end up causing suffering, personal responsibility may be mitigated to some degree. My thanks to Brian Vos for his insights into this type of suffering.

was a multiplication of suffering for others. Through a combination of factors beyond our control, poor choices on our part, and the irresponsible actions of others, the coronavirus pandemic has caused widespread, intense suffering.

Christians face another type of suffering: persecution for the sake of the gospel of Jesus Christ. Such suffering may express itself in the physical realm in terms of having property confiscated, loss of a job, imprisonment, and even death by martyrdom.

In summary, we suffer in a variety of ways: suffering beyond our control, self-imposed suffering, suffering from others, suffering persecution. We urge caution, however, that this list not be misused in an attempt to understand and thus master our afflictions by categorizing them. As the story of Job underscores, suffering is ultimately mysterious. For this reason, we aren't called to figure it out but to place our faith in the sovereign, good, and wise God and his will for us.

Biblical Affirmations

Because of its uniqueness for Christians, and because Scripture focuses on it, we will concentrate on biblical affirmations about the reality of suffering for the gospel. Of course, such religious suffering didn't originate with Jesus and his followers. The New Testament is clear that prior to Christ's coming the prophets were the target of intense suffering and persecution, even at the hands of the so-called people of God (Matt. 5:12; Acts 7:52). In keeping with this trend, Jesus underscores the cost of discipleship: "Peter began to tell him [Jesus], 'Look, we have left everything and followed you.' 'Truly I tell you,' Jesus said, 'there is no one who has left house or brothers or sisters or mother or father or children or fields for my sake and for the sake of the gospel, who will not receive a hundred times more, now at this time—houses, brothers and sisters, mothers and children, and fields, with persecutions—and eternal life in the age to come'" (Mark 10:28–30).

Jesus appears to promise an almost one-to-one correlation between giving up and getting back blessings. Give up houses, brothers, sisters, mother, father, children, and fields. Get back houses, brothers, sisters, mother, father, children, and fields. Clearly, these two groups aren't one and the same, otherwise the trade would seem trivial. So, while the two groups share the same vocabulary, the second group, as the community of Jesus and his followers, goes beyond the bond of family blood to the bond of Messiah's blood-bought family. His disciples form the blessing of a new community with bonds that are deeper and stronger than those of a natural community.

Beyond this point are the specific listed differences in the "get back" category: persecutions and eternal life. Along with membership in a new community, Jesus's followers are promised sufferings for the sake of the gospel in this life and, when it is over, life that will endure forever. From one perspective, Jesus's disciples give up much in this life to follow him and get persecutions in the present. From another perspective, what they give up pales in comparison to what they get back. And even the persecutions aren't a deterrent to making the exchange.

Jesus ties the sufferings that his disciples encounter to the fact that he himself suffered for the same reason: the persecutors hated him first.

> "If the world hates you, understand that it hated me before it hated you. If you were of the world, the world would love you as its own. However, because you are not of the world, but I have chosen you out of it, the world hates you. Remember the word I spoke to you: 'A servant is not greater than his master.' If they persecuted me, they will also persecute you. If they kept my word, they will also keep yours. But they will do all these things to you on account of my name, because they don't know the one who sent me." (John 15:18–21)

As Jesus suffered persecution, so his followers suffer persecution.

Paul affirms the same idea: "It has been granted to you on Christ's behalf not only to believe in him, but also to suffer for him" (Phil. 1:29). Paul himself was a paradigm of such affliction, which included lashes, beatings, stoning, sleeplessness, lack of the basic necessities of life, imprisonment, and ultimately martyrdom (2 Cor. 11:23–33). We in our comfortable Western world are relatively unfamiliar with this kind of suffering. Our secular culture works against this perspective, emphasizing the pursuit of happiness, peace, pleasure, and a pain-free life. So too does the increasingly popular health, wealth, and prosperity gospel. It wrongly assures its followers that God's will never includes pain, suffering, poverty, sickness, and persecution. Both influences contradict Scripture's clear and repeated emphasis on suffering for the sake of the gospel.

These anti-suffering perspectives steer Christians away from dependence on divine grace to support and comfort them during their hardships. Paul underscores this perspective:

> Therefore, so that I would not exalt myself, a thorn in the flesh was given to me, a messenger of Satan to torment me so that I would not exalt myself. Concerning this, I pleaded with the Lord three times that it would leave me. But he said to me, "My grace is sufficient for you, for my power is perfected in weakness." Therefore, I will most gladly boast all the more about my weaknesses, so that Christ's power may reside in me. So I take pleasure in weaknesses, insults, hardships, persecutions, and in difficulties, for the sake of Christ. For when I am weak, then I am strong. (2 Cor. 12:7–10)

As believers encounter suffering and persecution for the sake of the gospel of Christ, they are buoyed up by powerful divine favor. At all times, God's grace is sufficient to sustain his people. At some times, he will rescue them from persecution or physically heal them.

Persecution

As an example of rescue from persecution, we have Peter's escape from prison:

When Herod was about to bring him out for trial, that very night Peter, bound with two chains, was sleeping between two soldiers, while the sentries in front of the door guarded the prison. Suddenly an angel of the Lord appeared, and a light shone in the cell. Striking Peter on the side, he woke him up and said, "Quick, get up!" And the chains fell off his wrists. "Get dressed," the angel told him, "and put on your sandals." And he did. "Wrap your cloak around you," he told him, "and follow me." So he went out and followed, and he did not know that what the angel did was really happening, but he thought he was seeing a vision. After they passed the first and second guards, they came to the iron gate that leads into the city, which opened to them by itself. They went outside and passed one street, and suddenly the angel left him.

When Peter came to himself, he said, "Now I know for certain that the Lord has sent his angel and rescued me from Herod's grasp and from all that the Jewish people expected." (Acts 12:6–11)

It may be difficult to believe that God will at times rescue his people from persecution. As the continuation of the above narrative makes clear, not even the Christians who were praying for Peter's release believed it when he presented himself to their gathering (12:12–17)! But God may will to intervene in such a miraculous way.

At all times, God's grace is sufficient to sustain his people. At some times, he will rescue them from persecution. When he doesn't, Jesus promises to give his persecuted people the kingdom as their blessing (Matt. 5:10) and the affliction of their persecutors as their vindication (2 Thess. 1:6–8).

Healing

At all times, God's grace is sufficient to sustain his people. At some times, he will physically heal them. As an example of healing from physical suffering, we can appeal to the miraculous interventions during Jesus's ministry. He released demonically influenced people from that oppression. One example is the demon-possessed man (Matt. 12:22–32). Another is the Gerasene demoniac (Mark 5:1–20). Jesus healed the sick and raised the dead. Beneficiaries included the official's son (John 4:46–54), the paralytic (5:1–15), the blind man (9:1–7), and Lazarus (11:1–45). The first disciples continued this miraculous work throughout the book of Acts as seen with the lame man (Acts 3:1–16), sick and demonically tormented people (5:12–16; 8:4–13), and Aeneas and Dorcas (9:32–43). The church throughout its history has recorded similar miraculous interventions.[4] Such healings continue today.

Beyond these examples of healing from physical suffering, we have instructions in Scripture about praying for such healing as part and parcel of the life of the church (James 5:13–16). When someone is sick, the pastors are to gather with the ill person (v. 14). Though all Christians are to pray, the leaders of the church bear a particular responsibility to pray for the sick. Next, the pastors anoint the sick person with oil. This application of oil isn't a symbol of the infusion of grace as it is with the Roman Catholic sacrament of the anointing of the sick.[5] Moreover, it isn't a medicinal solution.[6] Furthermore, anointing with oil isn't a talisman, like a good luck charm. Rather, oil is a sign of consecration, marking the sick person for God's particular attention.

This action is done as the pastors call on the name of the Lord. This invocation acknowledges that the church is impotent to do any healing and recognizes that all healing comes from the

---

4. For extensive discussion see Stanley M. Burgess, "Holy Spirit, Doctrine of: The Ancient Fathers"; "Holy Spirit, Doctrine of: The Medieval Church"; and "Holy Spirit, Doctrine of: Reformation Traditions," in *The New International Dictionary of Pentecostal and Charismatic Movements*, rev. and expanded ed., ed. Stanley M. Burgess and Eduard M. van der Maas (Grand Rapids: Zondervan, 2002), 730–69.

5. The Roman Catholic sacrament of anointing of the sick is treated in the *Catechism of the Catholic Church* §1499–1523.

6. Though extra-virgin olive oil contains oleocanthal, an anti-inflammatory compound (like ibuprofen), the amount that one would have to consume for any kind of health benefit is enormous. And it would help only in certain cases of sickness, not all cases. My thanks to Luke Allison for his research on oleocanthal.

authority and power of the Lord of the church. The pastors pray that God will heal the sick person; they don't pray that God will take the sick person to heaven. While that may be the ultimate healing, it isn't the content of this healing prayer. Nor do they pray merely (though rightly) that God's will may be done. That is the presupposition of all prayer (as we will see in next point).

The pastoral prayer is something like, "Lord, in the name of Jesus, we ask that you heal Rebecca of her cancer and restore her to the fullness of life." Admittedly, some Christians disagree with this prayer. For example, John Calvin argued that this activity was no longer effective because it continued only for a time in the early church. Still others insist that the prayer should be only, "Lord, may your will be done." The problem is that this prayer isn't in step with the promise in James 5:15: "The prayer of faith will save the sick person, and the Lord will raise him up." Accordingly, the pastoral prayer isn't about the fact that God *can* heal Rebecca but is in line with the promise that God *will* heal Rebecca. So the elders pray for healing.

In accordance with a theme of James's letter, prayer must be done in faith (James 1:5–8) with the full conviction that the sovereign God will accomplish his good will (4:13–17). How do the pastors know if they are praying in faith and with full conviction? A simple diagnostic question may be put to them: How would they react if God miraculously healed Rebecca? If some pastors respond with incredulity or fear, it probably exposes their lack of faith. In such cases, and so as not to short-circuit the work of God who demands praying in faith, those pastors who don't believe that God will heal Rebecca should be asked to step outside the circle and observe what praying in faith for her healing entails.

The results of this prayer for healing are varied. The sovereign Lord may answer the prayer negatively because his will is that the sick person not recover from their illness. The sovereign Lord may use secondary causes, such as surgical intervention and/or medicine, to bring healing to the sick person. The sovereign Lord may miraculously heal the sick person. Whatever the response may be, all those involved rightly give thanks to the Lord, for he is good. At all times, God's grace is sufficient to sustain his people. At some times, he will physically heal them.

Suffering and Hope

Up to this point we have addressed specific instances of suffering, rescue from persecution, and healing of illness. Scripture also provides an overall viewpoint on suffering and ultimate release from it. Again, focusing on Christians, Paul directs them to consider the general suffering they experience and where their ultimate hope should rest (2 Cor. 4:7–18).

Paul first presents the *message* of the gospel as a lighted treasure invading the darkness of the Satanic veiling of unbelievers (2 Cor. 4:1–6). He then switches his attention to the *messengers* of the gospel:

> Now we have this treasure in clay jars, so that this extraordinary power may be from God and not from us. We are afflicted in every way but not crushed; we are perplexed but not in despair; we are persecuted but not abandoned; we are struck down but not destroyed. We always carry the death of Jesus in our body, so that the life of Jesus may also be displayed in our body. For we who live are always being given over to death for Jesus's sake, so that Jesus's life may also be displayed in our mortal flesh. So then, death is at work in us, but life in you. And since we have the same spirit of faith in keeping with what is written, 'I believed, therefore I spoke,' we also believe, and therefore speak. For we know that the one who raised the Lord Jesus will also raise us with Jesus and present us with you. Indeed, everything is for your benefit so that, as grace extends through more and more people, it may cause thanksgiving to increase to the glory of God. (2 Cor. 4:7–15)

In comparison with the surpassing magnitude of the message, its messengers are astonishingly meager. The treasure of the gospel is glorious, powerful, enduring, and exalted, but the treasure-bearers are feeble, impotent, fragile, and paltry. This stark contrast between the two is divinely designed. It has the purpose of manifesting the fact that it is God's extraordinary power that is at work through his people and not something in them or about them that advances the gospel.

Through a series of four parallels, Paul highlights the reality of the suffering and persecution endured by gospel heralds. They are squeezed tightly but never crushed; confused but not confounded; harassed but not deserted; knocked down but not knocked out. The messengers regularly face death for the sake of Jesus. As they do, however, the life of Jesus becomes manifested in and through them, sustaining them in existence and protecting them as they communicate the gospel. Because of their union with Christ, because they are servants of Jesus, they are identified with him in both life and death. While they don't seek out trials and tribulations, the outcome is life in the midst of death, preservation in the midst of persecution, power in the midst of weakness, and—ultimately—resurrection from the dead.

But there is more than personal benefit. As the messengers believe the good news and speak it to others, more and more unbelievers are graciously brought to belief through their message. Even more, thanksgiving for salvation embraced is increased to the glory of God.

Paul concludes with the takeaway, "Therefore we do not give up. Even though our outer person is being destroyed, our inner person is being renewed day by day. For our momentary light affliction is producing for us an absolutely incomparable eternal weight of glory. So we do not focus on what is seen, but on what is unseen. For what is seen is temporary, but what is unseen is eternal" (2 Cor. 4:16–18). The weak, frail, mortal treasure bearers—relentlessly pursued by suffering, persecution, trials, and tribulations— refuse to give up. Instead, they count it all worthwhile because the treasure itself—the light of the gospel, the life of Christ—is at work in them and in others:

Disaster for us	Deliverance for others
Suffering for us	Salvation for others
Humiliation for us	Hope for others
Persecution for us	Promise for others

Moreover, the messengers develop the proper perspective on their rough and deteriorating life. It's not about what is visible and tangible. It's not about the pining away of their embodied being. Not just their body but everything about them as an embodied person is moving toward dissolution and death. It's not about the affliction of their trials and tribulations. It's not about the temporariness of their earthly existence. From an outward or external perspective, the messengers of the gospel are wasting away. The decay of their life is a steady, inevitable, irreversible process.

Rather, it's about what is invisible and intangible. It's about the daily renewal of their embodied being. Not just their soul or immaterial aspect, but the entirety of their embodied person is being transformed. It's about the value added to their trials and tribulations. Gospel messengers consider their sufferings as momentary and light in comparison with the eternal and weighty glory that is to come. It's about the eternality of their future existence. From an inward or internal perspective, the messengers of the gospel are being transformed steadily into the image of Jesus Christ, a renewal of their entire existence.

Scripture calls us to develop and focus on an eternal perspective. Certainly, this perspective is counter to our culture's emphasis on present happiness, comfort, security, and painlessness. As servants of Christ, this perspective can also be confusing. Can we or should we enjoy the comfort and security that life in our American society affords us? As Scripture reminds us elsewhere (1 Tim. 6:17–19), we can be blessed by such riches as we also engage in the following: We are to be on the alert to thank God as the giver of such good gifts. We are to be quick to share with others from our abundance. We are to hold these gifts loosely in our hands, offering them back to God as privileges we can live without. We are to avoid becoming inordinately attached to security and comfort. We are to receive these luxuries as blessings from God and never demand them as our rights. Finally, we are to be aware that such blessings can too easily and quickly become curses, promoting our sinful tendencies toward lukewarmness, worldliness, and compromise.

In light of this eternal perspective, what is the proper view of suffering? We don't consider suffering as just something to be endured passively and patiently with the hope that everything will get better in this life. Rather, suffering should be embraced as divinely operative to produce greater conformity to the image of Christ, to augment hope in the return of Christ, to prompt greater dependence on the gracious presence and power of God, and to provide opportunities for communicating the gospel.

Only by developing this eternal perspective on suffering may we live as whole people in a fractured world.

In summary, suffering is part and parcel of embodied existence, and suffering may persist, worsen, improve, or perhaps even be healed. God's design for his embodied image bearers after the fall is to permit us to suffer the physical consequences of living in a fallen world. Moreover, he calls Christians to suffer for the sake of Christ, even to the point of martyrdom. At all times, God's grace is sufficient to sustain his people, and sometimes he will rescue them from persecution or physically heal them.

Application

As an embodied Christian, how should you face suffering? How should you seek healing?

Focusing on our theme of embodiment, in what ways have you suffered or are you suffering?

Is your suffering due to factors outside your control, part and parcel of living in a fallen world? Examples include your genetic makeup or receiving ill-advised medical counsel.

Is your suffering self-inflicted, the result of your own poor choices or the downward addictive spiral on which you find yourself? Examples include poor nutrition, neglecting to exercise, irregular patterns of rest and sleep, or overconsumption of alcohol.

Are other people the cause of your suffering? Examples include abuse when you were a child or physical violence at the hands of your spouse.

Are you persecuted for your faith in Jesus Christ and thus suffer? Examples include loss of your job or confiscation of your property.

With each of these four types requiring different approaches, how can you best face your suffering?

Finally, how can the first question and answer from the Heidelberg Catechism help you to develop an eternal perspective?

Q: What is your only comfort in life and in death?

A: That I am not my own, but belong—body and soul, in life and in death—to my faithful Savior, Jesus Christ.

For the Curious

Disabilities

Our discussion of physical suffering raises an important question about disabilities. "A disability is defined as a condition or function judged to be significantly impaired relative to the usual standard of an individual or group. The term is used to refer to individual functioning, including physical impairment, sensory impairment, cognitive impairment, intellectual impairment, mental illness, and various types of chronic disease."[7] In many cases,

---

7. "What Is a Disability?" Disabled World, last revised December 14, 2019, https://www.disabled-world.com/disability/types/.

disabilities are the result of living in a fallen world, the first type of suffering that we discussed. In very broad strokes, we offer this theology of disability.

We affirm that all human beings are divine image bearers. As the sovereign, good, and wise God is the Creator of all people, he didn't make a mistake in his formation of disabled people. Furthermore, we deny any notion of merit before God. No one deserves to be created, nor does anyone deserve to be created without disabilities. Thus disabled people aren't somehow deficient in image bearing, nor do they possess less merit before God because they are perceived as inferior or did something wrong to cause their disability.

Being created in the divine image, "People with disabilities are people first who shouldn't be defined solely by their disabilities. More particularly, people with disabilities are agents in their own right. . . . People with disabilities should be allowed to define their own needs and wants, to the extent that such is possible, and should be consulted rather than cared for paternalistically as if they were completely helpless creatures."[8]

A theology of disability acknowledges that a theology of power and prosperity is a worldly, cultural construction that is at odds with Scripture's emphasis on humility, weakness, dependence, and self-sacrifice. In our American context, an emphasis on status, position, authority, power, prestige, wealth, success, and health fosters an environment in which disabled people are considered second-class citizens and thus are marginalized and even mistreated. The world regards disability with shame, doubt, fear, discomfort, and disgust. Sadly, many Christians and churches

---

8. Amos Yong, *The Bible, Disability, and the Church: A New Vision of the People of God* (Grand Rapids: Eerdmans, 2011), 13. Other helpful books on disability from a Christian perspective include Michael S. Beates, *Disability and the Gospel: How God Uses Our Brokenness to Display His Grace* (Wheaton: Crossway, 2012); Brian Brock, *Wondrously Wounded: Theology, Disability, and the Body of Christ* (Waco: Baylor University Press, 2019).

have fallen prey to this culture of disrespect. Accordingly, we need to work hard to repulse this worldly viewpoint and to embrace disabled people with love and honor.

As concerned church members, we should advocate for the inclusion of disabled people in the life and ministry of our church. "I envision a fully inclusive church . . . to be one in which people with disabilities are honored and in which they are fully ministers alongside nondisabled people. To be sure, in many cases accommodations will need to be provided, but the point is that the Spirit empowers willing vessels, not only those who fit some kind of conventional norm about what it means to be a minister of the gospel."[9] It isn't that the church is unfamiliar with such compassionate inclusion. From its earliest days, the church has cared for the sick, the poor, the widows, the abandoned, and the disabled. In this and many other ways, the church differentiated itself from the pagan society in which it ministered. It may recover its distinguished past and be salt and light in the world: "The church should be at the vanguard of showing the world how to value all people, how to receive the full spectrum of gifts, and how to channel what each of us with our diverse abilities has to offer."[10]

Relieving Suffering

Our discussion of physical suffering raises an important question about interventions to relieve or even remove suffering. We begin with a discussion of plastic and cosmetic surgery.[11]

By way of definition, plastic surgery is "a surgical specialty dedicated to reconstruction of facial and body defects due to birth disorders, trauma, burns, and disease. Plastic surgery is intended to correct dysfunctional areas of the body and is reconstructive in

---

9. Yong, *Bible, Disability, and the Church*, 146.
10. Yong, *Bible, Disability, and the Church*, 146.
11. For a history of these surgeries, see Ellen Feldman, "Before & After," *American Heritage*, March 2004, 60–71.

nature."[12] The key idea of plastic surgery is that of reconstruction or restoration. Relatedly, cosmetic surgery focuses on "enhancing appearance through surgical and medical techniques. Cosmetic surgery can be performed on all areas of the head, neck and body. Because treated areas function properly but lack aesthetic appeal, cosmetic surgery is elective."[13] The key idea of cosmetic surgery is aesthetic (and elective) improvement.

America has "an insatiable obsession with cosmetic surgery."[14] Over sixteen million cosmetic surgery procedures are carried out annually, with over 90 percent being done on women and over 80 percent being done on Caucasians. As you can imagine, the industry brings in billions of dollars annually.[15] "The proliferation of procedures goes hand in hand with the individual quest for self-realization and society's relaxation of strictures against vanity and self-indulgence. . . . Most aesthetic procedures are designed to enable the patient to pass as something he or she does not feel, whether it be younger, sexier, or more Anglo-Saxon than nature and birth have determined."[16]

Beyond plastic and cosmetic surgery, all of us are aware of medical interventions that have become so commonplace that we forget how they regularly ease pain, repair injuries, correct serious physical problems, and even save lives. The list is extensive. Nearly every body part can be repaired or replaced. From simple procedures such as cataract removal and setting a broken bone, to quadruple bypass surgery and liver transplant, we live in a society

12. "About Us," American Academy of Cosmetic Surgery, https://www.cosmeticsurgery.org/page/About.
13. American Academy of Cosmetic Surgery, "About Us."
14. Feldman, "Before & After," 60.
15. The three predominant cosmetic surgical procedures are rhinoplasty, face-lifts, and breast surgery. Other common interventions include tummy tucks, liposuction, eyelid surgery, abdominoplasty, hair transplantation, foreskin reconstitution, labiaplasty and hymenorrhaphy, collagen and Botox injections, pectoral implants, buttock lifts, laser hair removal, wrinkle reduction, lip enhancement, ear surgery, arm lifts, and cheek augmentation.
16. Feldman, "Before & After," 65–66.

that embraces medical interventions and accepts them as a way of life. And procedures that even a few years ago seemed impossible are now becoming mainstream interventions.

How do we determine which of these interventions are legitimate and which are illegitimate? We propose several principles to help in the deliberation.

First, the procedure is *designed to maintain life and not cause death*. While most surgical interventions incur risks, an acceptable procedure holds a reasonably high degree of promise for successful healing of the disease or containment of the illness. Moreover, the intervention isn't a desperate overtreatment prompted by an inordinate fear of death.

Second, the intervention is *designed to alleviate intense pain and suffering*, though it may hasten death as a by-product. This isn't a matter of simple unintended consequences, for the probability of them occurring is fairly high, but of foreseeable unintended consequences. An example is the medical use of morphine. The primary objective in administering the medication is to provide comfort from distress. In so doing, it's well known that the morphine may hasten the shutting down of respiratory functions, leading to death. These negative consequences aren't intended; on the contrary, the intention is right and admirable. They are, however, foreseen. An example in Scripture is the recommendation of strong drink for relief from misery (Prov. 31:6–7). There are foreseeable unintended consequences, some of which (e.g., drunkenness) would be condemned elsewhere in Scripture. Still, strong drink is prescribed, and appropriately so.

Third, the procedure *has the consent of the suffering person* through, for example, a living will. Alternatively, it has been approved by the designated power of attorney who makes an informed and final decision on the sufferer's behalf. Such structures are needed in cases involving insurance companies or family members who don't have the best interests of the suffering person at heart. We may be aware of instances of deplorable and culpable under- or overtreatment prompted by insurance companies to avoid having to pay for procedures. Sadly, this is managed death, not managed care. Even more disconcerting are cases of poor treatment due to the financial considerations of family members who greedily aim to hasten the collection of their inheritance.

Fourth, the procedure *may be initiated, then terminated*. An example is the use of life support systems—for example, a mechanical ventilation machine—to provide time for family and friends to find closure with the dying person. The extraordinary measure is terminated if death is indeed imminent. Importantly, while extraordinary measures are optional, we should ensure the provision of all necessary nutrients and liquids to maintain physical existence (e.g., IV feeding). Any nonintervention in such a situation constitutes immoral neglect.

Finally, the intervention *seeks to repair or restore what sin and the fall has destroyed or partially ruined*.[17] Examples include heart bypass surgery, breast reconstruction after a mastectomy, and kidney transplants. Such procedures are curative medical interventions to mend that which is diseased or destroyed. These are substantive measures, not superfluous cosmetic surgeries for vain appearance purposes only. According to this principle, there are limits to surgical procedures and medical prescriptions. An intervention must not be an encroachment on God's role as Creator, usurping his place as the designer of life. It is one thing to reverse the curse of the fall; it is quite another matter to circumvent what has been limited or inhibited by human nature as designed by God. As Mary Shelley warned in *Frankenstein*, "Frightful must it be; for supremely frightful would be the effect of any human

---

17. Some of this discussion is influenced by Oliver O'Donovan, *Begotten or Made? Human Procreation and Medical Technique* (Oxford: Oxford University Press, 1984).

endeavor to mock the stupendous mechanism of the Creator of the world."[18] The specter of transhumanism looms large.[19]

In summary, we've explored both disabilities and measures for relieving suffering, including cosmetic and plastic surgery. While not easy matters to discuss, they are becoming more and more pressing due to advances in medical and other scientific fields. Importantly, a theology of human embodiment can be the foundation for such discussions and can help us live as whole people in a fractured world.

---

18. Mary W. Shelley, "Introduction," *Frankenstein* (London: Colburn & Bentley, 1831), x.

19. For further discussion, see Jacob Shatzer, *Transhumanism and the Image of God* (Downers Grove, IL: IVP Academic, 2019).

CHAPTER 12

THE DEAD BODY

"It's so morbid and frightening that I rarely if ever contemplate my death." Do you agree or disagree with this statement, and why?

Big Idea

Human existence plays itself out from conception through eternity. Death is an enemy intruder that, at the end of our earthly existence, results in the cessation of the body's proper functioning. God's design for his embodied image bearers after the fall is to permit us to die as a physical consequence of living in a fallen world.[1] Because of their salvation through Christ, Christians are able to face death with hope and not fear.

Application Question

How should you face death?

---

1. As we will discuss, death is the penalty for sin. In the case of unbelievers then, death isn't only the consequence of living in a fallen world but primarily a punishment for sin. By contrast, in the case of believers for whom Christ has fully paid the penalty for sin, death isn't imposed as a punishment but happens as a consequence of living in a fallen world.

A Near-Death Experience

In 1989 my wife and I moved our family to Ticino, Switzerland, to launch a ministry with Campus Crusade for Christ (now called Cru). The difficulty of moving overseas, the burden of trying (unsuccessfully) to find a place to live, the uneasiness of living in someone else's house, and the struggle to start up a ministry from scratch—these and other points of tension contributed to rising stress in our life. One evening, Nora and I were sitting at the dining room table in our temporary living quarters. We were calmly discussing what kind of furniture we would purchase for our girls' bedroom once we found a place of our own. Suddenly, I rose out of my seat, looked at Nora, and told her to call 911 (the Swiss equivalent, that is). As she took one look at my ashen face and hurried to make the call, I walked out into the garden area of the property, kneeled down, and told the Lord that I was going to meet him. My heart was racing—150, 200, 300 beats per minute? It was so fast that I couldn't accurately count. Add to that arrhythmia, and at times I couldn't detect any pulse. I was convinced that I was having a heart attack and was about to die.

Thinking back on that event, I should have known I wasn't having a heart attack. There were none of the typical signs like pressure in my chest or pain shooting down my left arm. But I wasn't in my right mind at the time! I felt sure I was going to die.

In under ten minutes the emergency medical team arrived and hooked me up to an EKG monitor. I was already sensing a slowing down and regulating of my heart rate. For their part, the EMTs assured me that I wasn't having a heart attack and that my vital signs were stabilizing. By thirty minutes from its onset, the event was over and my heart returned to its normal pace.

Per the EMTs' instructions, I took the EKG record to a doctor the next day. He explained that I'd had an incident of tachycardia—literally, fast heart. My brain had sent a false signal to my heart, it sped up and became irregular, and—as in the vast majority of such cases—rectified itself. He tried to comfort me with the fact that tachycardia is common among men my age who are under a lot of stress. And he gave me some steps to take if or when it occurred again. Then he finished with what I certainly knew to be true: tachycardia is accompanied by a dreadful fear of death!

I learned that night that death is only a snap of the fingers away. Though I was young and energetic and in very good heath, I realized that such a profile is no safeguard against death. I live with the lurking reality that another incident could occur at any moment, my cardiac system could fail to right itself, and I could die. I have faced the reality of death, and its inevitability looms large.

Have you ever had an experience like mine? Perhaps it was tachycardia, or maybe you've had an actual heart attack. Have you ever had a near-death experience? What was it like? Did it result in any change in your life?

Like an unwanted visitor, death forces itself upon us and compels us to face its inevitability.

Facing Death

Death is inevitable. As Ecclesiastes laments:

> Everything is the same for everyone: There is one fate for the righteous and the wicked, for the good and the bad, for the clean and the unclean, for the one who sacrifices and the one who does not sacrifice. As it is for the good, so also it is for the sinner; as it is for the one who takes an oath, so also for the one who fears an oath. This is an evil in all that is done under the sun: there is one fate for everyone. In addition, the hearts of people are full of evil, and madness is in their hearts while they live; after that they go to the dead. (Eccles. 9:2–3)

Death is one of those common human experiences: "There is an occasion for everything, and a time for every activity under heaven: a time to give birth and a time to die" (Eccles. 3:1–2).

Despite the inevitability of death, attempts are made to deny it. A fundamental Hindu concept is *maya*, or illusion. Just as the world we experience isn't real, so too death is an illusion. Christian Scientists deny the reality of death. Just like sickness and pain, death is due to "bad faith" and is illusory: "Life is real, and death is the illusion."[2] More subtle is the view that death, while inevitable, is natural, something to be embraced. The idea is that when God created Adam and Eve, he created them good, with full integrity, but also mortal. At some point, both would die as a natural consequence of being finite human beings. Sadly, this view fails to understand that death is a penalty for sin. It is not natural.[3]

Despite its inescapability, people often try to avoid death. As some people approach the end of their life, they fight hard against dying. They try doing anything and everything within their power and financial wherewithal to stave off the inevitable. This frenzy is often due to anxiety about the pain and suffering that lead up to death, as well as fear about what lies on the other side of this life. Other people go to extremes like neuro-cryopreservation. Cryonics is the belief that a person's body or body parts (e.g., one's head) can be frozen at death, stored at extremely low temperatures in a cryogenic vessel, and later brought back to life.[4] It is viewed as

2. Mary Baker Eddy, *Science and Health with Key to the Scriptures* (Boston: Christian Science Publishing, 1934), 428. Similarly, "the cardinal point in Christian Science [is] that matter and evil (including all inharmony, sin, disease, death) are *unreal*." Eddy, *Miscellaneous Writings* (Boston: Christian Science Publishing, 1924), 27.

3. A secular spin on this idea is that human beings, whether as the product of evolutionary development or some other pathway, are naturally mortal. This view is very common among unbelievers. My thanks to Laura Wierenga for her contribution to this point.

4. For further discussion, see the Cryonics Institute website: "Imagine a world free of disease, death and aging. At the Cryonics Institute, we believe that day is inevitably coming, and cryonics is presently our best chance of getting there. Our mission is to extend human lifespans by preserving the body using existing cryogenic technologies—with the goal of revival by future science." https://www.cryonics.org/. In terms of affordability, the possible cost of such technology is a one-time fee of $28,000, due at the time of death. Neuro-cryopreservation may cost $80,000.

a form of life support and eventual resuscitation, not resurrection from the dead, but it is an extreme attempt to avoid death's inevitability.

Against such attempts to deny and avoid death, the truth is that all people face an engagement with death: "It is appointed for people to die once—and after this, judgment" (Heb. 9:27). We most readily link death with sin, as death is the penalty for sin (Rom. 6:23). Additionally, the usual connection we draw is between personal sin and death. Each of us dies because each of us personally sins. While this bond is certainly true, it overlooks another important association: we die because of our identification with Adam and his sin.

Paul makes this connection in Romans 5:12–21, emphasizing it several times for good effect:

- "by the one man's trespass the many died" (v. 15)
- "from one sin came the judgment, resulting in condemnation" (v. 16)
- "by the one man's trespass, death reigned through that one man" (v. 17)
- "through one trespass there is condemnation for everyone" (v. 18)
- "through one man's disobedience the many were made sinners" (v. 19)

Thus "sin entered the world through one man, and death through sin, in this way death spread to all people, because all sinned" (v. 12). There is a clear link between the "one" and the "all." On the one hand is Adam's one trespass/sin/act of disobedience and its consequences of death, judgment, condemnation, and being constituted a sinner. On the other hand is the spread of those consequences to all people. As Paul underscores elsewhere, "For since death came through a man, the resurrection of the dead also comes through a man. For just as in Adam all die, so also in

Christ all will be made alive" (1 Cor. 15:21–22). It is through our identification with Adam and his one act of sin that all human beings are constituted sinners and become susceptible to death along with judgment and condemnation.

In light of death's inevitability, Scripture exhorts us to contemplate our own death: "It is better to go to a house of mourning than to go to a house of feasting, since that is the end of all mankind, and the living should take it to heart. . . . The heart of the wise is in a house of mourning, but the heart of fools is in a house of pleasure" (Eccles. 7:2, 4). The biblical challenge is clear: it is better to go to a funeral parlor than to a frat party. This isn't an invitation to morbid introspection or an obsession with death. Rather, it is a reminder that death comes to all: "For you are dust, and to dust you shall return" (Gen. 3:19 ESV). Such contemplation may lead us to an honest evaluation of our life, a readjustment of our priorities, a valuing of people and relationships over possessions and achievements, and a plea to the Lord to "teach us to number our days carefully so that we may develop wisdom in our hearts" (Ps. 90:12).

The Nature of (Physical) Death

In our discussion, we have assumed an idea of death. But it's important that we understand death according to its several definitions. In one sense, it is the death of the material aspect of human nature, the cessation of the functioning of a person's material element (i.e., body). In surrendering to cancer or being involved in a fatal car crash, a person's physiological functioning ceases and their body dies. In another sense, death is the temporary separation of the material and the immaterial aspects of human nature. It is an unzipping of a person's being, resulting in a temporary disembodiment. The body-soul unity is interrupted for a time. A person's immaterial element continues to exist while their material element is sloughed off, laid in a grave or tomb, buried at sea, cremated, or disposed of in some other form. They become a disembodied person.

Scientifically, a distinction is made between two types of brain death. According to the Uniform Determination of Death Act, *whole brain death* means either "irreversible cessation of circulatory and respiratory functions, or irreversible cessation of all functions of the entire brain, including the brain stem."[5] As application, a common but imprecise attempt to determine if someone is alive or dead is to feel for a pulse and listen for breath sounds. In the absence of these indicators, we say the person is dead. A more recent measure focuses on *higher brain death* or *neocortical death*, which is the loss of capacity for consciousness (self-awareness), social interchange, and financial contribution. While biological life continues (whether sustained, for example, by a life-support apparatus or not), biographical life no longer exists. It is frightening to imagine how this definition of death could be easily abused, for example, with victims of Alzheimer's disease.

The Ways We Die

Surprisingly, the ways we die are quite limited in number. The following diseases are generally not isolated causes of death but are accompanied by pneumonia, infection, kidney and/or liver failure, septicemia, and other complicating factors:

Heart disease

Cancer

Stroke

Respiratory failure

Alzheimer's disease

5. "Uniform Determination of Death Act," National Conference of Commissioners on Uniform State Laws, http://www.lchc.ucsd.edu/cogn_150/Readings/death_act.pdf, 7.

Hemorrhage

Diabetes

Murder, including abortion[6]

Death by accident, especially a vehicular incident in which
alcohol is involved

Suicide

Acquired immunodeficiency syndrome, or AIDS, often in
conjunction with Kaposi's sarcoma

Old age

Though not recognized as an official "category" of death by the
biomedical community, the "wearing out" of the body brings
about death.[7]

These are the ways we die.

The Art of Dying

The Middle Ages witnessed the development of *ars moriendi*,
or the art of dying. Paintings and woodcuts portrayed the inevitability of death. One such artistic piece pictured death as a
skeleton at the head of a long line of people. These characters
were ordered according to their status in life. At the head of
the parade were monarchs, wealthy landowners, and religious
leaders. At the end of the line were peasants, the poor, the sick,
and the lame—those who couldn't earn a living and were thus

6. While most people know about death due to heart disease and cancer, the
number of deaths from those leading causes of death pales in comparison to the
number of abortions. In the United States alone since Roe v. Wade in 1973, there
have been over 60 million abortions. If that figure isn't shocking enough, the
number of abortions worldwide is staggering, totaling well over 1.5 billion since
1973. These are babies who were never allowed to be born. Whereas all the rest
of us will experience death after birth, they never had that basic human right.

7. All except diabetes are causes listed in Sherwin B. Nuland, *How We Die:
Reflections on Life's Final Chapter*, new ed. (New York: Vintage Books, 1995).
The CDC's list includes diabetes, so we have added it here.

destitute. In the middle of the procession were tradespeople, priests, and lesser royalty. The point was clear: no matter one's station in life, all people follow in the train of death and move inexorably toward their final demise. A similar idea was communicated by paintings in which an hourglass was included in a lower corner. As the sands of time slip away, everyone moves toward their appointment with death.

Religious art also portrayed how religious folk die. One example is an elaborate sketch that portrays death in a series of scenes. A dying man is tormented by demons, who remind him of the many sins he has committed: murder, adultery, embezzlement, and other crimes. Undone, he calls to mind the religious symbols of his day to find comfort in his torment. Saint Peter with the keys, Mary and the saints, the cross of Jesus Christ—these religious icons help ease the dying man's misery. As his life slips further away, he is again tormented by evil spirits. The demons show him what will happen to his hard-earned possessions once he dies. They will be divided up among his heirs, who will in turn squander them. In reaction, the man banishes these ingrates from his presence. In the final scene, the dying man is again comforted by religious figures. His soul, emerging out of his head, is borne by the angels into heaven to be with God.

If this is the medieval *ars moriendi*, what is a biblical art of dying? Several elements compose such an art. First, we should avoid two extremes. On the one hand is the extreme of doing everything we possibly can to avoid death. We become willing to pay any cost—extreme medical intervention, risky experimental drug treatment—to postpone what is ultimately inevitable. On the other hand is the extreme of downplaying the tragedy, horror, and evil of death. Under no circumstance should death be welcomed as a friend, even if what awaits on the other side of death—blessing in the presence of the Lord—is anticipated. While the good to come is a proper hope, death itself is wicked and disgusting. We should not confuse our homecoming with the evil gauntlet of death through which we must run to get there. For similar reasons, death must not be hailed.[8]

Second, death is the gateway between our current existence and an eternal existence of either blessedness in the Lord's presence or misery and torment away from that blessed presence. As already discussed, this gateway of death is the result of sin and not part and parcel of the created human order. We don't applaud the gateway. We mourn for those who, upon passing through it, experience eternal condemnation away from the Lord. And we welcome the eternal life that is to come for believers through what Christ has accomplished and the Spirit has applied.

Christians should view their own death with the assurance of faith and not with fear. As for the former posture of faith, Paul writes that "we are confident, and we would prefer to be away from the body and at home with the Lord" (2 Cor. 5:8). Why? "My eager expectation and hope is that I will not be ashamed about anything, but that now as always, with all courage, Christ will be highly honored in my body, whether by life or by death. For me, to live is Christ and to die is gain" (Phil. 1:20–21). As for the latter posture of rejecting fear: "Now since the children have flesh and blood in common, Jesus also shared in these, so that

8. As John Donne voiced in his poem "Death, Be Not Proud" (Holy Sonnet 10; 1633):
Death, be not proud, though some have called thee
Mighty and dreadful, for thou are not so;
For those whom thou think'st thou dost overthrow
Die not, poor Death, nor yet canst thou kill me.
From rest and sleep, which but thy pictures be,
Much pleasure; then from thee much more must flow,
And soonest our best men with thee do go,
Rest of their bones, and soul's delivery.
Thou art slave to fate, chance, kings, and desperate men,
And dost with poison, war, and sickness dwell,
And poppy or charms can make us sleep as well
And better than thy stroke; why swell'st thou then?
One short sleep past, we wake eternally,
And death shall be no more; Death, thou shalt die.

through his death he might destroy the one holding the power of death—that is, the devil—and free those who were held in slavery all their lives by the fear of death" (Heb. 2:14–15). Christians have been freed from the fear of falling prey to the schemes of the evil one. Because of Jesus's incarnation and redemption, believers have this hope: "For I am persuaded that neither death nor life, nor angels nor rulers, nor things present nor things to come, nor powers, nor height nor depth, nor any other created thing will be able to separate us from the love of God that is in Christ Jesus our Lord" (Rom. 8:38–39).

Christians view the death of other Christians with sadness and express sorrow. They have been temporarily separated from these brothers and sisters. While other believers may become dear friends and ministry partners, they can't take the place of the deceased. But such grief due to loss is mitigated by the knowledge that these brothers and sisters are now with Christ in heaven. Because of this truth, "Within the Christian tradition funerals aren't simply ways of disposing of dead bodies, nor are they about remembering the departed or expressing grief. Rather, for believers, funerals ought to be Christ-centered events, testifying throughout to the message and hope of the gospel."[9]

Furthermore, Christians view the death of non-Christians with great sorrow that is not intermingled with joy, for unbelievers face eternal, conscious punishment in hell. At the same time, Christians may face the death of non-Christians with hope that their impending death prompted serious reflection leading to repentance. Still, they must avoid giving false assurance of salvation. Pastors and other officiants at funerals must resist well-intentioned demands

9. David Jones, "To Bury or to Burn? Cremation in Christian Perspective," The Gospel Coalition, January 23, 2013, https://www.thegospelcoalition.org/ article /to-bury-or-to-burn-cremation-in-christian-perspective/. For further discussion, see Jones, "To Bury or Burn? Toward an Ethic of Cremation," *JETS* 53, no. 2 (June 2010): 335–47. Available at https://www.etsjets.org/files/JETS-PDFs/53/53-2/ JETS_53-2_335-347_Jones.pdf.

that they "preach the deceased into heaven" by portraying them as something they weren't in this life.[10]

In summary, human existence plays itself out from conception through eternity. Death is an enemy intruder that, at the end of our earthly existence, results in the cessation of the body's proper functioning. God's design for his embodied image bearers after the fall is to permit us to die as a physical consequence of living in a fallen world. Because of their salvation through Christ, Christians are able to face death with hope and not fear.

Application

How should you face death?

Think first of your own death. Are you frightened by the prospect? To what can you attribute that fear? How do the truths about salvation calm your fears?

Next, think of the death of other Christians. How have you experienced grief at their loss? What have you done to comfort their loved ones at the wake, the funeral, and afterward? How does knowing that you will see them again and spend eternity with them round out your perspective on their death?

Finally, think of the death of unbelievers. How have you experienced grief at their loss? How has that sorrow been different from the heartache you've felt at the loss of a brother or sister in Christ? As you think about non-Christian family members, colleagues, and friends who are alive, does your role as an ambassador for Christ compel you to communicate the gospel to them?

---

10. At a recent funeral I attended, a relative of the deceased man used the audience sharing time to preach him into heaven. He spoke of the deceased's commitment to Christ, love of others, servant heart, and more. Afterward, the parents of the deceased wondered incredulously, "Who was our relative speaking about? Surely it wasn't our son, was it?"

For the Curious

Following death and before the funeral, the family of the deceased holds a wake or viewing. The funeral home puts the deceased person's lifeless body on display in an open casket. In some cases the casket is closed. Relatives, friends, and colleagues come to pay their last respects. On these occasions, statements such as the following are often made: "He's not really here." "Her true self is still alive." "His best part continues to live." "She's in a better place." "He's united once again with his wife." "She's in heaven with Christ." These comments reflect a hope—confused as it might be—in something after death.[11] But confusion and angst come in what to think about and how to view the lifeless body. Often the most comforting thing to do is simply be with those who are mourning, grieve with them in their loss, hold them tightly, and avoid offering platitudes.

Important questions arise about the proper way to dispose of the body. Two common modes are traditional burial and cremation.

Traditional Burial

We start with arguments for and against the traditional mode. Burial shows reverence for the body. As we have frequently emphasized, the body isn't vile or evil as Gnosticism holds and has corrupted us to think. Thus the showing of the body at the wake or viewing and preserving it by burial express the goodness of the body. Additionally, burial underscores resurrection from the dead. With what expectation is the body lowered into the grave? Bodily resurrection. Furthermore, burial enjoys historical precedent: from Sarah and Abraham's burial (Gen. 23; 25:7–10) to Lazarus's grave (John 11:17), to Jesus's tomb (Matt. 27:57–66); from Augustine to Martin Luther, to John Calvin, and even to present day, burial of an intact body has been the norm in Christian circles. Finally, burial

---

11. The next chapter will treat the hope of the resurrection.

emphasizes the end of mortal beings. Cemeteries, with bodies buried in traditional fashion, underscore human mortality. They provide a constant reminder to those driving or walking by that sooner or later everyone dies.[12]

Arguments against burial include the following. Though Scripture overwhelmingly supports the traditional mode of burial,[13] it doesn't rule out cremation. Amos 2:1–3 and 6:8–11 may address cremation, but the details are minimal. More clearly, the Mosaic law states that in cases of sexual immorality, the perpetrators are to be put to death, and in one particular case, burning with fire is the penalty: "If a man marries a woman and her mother, it is depraved. Both he and they must be burned, so that there will be no depravity among you" (Lev. 20:14). We wonder, however, whether this provision is actual support for cremation. It seems rather to underscore the heinousness of such a crime and the necessity of removing even the physical remains of it from proximity to the people for the sake of their holiness.

Another argument depends on a possible cultural background. It may be the case that Roman society cremated their dead in light of their denial of an afterlife. Thus Christians were countercultural in their choice of burying their dead.[14] Once the cultural denial of an afterlife is removed, Christians may opt to cremate rather than bury the dead.

The most common argument against disposing of the body by burial is that it's relatively expensive. Some people aren't able to afford a traditional burial or, if they choose this option, go

12. For further discussion, see Mark Coppenger, "What about Cremation?" *Baptist Press News*, October 12, 2005.

13. The Old Testament contains about 200 references to the burial of human remains (e.g., 1 Sam 31:8–13).

14. For a historical discussion see Tertullian, *On the Resurrection of the Flesh*, 1; *A Treatise on the Soul*, 51. *Ante-Nicene Fathers*, ed. Alexander Roberts, James Donaldson, Philip Schaff, and Henry Wace, 10 vols. (Peabody, MA: Hendrickson, 1994), 3:85, 228–29.

into debt to pay for it. This economic factor makes the option of cremation attractive to a growing number of people.

Cremation

Turning to arguments for and against cremation, this last argument against burial becomes the primary argument for cremation: it is relatively inexpensive.[15] Probably for this reason (there may be other reasons also), today well over 50 percent of North Americans select cremation as the mode for disposing of the body. Additionally, it's claimed that cremation is more sanitary than burial, and it resolves the problem of overcrowded cemeteries. Finally, unlike traditional burial, about which decisions must be made very quickly, the decision about what to do with a person's ashes isn't a rushed one. Cremation minimizes the stress that surrounds the death of a loved one.

In terms of arguments against cremation, the Roman Catholic Church historically banned it because cremation seems to communicate disbelief in the resurrection of the body. In 1963, however, Pope Paul VI lifted the ban, expressing the Catholic church's earnest recommendation for traditional burial but permitting cremation as long as it isn't "chosen for reasons contrary to Christian doctrine."[16] Additionally, one argument offered against cremation confuses two matters. It is argued—and it certainly is the case—that the Bible presents "the dreadfulness of fire as it relates to the human body, especially after death"; thus this truth points us

15. Unnecessary additional services can add significantly to the cost of cremation.

16. Pope Paul VI, *Piam et constantem*, July 5, 1963. The pope's permission for cremation was codified in the 1983 Code of Canon Law 1176 §3 (from which this discussion is taken), http://www.vatican.va/archive/ENG1104/__P4A.HTM. For particular instructions for US Catholics, see "Cremation and the Order of Christian Funerals," United States Conference of Catholic Bishops, January 2012 Newsletter, http://www.usccb.org/prayer-and-worship/bereavement-and-funerals/cremation-and-funerals.cfm.

away from cremation.[17] However, this argument doesn't address the selection of the manner of the disposal of the body. "Fire" as a symbol of divine, eternal judgment following death (Matt. 5:22; 10:28; James 3:6) is much different from cremation as a way of disposing the body at death. A final opposing argument is rooted in the misconception that cremation is merely a way of getting rid of a body and doesn't allow for mourners to pay their proper respect for the deceased. To clarify this misconception: even with cremation, there can be a funeral or memorial service (either before or after cremation). This answers the concern of those who urge caution about cremation.

In summary, there are arguments both for and against each mode of disposing of a lifeless body. What then should we conclude about burial and cremation? In the end, whether through a relatively quick process of cremation or through a relatively long process of decay, all bodies return to the dust from which they were taken (Gen. 3:19). Additionally, no matter which mode is chosen, God will raise up the body at the resurrection. Believers whose bodies have been buried at sea, burned to ashes as martyrs, beheaded, eaten by wild beasts during persecution, buried in a grave, or cremated will be given glorified bodies at the return of Jesus Christ. It seems then that the matter of disposition of the body after death is adiaphora, a matter left up to one's conscience.[18] If so, we should be careful to avoid becoming dogmatic and causing distress to fellow Christians over the matter, especially at their time of loss.[19]

17. John Piper, "Should Christians Cremate Their Loved Ones? A Modest Proposal," Desiring God, April 26, 2016, https://www.desiringgod.org/articles/should-christians-cremate-their-loved-ones.
18. For a discussion of adiaphora, see chap. 10, n. 24.
19. Importantly, donation of our organs for transplantation, or donation of our body for scientific research, is virtuous in some cultures.

CHAPTER 13

THE FUTURE BODY

Consider

"I occasionally think about what eternal life in the new heaven and new earth will be like, and it motivates me to love the Lord and do good now." Do you agree or disagree, and why?

Big Idea

After death, which is a temporary separation from our body, we live in an abnormal condition of disembodiment. At the return of Christ and the accompanying event of bodily resurrection, we will be re-embodied. God's design for his embodied image bearers is that as we are in this earthly life, so we will be for all eternity: embodied.

Application Question

How does the resurrection (with eternal physical life) confirm our first big idea that embodiment is the proper state of human existence?

Disembodiment in the Intermediate State

The intermediate state is the condition of people between their physical death and the return of Jesus Christ (with the accompanying event of bodily resurrection). Importantly, this state of disembodiment is abnormal for human beings created as embodied image bearers of God. This disembodiment is so aberrant that Paul shudders in horror at the thought of such an existence: "For we know that if our earthly tent we live in is destroyed, we have a building from God, an eternal dwelling in the heavens, not made with hands. Indeed, we groan in this tent, desiring to put on our heavenly dwelling, since, when we are clothed, we will not be found *naked*. Indeed, we groan while we are in this tent, burdened as we are, because we do not want to be *unclothed* but clothed, so that mortality may be swallowed up by life" (2 Cor. 5:1–4).

Using the metaphors of nakedness and being unclothed, Paul underscores how wrong human disembodiment is. In this context, the two metaphors grate against human sensitivity that people are to be clothed for the purpose of covering their nakedness (discussed in chap. 10). Every culture in the world insists on its citizens being clothed and considers it shameful to uncover oneself before any person of the other gender other than one's spouse.[1] Thus for Paul it's proper for people to be clothed, or embodied, whether that has reference to their earthly body or, following the return of Christ, their resurrection body. In contrast, the idea of being naked/unclothed, or disembodied in the intermediate state, provokes Paul's unease, even distress.

Some people offer this objection: because the destiny of all human beings is disembodiment after death, that state actually defines human nature. Our true self is our soul or spirit, with our body as an additional element that isn't essential.

This view is wrong on three accounts. The first is the biblical discussion immediately above. Paul looks on the state of disem-

---

1. For example, "clothing the sexual organs was a universal practice" in ancient Near Eastern cultures. The lone exception was the limited nudity approved by the Greeks during athletic competition. Ryan Hanley, "Nakedness Imagery as Theological Language in the Old Testament" (PhD diss., The Southern Baptist Theological Seminary, 2019), 51–78 (quote from p. 76).

bodiment as abnormal. Thus we can't determine what human nature is essentially by appealing to an irregularity in human existence.

The second reason is that the view reflects the influence of Gnosticism. To the extent that it represents the prioritization of the immaterial/spiritual aspect over the material/physical aspect of human nature, is both wrong and dangerous.

The third reason is a theological consideration. If Adam and Eve had remained upright and not disobeyed the Lord's prohibition in the garden, would they have died? No. Death is the penalty for sin. If they hadn't sinned, they wouldn't have died.[2] In that case, Adam and Eve wouldn't have existed in the intermediate state as disembodied people. We can surmise, then, that both death and the condition of disembodiment are the result of sin, not the way things are supposed to be. Embodiment, not disembodiment, is the proper state of human existence.

What happens after death? Believers (disembodied) go immediately into the presence of Christ. They are "away from the body and at home with the Lord" (2 Cor. 5:8; cf. Phil. 1:23–24). According to Hebrews, a vision of heavenly worship includes participation by "the spirits of righteous people made perfect" (Heb. 12:23). Oppositely, unbelievers (disembodied) go immediately into misery, torment, and punishment. In the parable of the rich man and poor Lazarus, Jesus recounts the postmortem condition of the two characters. The poor man experiences comfort; the rich man is "in torment in Hades" and cries out for relief "because I am in agony in this flame!" (Luke 16:22–26). While sensitive to the parabolic nature of this story, we glean from Jesus's account that unbelievers suffer immediate misery and torment upon their entrance into the intermediate state. Additionally, believers await the resurrection of their bodies. So too do unbelievers (Dan. 12:1–2;

---

2. How they would have been sustained in eternal life is another matter. Scripture seems to indicate that they would have eaten from the tree of life and thus lived forever (Gen. 2:9; confirmed by Rev. 22:2, 14).

Rev. 20:13–15). Soberly, there is no "second opportunity" to accept Christ postmortem, in the intermediate state.

Sadly, there is a good deal of confusion about this state between death and the Lord's return. The historical view of the church as just presented has been challenged by two inadequate views.

Inadequate Views of the Intermediate State

The first inadequate view of the intermediate state is called "soul sleep":

> Seventh-day Adventists and Jehovah's Witnesses believe that people exist in an unconscious condition in the intermediate state. Supposed biblical support includes the biblical descriptions of death as "sleep" (1 Kings 2:10; John 11:11; Acts 7:60; 13:36; 1 Thess. 4:13), which is characterized by the absence of memory, praise, and hope (Ps. 6:5; 115:17; Isa. 38:18). This view misunderstands that Scripture uses "sleep" as a euphemism for death itself. It is not a description of what happens after death. Moreover, the biblical presentation of inactivity after death refers to the condition of people in Sheol, part of Old Testament eschatology that has been clarified in the further revelation of the New Testament. Finally, this position cannot account for the biblical passages that present believers being in the presence of Christ after their death.[3]

Like the church has always done, I reject the position of soul sleep.

A second inadequate view of the intermediate state is the doctrine of purgatory. "According to Roman Catholicism, purgatory is the temporary state of purification of the Catholic faithful who were not fully obedient during their earthly existence. Bearing the stain of sin, these faithful experience the temporary punishment for sin in purgatory. When their purification is completed, they will go to heaven."[4]

---

3. Gregg R. Allison, *50 Core Truths of the Christian Faith* (Grand Rapids: Baker, 2018), 360–61.

4. Allison, *50 Core Truths*, 361.

Key support for the doctrine of purgatory comes from the noncanonical book 2 Maccabees. After a battle between pagan troops and the Jewish army, the Jewish leader Judas Maccabeus and his men discover the reason why some of the Jewish soldiers had died in the conflict: they had committed the sin of idolatry, so God punished them with death. The story continues with the response of Judas and his troops:

> Turning to supplication, *they prayed that the sinful deed might be fully blotted out.* The noble Judas exhorted the people to keep themselves free from sin, for they had seen with their own eyes what had happened because of the sin of those who had fallen. He then *took up a collection* among all his soldiers, amounting to two thousand silver drachmas, which he sent to Jerusalem *to provide for an expiatory sacrifice.* In doing this he acted in a very excellent and noble way, inasmuch as *he had the resurrection in mind;* for if he were not expecting the fallen to rise again, it would have been superfluous and foolish to *pray for the dead.* But if he did this with a view to the splendid reward that awaits those who had gone to rest in godliness, it was a holy and pious thought. Thus, *he made atonement for the dead that they might be absolved from their sin.* (2 Macc. 12:38–45)

Prayers for the dead, that God might forgive them. A collection of money for the purpose of offering atonement for their sin of idolatry. An expectation that the Lord would raise these sinful men from the grave. From this text (which Protestants rightly reject because it isn't part of inspired, authoritative Scripture) the Roman Catholic Church has developed its doctrine of purgatory and the practices of praying for the souls in purgatory, paying money for the celebration of masses on behalf of those souls, and expecting that those souls will one day enter into heaven.

Other alleged support from Scripture includes 1 Corinthians 3:10–15 and Matthew 12:22–32. In the first passage, Paul discusses the Lord's evaluation of the works of people who build the church: "Each one's work will become obvious. For the day [of judgment] will disclose it, because it will be revealed by fire; the fire will test the quality of each one's work. If anyone's work that he has built survives, he will receive a reward. If anyone's work is burned up, he will experience loss, but he himself will be saved—but only as through fire" (1 Cor. 3:13–15). The Roman Catholic interpretation understands the reference to fire as the flames of purgatory removing the stain of sin from the souls present there. However, this interpretation is flawed. The purging with fire refers to the final judgment of believers, especially leaders, in regard to their poor work in the church. It has nothing to do with the purification of Catholic faithful in purgatory, readying them for heaven by smelting the dross from them.

In the second text, Jesus speaks about blasphemy against the Holy Spirit: "I tell you, people will be forgiven every sin and blasphemy, but the blasphemy against the Spirit will not be forgiven. Whoever speaks a word against the Son of Man, it will be forgiven him; but whoever speaks against the Holy Spirit, it will not be forgiven him, either in this age or in the one to come" (Matt. 12:31–32). The Roman Catholic Church finds an implication in Jesus's words: though there is one sin that cannot ever be forgiven, other sins can be forgiven even after death. "The (mis)interpretation is that, whereas blasphemy against the Spirit can never be forgiven, other sins, if they are not forgiven in this age, can be forgiven in the age to come. But Jesus is emphasizing the unforgiveable seriousness of blasphemy against the Spirit without implying anything about other, less serious sins."[5]

By appealing to these texts, Roman Catholicism developed its doctrine of purgatory, which is the destiny for the souls of the Catholic faithful who aren't perfectly pure during their lifetime. As a temporary state of purgation, purgatory removes the stain of sin and satisfies divine justice through the punishment suffered.

5. Allison, *50 Core Truths*, 361.

Purgatory thus prepares those souls for their final destination of heaven.[6]

Protestants disagree sharply with this doctrine for at least two reasons. First, it has a poor biblical basis, along with an errant appeal to the noncanonical book of 2 Maccabees. Second, in terms of salvation there's no need for a final purging of the taint of sin after death, because God has justified his people. His declaration that we are no longer guilty but are instead fully righteous—clothed in the perfect righteousness of Christ—means that we stand before God without any need of further cleansing from the guilt and corruption of sin.

Re-embodiment, or Resurrection, at the Second Coming of Christ

Over and over again, Scripture affirms the resurrection of the body. Jesus himself promises, "Do not be amazed at this, because a time is coming when all who are in the graves will hear his [the Son of man's] voice and come out—those who have done good things, to the resurrection of life, but those who have done wicked things, to the resurrection of condemnation" (John 5:28–29). Jesus also pledged himself to this end:

> Everyone the Father gives me will come to me, and the one who comes to me I will never cast out. For I have come down from heaven, not to do my own will, but the will of him who sent me. This is the will of him who sent me: that I should lose none of those he has given me but should raise them up on the last day. For this is the will of my Father: that everyone who sees the Son and

6. The official decrees about purgatory come from the Council of Trent: "If anyone says that after the grace of justification has been received the guilt is so remitted and the debt of eternal punishment so blotted out for any repentant sinner, that no debt of temporal punishment remains to be paid, either in this world or in the other, in purgatory, before access to the kingdom of heaven can be opened (to him), let him be anathema." Canon 30 from the *Decree on Justification*; Council of Trent, 6th session, 1547. For further discussion, see "Concerning Purgatory," First Decree; Council of Trent, 25th session, 1563.

believes in him will have eternal life, and I will raise him up on the last day. (John 6:37–40)

Furthermore, Paul explains that our resurrection, just like that of Jesus himself, will come about by the Holy Spirit: "If the Spirit of him [the Father] who raised Jesus from the dead lives in you, then he [the Father] who raised Christ from the dead will also bring your mortal bodies to life through his Spirit who lives in you" (Rom. 8:11).

Fittingly, because of Christ's work of salvation, our resurrection body will be like his: "Our citizenship is in heaven, and we eagerly wait for a Savior from there, the Lord Jesus Christ. He will transform the body of our humble condition into the likeness of his glorious body, by the power that enables him to subject everything to himself" (Phil. 3:20–21). Specifically, the nature of the resurrection body is fourfold:

Imperishable, unlike our current body that is moving inevitably toward death

Glorious, unlike our body during its earthly state of guilt, shame, and humiliation

Powerful, not in terms of superhuman strength, but as is fitting for divine image bearers

Spiritual, not as in immaterial, but as completely controlled by and submitted to the Spirit of God (1 Cor. 15:42–44, 49)

Anticipating, even longing for, our resurrection and being fully conformed to the image of Jesus Christ enables us to live as whole people in a fractured world.

The Physical Renewal of the Entire Creation

Depending on our eschatology, or view of the future, our bodily resurrection will be followed by either the thousand-year millennial rule of Christ on earth or the inauguration of the new heaven and new earth. In either case, at some future point a total renewal of the entire creation will take place. Paul links this marvelous transformation to our resurrection: "The creation eagerly waits with anticipation for God's sons to be revealed. For the creation was subjected to futility—not willingly, but because of him who subjected it—in the hope that the creation itself will also be set free from the bondage to decay into the glorious freedom of God's children" (Rom. 8:19–21). We Christians will be revealed, liberated as God's children from sin, and granted the fullness of our salvation with the resurrection of our bodies. When that all-transforming event occurs for us, the creation itself will be completely and eternally transformed.[7] In the physically new heaven and new earth, we will worship the triune God as physically new people.

Accordingly, at the resurrection of our body and for the rest of eternity, our first big idea will be confirmed. God's design for his image bearers is that we are embodied human beings. Embodiment is the proper state of human existence, both during this earthly life and in the new heaven and new earth.

In summary, after death, which is our temporary separation from our body, we live in an abnormal condition of disembodiment. At the return of Christ and the accompanying event of bodily resurrection, we will be re-embodied. God's design for his embodied image bearers is that as we are in this earthly life, so we will be for all eternity: embodied.

Application

How does the resurrection (with eternal physical life) confirm our first big idea that embodiment is the proper state of human existence?

---

7. This renovation *may* involve the destruction of the current cosmos, followed by its re-creation (2 Pet. 3:10–13; Rev. 21–22).

To press in a bit more, do you look forward to the resurrection of your body? If so, what prompts you to long for it? If not, why is this future event not of much importance to you?

How does thinking about the resurrection affect the decisions you make and the way you live today? How does it help you live as a whole person in a fractured world?

Why is it difficult to imagine living as disembodied believers in heaven during the intermediate state? And how do we know that our resurrected body will fit well over our disembodied being and truly be *our* body though glorified?

For the Curious

Accounting for postmortem existence as disembodied human beings is problematic from a physiological point of view and is a common argument against the Christian belief in the intermediate state. In addition, accounting for our resurrection body is fraught with problems. A key matter is that of continuity of identity between our present existence and our resurrection existence. If the two identities aren't in some manner the same, it seems we are dealing more with a completely new person rather than a glorified person. But how can there be any continuity of personhood in the three stages: embodiment in this earthly life, disembodiment in the intermediate state, and re-embodiment at the resurrection?

Let's push the envelope a bit. Philip Rolnick refers to the physical changes we undergo from infancy to adolescence, adulthood, and old age "without becoming what we would call a different body." Though there is change to our embodied existence over time, there is also continuity. Our embodiment is also stationary. Rolnick offers, "Since an unchanging material identity is not present in this life, neither should a completely unchanged material identity be required in resurrection, only some form of continuity." That is, what we should expect isn't a physical sameness but a resurrection body that is proportional to our former one. The latter, glorified body will correspond to the former, earthly body. Rolnick continues, "Whatever body is given, it must be experienced as my own. Its belongingness cannot be like that of an external object, but rather, like that of seamless continuity with myself, now functioning in the resurrected environment."[8] We need a sense of fittingness to our resurrected body.

Perhaps help in understanding this comes from an unlikely corner: phantom limbs. "The phenomenon of phantom limbs [is] the experience of sensations where a limb has been amputated or is missing. . . . A crucial part of what is involved—a necessary condition for phantom limbs—is the establishment of bodily integrity, and in particular, the existence of a faculty which acts to constantly check our bodily integrity. It is something amiss in this faculty that gives rise to the peculiar phenomenology of phantom limbs."[9] To take an example, a soldier who lost his left leg in war returns home and continues to have the sensation of a left leg. He experiences soreness and pain where the leg would be, but it is missing. Remarkably, phantom limb syndrome makes it possible for the man to be fitted for a prosthetic leg, and it will function well.

This idea of "a faculty which acts to constantly check our bodily integrity" may supply some help. Could it be that in the intermediate state, this faculty (which is somehow preserved in our immaterial self) anticipates the reestablishment of bodily integrity that will be actualized when we are clothed with our glorified body? At that time, our resurrection body will be felt to fit neatly over our "phantom" body. We will feel it to be the very body that we once had but that is now reconstituted as imperishable, glorious, strong, and dominated by the Spirit.

8. Philip A. Rolnick, *Person, Grace, and God* (Grand Rapids: Eerdmans, 2007), 254.

9. Stephen Gaukroger, "Phantom Limbs," in *Embodiment: A History*, ed. Justin E. H. Smith (New York: Oxford University Press, 2017), 307, 310.

In the intermediate state, something will indeed be amiss—we will be missing our body. Parallel in some way to the phenomenon of phantom limbs, our experience in the intermediate state will be that of a *phantom body*: we will continue to have the sensation of the reality of our body after it has been sloughed off at our death. Even then, something will be amiss as we anticipate our resurrection body and long for our re-embodiment. When that miracle occurs, the glorified body with which we will be reclothed will appropriately correspond to the contours of our immaterial self and fit over us fittingly.

"I am my body."

CONCLUSION

I conclude with an invitation based on these words: "The way we feel about our embodiedness significantly conditions the way we feel about the world."[1] If my first big idea is correct—by God's design, the proper state of human existence is embodiment—then I invite you to adopt it as a new perspective on the world. Renounce the infection of Gnosticism and its prioritizing of the immaterial/spiritual over the material/physical aspects of your life. Stop viewing your body as an instrument to use and steward like you do your time, your treasures, and your talents. Reject the notion that "the fact that we have bodies is the oldest joke there is."[2] Don't think and live like my former student Drake, mentioned in the introduction to this book.

Instead, embrace the statement, "I am my body." Affirm the idea, "I am who I am principally in virtue of the fact that I have the body I have."[3] That is, realize that if you had a different body—say, that of your spouse or that of your best friend—you would be a

---

1. James B. Nelson, *Body Theology* (Louisville: Westminster/John Knox, 1992), 43.
2. C. S. Lewis, *The Four Loves* (New York: Harcourt Brace, 1960), 101.
3. Justin E. H. Smith, "Introduction," *Embodiment: A History*, ed. Justin E. H. Smith, (Oxford: Oxford University Press, 2017), 2. Originally in the form of a question, I've changed it to a statement.

different person altogether. Consider as truth "without this body
I do not exist, and I am myself as my body."[4]

If you accept my invitation, it will radically alter your view
of your createdness, your genderedness, your particularity, your
sociality, your sexuality, your sanctification, your blessedness and
discipline, your worship, your clothes, your suffering and healing, your death, and your eternal future. It will decisively enable
you to live as a whole person in a fractured world. And I think it
will give new meaning to your relationship with Jesus Christ. As
it is written of him, "the Word"—the preexisting Son of God,
who was always with God and was himself fully God—"became
embodied." And as the Nicene Creed announces the gospel, "For
us [who are embodied] and for our salvation he came down from
heaven. He became incarnate by the Holy Spirit and the virgin
Mary, and he was made [an embodied] man."

As God the Son was embodied and is re-embodied, so too we
are embodied and will be re-embodied.

The proper state of human existence—both now and then—is
embodiment.

4. As expressed by the Russian philosopher Vladimir Iljine. Quoted without
bibliographic detail in Elisabeth Moltmann-Wendel, *I Am My Body: A Theology
of Embodiment*, trans. John Bowden (New York: Continuum, 1995), 2.

Gregg R. Allison (PhD, Trinity Evangelical Divinity School) is professor of Christian theology at The Southern Baptist Theological Seminary in Louisville, Kentucky. Additionally, he is secretary of the Evangelical Theological Society and a pastor at Sojourn Community Church East. He and his wife, Nora, have three adult children and ten grandchildren. Being from Chicago, he's a big fan of the Cubs, Blackhawks, Bears, and Bulls (and hates the White Sox).

Allison is the author of numerous books, including *The Baker Compact Dictionary of Theological Terms* and *50 Core Truths of the Christian Faith: A Guide to Understanding and Teaching Theology*.

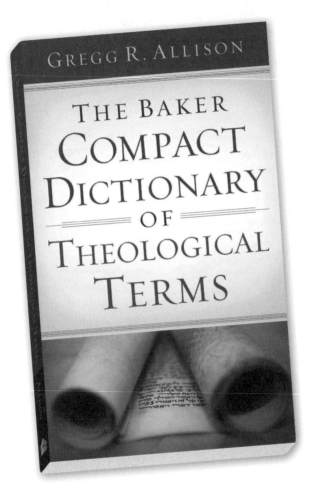

50 ESSENTIAL DOCTRINES,
Clearly and Succinctly Explained

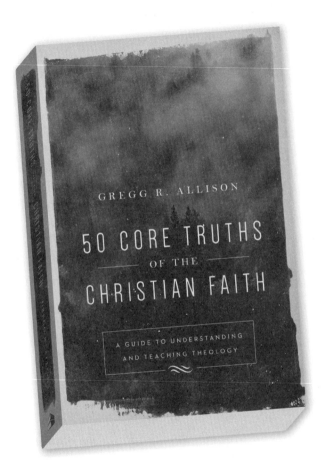

Theologian Gregg R. Allison unpacks fifty key doctrines of the Christian faith
in a clear, engaging way and provides guidance for how to accurately teach them.
This is an indispensable resource for anyone who desires to form believers in
sound doctrine and transform lives for the glory of God.